EDWARD W. SAID

COVERING ISLAM

Edward W. Said was born in Jerusalem, Palestine, and attended lower and secondary schools there and in Egypt. He received his B.A. from Princeton, and his M.A. and Ph.D. from Harvard, where he won the Bowdoin Prize. In 1974 he was Visiting Professor of Comparative Literature at Harvard, and during 1975–76 was a fellow at the Center for Advanced Study in the Behavioral Sciences at Stanford. In 1977 he delivered the Gauss Lectures in Criticism at Princeton, and in 1979 he was Visiting Professor of Humanities at Johns Hopkins. Currently he is University Professor of English and Comparative Literature at Columbia University.

Mr. Said's work has been translated into twenty-four languages and published throughout Europe, Africa, Asia, and Australia. His book *Beginnings: Intention and Method* won the first annual Lionel Trilling Award, given at Columbia University. In 1978 his book *Orientalism* was a runner-up in the criticism category of the National Book Critics Circle Award. He is also the author of *The World, the Text, and the Critic*; *After the Last Sky*; and *Culture and Imperialism*.

ALSO BY EDWARD W. SAID

Joseph Conrad and the Fiction of Autobiography
Beginnings: Intention and Method
Orientalism
The Question of Palestine
Literature and Society (ed.)
The World, the Text, and the Critic
After the Last Sky (with Jean Mohr)
Blaming the Victims
Musical Elaborations
Culture and Imperialism
The Politics of Dispossession
Representations of the Intellectual
Peace and Its Discontents

COVERING ISLAM

COVERING ISLAM

HOW THE MEDIA AND THE EXPERTS DETERMINE HOW WE SEE THE REST OF THE WORLD

REVISED EDITION

EDWARD W. SAID

VINTAGE BOOKS
A DIVISION OF RANDOM HOUSE, INC.
NEW YORK

First Vintage Books Edition, March 1997

The Library of Congress has cataloged the Pantheon edition as follows:
Said, Edward W.
Covering Islam.
Includes bibliographical references.
1. Islam—Public opinion.   2. Public opinion—United States.
3. Public opinion—Europe.   I. Title.
BP52.S24   909'.097671   80-8654
ISBN 0-394-50923-4
ISBN 0-394-74808-5 (pbk.)
Vintage ISBN 0-679-75890-9

Random House Web address: http://www.randomhouse.com/

Printed in the United States of America

B98765432

For Mariam

CONTENTS

CONTENTS

INTRODUCTION
TO THE VINTAGE EDITION

In the fifteen years since *Covering Islam* appeared there has been an intense focus on Muslims and Islam in the American and Western media, most of it characterized by a more highly exaggerated stereotyping and belligerent hostility than what I had previously described in my book. Indeed, Islam's role in hijackings and terrorism, descriptions of the way in which overtly Muslim countries like Iran threaten "us" and our way of life, and speculations about the latest conspiracy to blow up buildings, sabotage commercial airliners, and poison water supplies seem to play increasingly on Western consciousness. A corps of "experts" on the Islamic world has grown to prominence, and during a crisis they are brought out to pontificate on formulaic ideas about Islam on news programs or talk shows. There also seems to have been a strange revival of canonical, though previously discredited, Orientalist ideas about Muslim, generally non-white, people—ideas which have achieved a startling prominence at a time when racial or religious misrepresentations of every other cultural group are no longer circulated with such impunity. Malicious generalizations about Islam have become the last acceptable form of denigration of foreign culture in the West; what is said about the Muslim mind, or character, or religion, or culture as a whole cannot now be said in mainstream discussion about Africans, Jews, other Orientals, or Asians.

Of course there have been many provocations and troubling incidents by Muslims and such Islamic countries as Iran, Sudan, Iraq, Somalia, Afghanistan, and Libya during the past decade and a half. Consider the following abbreviated list of offenses. During 1983 in Lebanon about 240 United States Marines were killed by a bomb that was taken credit for by a Muslim group, and the United States embassy in Beirut was blown up by Muslim suicide bombers with considerable loss of life. In the 1980s numerous American hostages were taken by Shi'a groups in Lebanon and held for long periods of time. A number of plane hijackings—of which the most notorious was the TWA flight that was held in Beirut—between the 14th and 30th of June, 1985—were claimed by Muslim groups, as were several bomb atrocities in France at roughly the same time. The 1988 explosion of Pan Am flight 109 over Lockerbie, Scotland, was carried out by Islamic terrorists. Iran achieved a new prominence as the purported backer of and sympathizer with various insurgent groups in Lebanon, Jordan, Sudan, Palestine, Egypt, Saudi Arabia, and elsewhere. Afghanistan, following the end of the Soviet occupation, seemed to have descended into a cauldron of feuding Islamic parties and tribes; many of the Muslim insurgents—particularly the Taliban—armed, trained, and bankrolled by the United States have now overrun the country. Some of those earlier American-trained guerrillas have turned up elsewhere—like Sheikh Omar Abdel Rahman, who was convicted of masterminding the 1993 bombing of the World Trade Center—and now seem to be fomenting civil strife in Egypt and Saudi Arabia, important United States allies in the Middle East. Khomeini's *fatwa* against Salman Rushdie (February

14, 1989) and the multimillion dollar reward for the writer's assassination that accompanied it seemed to epitomize Islam's viciousness, its resolute war against modernity and liberal values, as well, of course, as its capacity of reaching across the oceans into the heart of the West in order to challenge, provoke, and threaten.

After 1983, Muslims declaring their faith in Islam were everywhere in the news. In Algeria they won municipal elections and were prevented from acceding to power by a military insurrection. Algeria is still in the throes of a truly appalling civil war, in which militants battle army groups, and thousands of intellectuals, journalists, artists, and writers have been killed. Sudan is now ruled by a militant Islamic party whose head, Hassan al-Turabi, is often represented as a brilliantly malevolent individual, a Svengali and Savonarola clothed in Islamic robes. Dozens of innocent European and Israeli tourists have been murdered by Islamic assailants in Egypt, where the power of the Muslim Brotherhood and the Jama'at Islamiya— one more violent and uncompromising than the other—seems to have grown enormously over the past decade. Once supported by Israel as a way of undercutting the PLO's authority during the Palestinian *intifada* (which began in December 1987) on the occupied West Bank and Gaza Strip, Hamas and with it Islamic Jihad have metamorphosed into the most feared and journalistically covered examples of Islamic extremism, with many suicide bombs, exploded civilian buses, and murdered Israeli civilians comprising their list of heinous acts. No less fearsome are the guerrillas—commonly referred to in the American media as terrorists—of Hizbollah (the Party of God), who identify themselves and are perceived locally as resistance fighters resisting the illegal Israeli occupation of a substantial so-called security strip in South Lebanon.

In March 1996, a major international conference attended by numerous heads of state, including President Bill Clinton, Prime Minister Shimon Peres, President Hosni Mubarak, and Chairman Yasir Arafat, was convened in the Egyptian port city of Sharm el-Sheikh to discuss "terrorism," a recent example of which had been three suicide attacks on Israeli civilians. In his speech, broadcast the world over, Peres left no doubt in the public's minds—as did the conference itself—that it was Islam and Iran's Islamic Republic which were to blame. So inflamed against Islam has the media environment in the United States and the West generally become that when the Oklahoma City bomb attack took place in April 1995 the alarm was sounded that the Muslims had struck once again; I recall (with residual chagrin) that I must have received twenty-five phone calls that afternoon from newspapers, the major networks, and several resourceful reporters, all of them acting on the assumption that since I was from and had written about the Middle East that I must know something more than most other people. The entirely factitious connection between Arabs, Muslims, and terrorism was never more forcefully made evident to me; the sense of guilty involvement which, despite myself, I was made to feel struck me as precisely the feeling I was meant to have. The media had assaulted me, in short, and Islam—or rather my connection with Islam—was the cause.

That certainly was the case with the Bosnian Muslims who were the victims of ethnic cleansing at the hands of their Serbian compatriots. But there, as David Rieff and others have shown, very little was done on their behalf by either the European powers or the United States until well after the worst atrocities had already been committed. A massive United Nations effort at humanitarian relief in Bosnia was a novelty, given that everywhere else Muslims were seen and treated as aggressors for whom the best treatment was abusive talk, threats, sanctions, quarantine, and, on occasion, air strikes. Consider also the bloody attempt by Russia at suppressing the Chechnyan Muslims. In the case of Libya and Iraq, the former was bombed by the United States in April 1986 during the prime time evening hours and the latter was the target of a full-scale war and subsequent United States air attacks in 1993 and 1996 (most of which were broadcast on CNN). People in the West felt that the strikes were justified even though huge numbers of innocent civilians were affected. No one seemed to object to the 1992 humanitarian intervention by the United States in Muslim Somalia, which, like the Lebanese expedition a decade earlier, ended in disarray. The Iraqi, Libyan, Chechnyan, and Bosnian cases are all different; but what they do have in common in the eyes of Muslims throughout the world is that it is Western, mostly "Christian" powers and peoples who are mobilized to fight a continuing war against Islam. Thus the polarity is deepened and the chance of dialog between cultures is postponed. Many Muslims have written and said that had the Bosnian, Palestinian, and Chechnyan victims not been Muslims, and had "terrorism" not emanated from "Islam," the Western powers would have done more. After all, Israel had occupied and annexed Arab Muslim territories and was never punished. Why should only the countries and peoples of Islam have been special objects of opprobrium and disproportionate hostility? To most Americans, Islam was nothing but trouble.

So the picture is a complicated one. There *has* been a resurgence of emotion throughout the Islamic world, and there have been a great many incidents of terrorism, organized or not, against Western and Israeli targets. The general state of the Islamic world with its decline in productivity and well-being, including such phenomena as censorship, the relative absence of democracy, the dismaying prevalence of dictatorships, and fiercely repressive and authoritarian states some of whom practice and encourage terrorism, torture, genital mutilation seems backward and cruel; this includes such basically Islamic countries as Saudi Arabia, Egypt, Iraq, Sudan, and Algeria, among others. In addition, the (to me) simplistic reductiveness of some numbers of people who have recourse to a hazy fantasy of seventh century Mecca as a panacea for numerous ills in today's Muslim world makes for an unattractive mix that it would be rank hypocrisy to deny.

My concern, though, is that the mere use of the label "Islam," either to explain or indiscriminately condemn "Islam," actually ends up becoming a form of attack, which in turn provokes more hostility between self-appointed Muslim and Western spokespersons. "Islam" defines a relatively small proportion of what actually takes place in the Islamic world, which numbers a billion people, and includes dozens of countries, societies, traditions, languages, and, of course, an infinite number of different experiences. It is simply false to try to trace all this back to something called "Islam," no matter how vociferously polemical Orientalists—mainly active in the United States, Britain, and Israel—insisted that Islam regulates Islamic societies from top to bottom, that *dar al-Islam* is a single, coherent entity, that church and state are really one in Islam, and so forth. My contention in this book is that most of this is unacceptable generalization of the most irresponsible sort, and could never be used for any other religious, cultural, or demographic group on earth. What we expect from the serious study of Western societies, with its complex theories, enormously variegated analyses of social structures, histories, cultural formations, and sophisticated languages of investigation, we should also expect from the study and discussion of Islamic societies in the West.

Instead of scholarship, we often find only journalists making extravagant statements, which are instantly picked up and further dramatized by the media. Looming over their work is the slippery concept, to which they constantly allude, of *"fundamentalism,"* a word that has come to be associated almost automatically with Islam, although it has a flourishing, usually elided, relationship with Christianity, Judaism, and Hinduism. The deliberately created associations between Islam and fundamentalism ensure that the average reader comes to see Islam and fundamentalism as essentially the same thing. Given the tendency to reduce Islam to a handful of rules, stereotypes, and generalizations about the faith, its founder, and all of its people, then the reinforcement of every negative fact associated with Islam—its violence, primitiveness, atavism, threatening qualities—is perpetuated. And all this without any serious effort at defining the term "fundamentalism," or giving precise meaning either to "radicalism" or "extremism," or giving those phenomena some context (for example, saying that 5 percent, or 10 percent, or 50 percent of all Muslims are fundamentalists).

Since 1991, in a massive five-volume study, by a group under its aegis, the American Academy of Arts and Sciences has been publishing its findings on "fundamentalism." My suspicion is that the project itself was started precisely with Islam in mind, although Judaism and Christianity are in fact discussed. Numerous distinguished academics were involved, with two general editors, Martin E. Marty and R. Scott Appleby, in charge. The net result is a compendium of often interesting papers, but, according to a perspicacious review of the series by Ian Lustick, no workable definition of fundamentalism emerges; on the contrary, Lustick adds, the editors and contributors "end up somewhat desperately suggesting that 'fundamentalism' [should] not be defined."[1] Thus, if specialists in the subject are unable to define it, no wonder then that a host of polemicists—spurred onward by zeal and a hostility to all things Muslim—do a good deal less well. They do succeed, however, in stirring up feelings of alarm and consternation in their readers.

Consider as a typical case in point former National Security Council member Peter Rodman, writing in the *National Review* of May 11, 1992. "Yet now the West finds itself challenged from the outside by a militant, atavistic force driven by hatred of *all* Western political thought, harking back to age-old grievances against Christendom," he states as a modest first premise. Note the absence of qualifiers, and the liberal use of sweeping, impossible-to-verify generalities like "harking back to age-old grievances against Christendom," the latter a word that sounds bigger, more impressive than the unadorned, but somehow truer, Christianity. Rodman plunges on: "Much of the Islamic world is rent by social divisions, frustrated by its material inferiority to the West, bitter at Western cultural influences, and driven by its resentments (what Bernard Lewis calls the 'politics of rage'). It's virulent anti-Westernism does not look like just a tactic." Lewis's role in this type of discourse is something that I shall give separate attention to a little later. Rodman provides no evidence for the allegations about Islamic inferiority, resentments, and rage: It is sufficient for him only to make the assertions because "Islam" as it is covered and (mis)represented in Orientalist thought and media stereotypes stands charged and convicted without the need for supporting arguments or modulating qualifications of the kind Rodman would routinely make for discussion of the "Western" world or even "Christendom." We want to ask, does every one of the billion Muslims in the world feel rage and inferiority, does every citizen of Indonesia, Pakistan, or Egypt resent "Western" influences? How would one set about getting answers to such basic questions? Or is it the case that "Islam" cannot be investigated as we would any other culture or religion because, unlike all the others, it stands outside "normal" human experience, a religion that one can talk about as if it, and everything within it, resembles a psychopathological human being?

Or consider Daniel Pipes, a perfervid anti-Muslim whose main characteristic is that as an Orientalist he "knows" Islam for the appallingly dreadful thing that it is. He delivers himself of some reflections in a "think" piece published in the Fall 1995 issue of *The National Interest* under the modest title "There are No Moderates: Dealing with Fundamentalist Islam." Nowhere in the piece does he absolve radical Islam—which he does not bother to define, but which his title lets us assume is the same as the non-radical variety—of its real nature which, he tells us right off, is "closer in spirit to other such movements (communism, fascism) than to traditional religion." A little later, he develops the analogy further: "While fundamentalist Islam differs in its details from other utopian ideologies, it closely resembles them in scope and ambition. Like communism and fascism, it offers a vanguard ideology; a complete program to improve man and to create a new society; complete control over that society; and cadres ready, and even eager, to spill blood." Pipes ridicules those experts who say that political Islam has run its course; no, he offers by way of counterargument, its heyday is upon us now. Violent, irrational, unappeasable, totally uncompromising, Pipes's "fundamentalist" Islam threatens the world, and especially "us," even though, according to State Department figures, terrorism originating in the Middle East is *sixth* in order of occurrence and frequency.

In short, fundamentalism equals Islam equals everything-we-must-now-fight-against, as we did with communism during the Cold War; in fact, Pipes says, the battle is graver, more profound and dangerous with Islam. Neither Pipes nor Rodman writes as an outsider, nor as a member of a lunatic fringe. Their work is thoroughly mainstream and is intended, with some realistic expectation, for the serious attention of policymakers. How widespread their views are can be gleaned from a *US News and World Report* item on July 6, 1987: "Unapologetic—and unbending—fundamentalism is riding a popular groundswell through much of the Islamic world. It has plainly caught the West off balance, especially when Islamic religious fervor and political objective join to create violent results. There is still little evidence that the majority of fundamentalists pledge obeisance to Khomeini's declared revolutionary objectives. But his message seems to be spreading." A little later, October 16, 1987, in the same magazine: "The martyr complex—integral to Iran's variety of Islam, the Shiite sect—now appears among the youth of the Sunni majority." The norms of rational sense are suspended when discussions of Islam are carried on. No one bothers to ask, for instance, how verifiable is the statement that martyrdom is spreading among Sunni youth, all several hundred million of them, from Morocco to Uzbekistan, and, if it is, what sort of evidence it is likely to be in the first place.

Small surprise then that the Sunday *New York Times* "Week in Review" headlined its January 21, 1996, issue with: "The Red Menace is Gone. But Here's Islam." Underneath was a long article by Elaine Sciolino which, though structured according to the on-the-one-hand/on-the-other-hand principle, gives an idea of what she called "one of the hottest, nastiest debates in academic circles today, mirroring the old debate on how well-organized and monolithic the

Communist menace was." Aside from its inflammatory title, Sciolino's article nudges the reader toward viewing Islam ("the green
menace") as a danger to Western interests, since a greater number
of witnesses for that position are cited (including NATO Secretary
General Claes, Newt Gingrich, Bernard Lewis, Shimon Peres, and
the ubiquitous, if not fully accredited, Steven Emerson); in addition, various American-linked heads of state, like Benazir Bhutto,
Hosni Mubarak, and Tansu Ciller are listed as proponents of a
worldwide conspiracy-menace thesis. As against all this only Professor John Esposito of Georgetown, whose sensible and cogently
argued book *The Islamic Threat: Myth or Reality?* (Oxford, 1992) patiently deflates the menace theory of Islam, is cited on the other
side. Clearly then, today's climate favors—one might even say requires—Islam to be a menace, notwithstanding the notion's impossible sweep and its unprovable, purely polemical essentials.

Islam has become, therefore, a central discussion in many policymaking, as well as media, circles. Most of these discussions elide the
fact that the major Islamic groupings today are United States allies
and clients, or within the United States orbit—such countries as
Saudi Arabia, Indonesia, Malaysia, Pakistan, Egypt, Morocco, Jordan, and Turkey where militant Muslims emerged to some degree
because the regimes are openly supported by the United States;
these often isolated minority governments, alienated from most
of their peoples, have been forced to accept United States tutelage
and influence because of a United States, not a Muslim, agenda.
The Council on Foreign Relations, a prestigious and influential
policy association, has recently set up a Muslim Politics Report and
study group which allows a wide range of opinions about Islam,
some of them salutary and informative. Yet in such publications as
Foreign Affairs, the Council's quarterly journal, the debate is often
set in polarized terms such as between Judith Miller and Leon
Hadar, the latter against, the former for, a positive answer to the
question, "Is Islam a Threat?" (*Foreign Affairs*, Spring 1993). With
some small degree of empathy it is not difficult to imagine that a

Muslim might be made uncomfortable by the relentless insistence—even if it is put in terms of a debate—that her or his faith, culture, and people are seen as a source of threat, and that she or he has been deterministically associated with terrorism, violence, and "fundamentalism."

A steady stream of such characterizations is inflated still more by contributions from pro-Israeli journals and books, in the hope that more Americans and Europeans will see Israel as a victim of Islamic violence. One Israeli government after another has resorted to the propagation of this self-image in the course of the information wars that have gone on since 1948 around the whole question of the Middle East. Although I have discussed this elsewhere, it is important to insist that such claims about Islam and, most of the time, the Arabs, are designed to obscure what it is that Israel and the United States, as "Islam's" main opponents, have been doing. Between them, the two countries have bombed and invaded several Islamic countries (Egypt, Jordan, Syria, Libya, Somalia, Iraq), they have (in Israel's case) occupied Arab-Islamic territory in four countries, and in the United States' case are seen in the United Nations as openly supporting the military occupation of these territories; to the overwhelming majority of Muslims and Arabs, Israel is therefore an arrogant regional nuclear power, contemptuous of its neighbors, heedless in the number and frequency of its bombings, killings (which far exceed the number of Israelis killed by Muslims), dispossessions, and dislocations, especially so far as the Palestinians are concerned. Defying international law and dozens of United Nations Resolutions, Israel has annexed East Jerusalem and the Golan Heights, has occupied South Lebanon since 1982, has had a policy of treating (and characterizing) Palestinians as sub-human—in effect a race apart—and has wielded its power over United States Middle Eastern policy whereby the interests of four million Israelis totally overshadow the interests of two hundred million Arab Muslims. It is all this, and not Bernard Lewis's quaint formulation that Muslims are enraged at Western "modernity," that has created an

understandable sense of Arab-Islamic grievance against powers
who, like Israel and the United States, proclaim that they are liberal
democracies but act against lesser peoples according to quite contradictory norms of self-interest and cruelty. When the United
States led a coalition of countries against Iraq in 1991, it spoke about
the need to reverse aggression and occupation. Had Iraq not been a
Muslim country that militarily occupied another such country in an
area of huge oil reserves that are considered to be the United States'
preserve, the invasion would not have taken place, just as Israel's invasion and occupation of the West Bank and Golan Heights, its annexation of East Jerusalem, and the implantation of settlements
were not seen by the United States as requiring its intervention.

I am not saying that Muslims have not attacked and injured Israelis and Westerners in the name of Islam. But I am saying that
much of what one reads and sees in the media about Islam represents the aggression as coming from Islam because that is what "Islam" is. Local and concrete circumstances are thus obliterated. In
other words, covering Islam is a one-sided activity that obscures
what "we" *do*, and highlights instead what Muslims and Arabs by
their very flawed nature *are*.

In what follows I am not going to be citing marginal, patently
crazy, or inconsequential writers on the Middle East and Islam, but
rather instances of otherwise well-known and mainstream journalism such as *The New Republic* and *The Atlantic*, the former owned
by Martin Peretz, the latter by Morton Zuckerman, both of them
great supporters of Israel, and therefore biased against Islam. Peretz
is a special case. No one in the American media has held forth for
so long (at least two decades) in accents of such racial hatred and
contempt against a given culture and people as he has about Islam
and the Arabs. Part of his venom is certainly derived from his relentless drive to defend Israel at all costs, but there is a great deal in
what he has said over the years that goes well beyond rational defense, and his columns of unadulterated, irrational, and vulgar
defamation are truly unsurpassed anywhere.

In his mind, Islam and the Arabs are one and can be attacked interchangeably. Here he is on May 7, 1984, describing a play he has seen:

> . . . a visiting German businessman, an American Jewess come as an immigrant, and an Arab Palestinian find themselves taking refuge in a bomb shelter in Jerusalem under Arab siege. If there is something a bit startling about the emerging empathy between the play's German and its Jew, even less have the universalist prejudices of our culture prepared us for its Arab—a crazed Arab, to be sure, but crazed in the distinctive ways of his culture. He is intoxicated by language, cannot discern between fantasy and reality, abhors compromise, always blames others for his predicament, and in the end lances the painful boil of his frustrations in a pointless, though momentarily gratifying, act of bloodlust. This is a political play and what makes it compelling is its pessimism, which is to say its truthfulness. We have seen this play's Arab in Tripoli and in Damascus, and in recent weeks hijacking a bus to Gaza and shooting up a street of innocents in Jerusalem. On the Rep. stage he is a fictional character, of course, but in the real world it is not he but his "moderate" brother who is a figment of the imagination.

This writing appears week after week in his magazine, which, to clarify, is a famous, once liberal, journal of opinion read by a large number of influential people in Washington and New York. Having assured us (June 24, 1991) that Israel was "the political expression of a people already formed, like Poland, Japan, or England," and that its political identity was secure (unlike India's or the Palestinians'), he then advances the thesis on September 6, 1993, that "to the Arabs, the Jews will always be usurpers and interlopers. Xenophobia in our time is not the disposition of the Arabs alone. But in an age when the state conflates politics with identity, Arab Islam, suffering from feelings of inferiority about Israel and the West, is especially xenophobic, thinking of its world and its world alone."

Peretz's extraordinary defamations are spun out so as to completely obscure the historical reality, that indeed it *was* the case that mostly-European Jews came to Palestine, a country already inhabited and settled by another people, destroyed their society, dispossessed them, and drove two-thirds of them out; in addition, Israel has been in military occupation of Palestinian (as well as Lebanese and Syrian) territory for several decades, has unilaterally annexed East Jerusalem, an act unrecognized by any country on earth, and has arrogated to itself the right to wage "pre-emptive" war against several Arab countries. Unable to deal with these facts except as right by virtue of Israel's superiority, Peretz displaces on to the Muslims and Arabs a theory of gratuitous violence and cultural inferiority. In the August 13, 1996, issue of his journal, Peretz first justifies Israeli Prime Minister Benjamin Netanyahu's brazen politics of force, then adds that, after all, Israel has to deal with Arab countries in which there is no "cultural disposition for scientific and industrial takeoff. Alas, these are societies which cannot make a brick let alone a microchip." Peretz pursues this idea (which of course resembles his views about African-Americans, that they are historically doomed to inferiority) to the following conclusion: "This widening gap will produce deep, perhaps intractable resentment against Israel. And while it may not lead to war in the traditional sense, it may well produce more of what Israel has experienced over the last years: terror and ongoing riot."

Peretz's habit of using vast, irrational generalizations to attack Islam and the Arabs for their sins against his favorite country, Israel, has its more benign counterpart in books, articles, television stories, and films that are either descriptive or entertaining. A writer of numerous articles on the Middle East for the *New Yorker*, Milton Viorst collected most of them in *Sandcastles: The Arabs in Search of the Modern World* (Knopf, 1994). A keen observer, Viorst is nevertheless hobbled by a whole arsenal of unexamined presuppositions about Islam that he delivers without any self-consciousness or skepticism. In hardly any of the reviews of this book was there criticism expressed of these dubious prepositions. One of the exceptions, Muhammad Ali Khalidi, writing in the *Journal of Palestine Studies* (Winter 1996), collected some of them together with devastating effect. He quotes Viorst as follows: "the traditional Islamic city shows little concern for exterior aesthetics; even now, Arabs seem not to notice their streets and cover them with litter. Some observers explain this indifference to public space as an outgrowth of Islamic culture's fixation on privacy, on conducting social life only inside the home." There is more. "Islam," says Viorst, ". . . succeeded where Christianity failed in shackling man's power of reasoning. . . . Arabs have often noted an intrinsic disposition to conservatism, if not to fatalism, within their culture. They are uncomfortable with intellectual challenge." Khalidi quite rightly reminds Viorst that Muslims, after all, adapted Greek philosophy for later European use, were pioneers in logic and astronomy, established medicine as a science, and invented algebra.

Viorst is undeterred by (or perhaps does not know about) any of this. He speaks assuredly about a "basic antagonism to creative thinking that has come increasingly to characterize Islam," and claims that "Muslims, both Arabs and Turks, readily acknowledge that, judged by a range of intellectual criteria, their civilization does not measure up to that of the West" because "intellectual rigor, the West's real gift to the modern world, has barely touched Arab civilization."

What I find depressingly symptomatic about these statements is that they seem to derive—rather defensively and even xenophobically—from self-appointed spokesmen like Viorst, Peretz, and others too numerous to mention, who attack Islam precisely for sentiments of free-floating hostility like these. Much in current representations of Islam is designed to show the religion's inferiority with reference to the West, which Islam is supposed to be hell-bent on opposing, competing with, resenting, and being enraged at.

Moreover, important journals of opinion such as the *New Yorker*, the *New York Review of Books*, and *Atlantic Monthly* never carry essays (or even literary works) in translation by Muslim and Arab authors but rely instead on experts such as Viorst to interpret political and cultural actualities shaped not by the facts but by unexamined presuppositions such as the above. Very rarely do critiques of these practices stray into the mainstream to challenge their hegemony.

One of the few recent critical assessments of the damage caused by clichés about Islam in the media, policy journals, and academia is by Zachary Karabell (*World Policy Journal*, Summer 1995), who starts from the premise that there has been undue attention paid to "fundamentalist" Islam since the end of the Cold War. The public media, he says quite rightly, has been filled with negative images of Islam. "Ask American college students, in the elite universities or elsewhere, what they think of when the word 'Muslim' is mentioned. The response is inevitably the same: gun-toting, bearded, fanatic terrorists hellbent on destroying the great enemy, the United States." Karabell notes, for instance, that ABC's 20/20, a prestigious, high-profile news program, "broadcast several segments discussing Islam as a crusading religion inculcating warriors of God; *Frontline* sponsored an investigation of the tentacles of Muslim terrorists around the world." He might also have mentioned Emerson's PBS film *Jihad in America*, cynically designed and promoted to exploit just this fear; or even the vogue of books with provocative titles like *Sacred Rage* or *In the Name of God*, which make the association between Islam and dangerous irrationalism firmer, more inevitable. "The same can be said of the print media," Karabell continues. "Stories about the Middle East are often accompanied by a picture of a mosque or large crowds praying."

All this, as I said earlier, marks a serious deterioration in the situation I described in the original edition of *Covering Islam*, published a decade and a half ago. There is now, for example, a new wave of large-scale feature films (one of them, *True Lies*, Karabell reminds us, "had as its villains classic Arab terrorists, complete with glinty eyes and a passionate desire to kill Americans") whose main purpose is to first demonize and dehumanize Muslims in order, second, to show an intrepid Western, usually American, hero killing them off. *Delta Force* (1985) began the trend, but it was carried forward in the Indiana Jones saga, and innumerable television serials in which Muslims are uniformly represented as evil, violent, and, above all, eminently killable. One of the changes from an old habit of exoticising the Orient in Hollywood films is that romance and charm have now been completely eliminated, as they have also been in the ninja films that pit a white (or even black) American against endless number of black-masked Orientals, all of whom get their just deserts.

Aside from the combination of hostility and reductionism offered by all these misrepresentations, there is the matter of how grossly they exaggerate and inflate Muslim extremism within the Muslim world. Karabell makes an excellent if ironically understated point when he says that "the forces of modernism and secularism are far from spent in the Middle East." In an essay originally published in 1993, and then collected in my book *The Politics of Dispossession* (Pantheon, 1994), I attempted to show how it was secularism, rather than fundamentalism, that held Arab Muslim societies together, despite the wild exaggeration of the sensationalist and ignorant American media, most of whose ideas were taken from anti-Islamic, careerist publicists who had found a new field for their skills in demonology. At the very least one should say that in the contest between the Islamists and the overwhelming majority of Muslims, the former have by and large lost the battle. *The Failure of Political Islam*, the French political scientist Olivier Roy called it in an excellent book by the same title (Harvard, 1994). Other scholars, such as John Esposito in his *The Islamic Threat: Myth or Reality?*, make the point in a different way, stressing the variety, complex expressions, and different traditions and historical experiences of Muslim societies over their putative mass-based unity and anti-Westernism.

But such reasoned, well-researched, alternative views have been barely in evidence; the market for representations of a monolithic, enraged, threatening, and conspiratorially spreading Islam is much greater, more useful, and capable of generating more excitement, whether for purposes of entertainment or of mobilizing passions against a new foreign devil. For every unusual book like Richard Bulliet's *Islam: The View from the Edge* (Columbia, 1994), there are many more books and articles expressing views like David Pryce-Jones in *The Closed Circle* (Harper, 1991), Charles Krauthammer's strident account of what he calls "the global *intifada*" (*Washington Post*, February 16, 1990), or any of A.M. Rosenthal's pieces in *The New York Times* (for example, his "The Decline of the West," September 27, 1996) in which Islam, terrorism, the Palestinians are routinely harangued together; these tend to be what passes for informed analysis and coverage in the United States' prestige media. The daily reader of the mainstream media is most unlikely to encounter, for instance, Yvonne Yazbeck Haddad's careful analysis of "Islamist Perceptions of US Policy in the Near East," which appeared, alas, in an obscure academic book, *The Middle East and the United States*, edited by David W. Lesch (Westview, 1996). By comparison with Rosenthal and Krauthammer, she carefully distinguishes among five different kinds of Islamists (preferring the use of that word instead of the inflammatory "radical" or "fundamentalist"), and even more usefully, collects a whole series of real incitements to Muslims that have exacerbated relationships between the world of Islam and the West. Among them are statements by Ben-Gurion ("We fear nothing but Islam"), Yitzhak Rabin ("The religion of Islam is our only enemy"), and Shimon Peres, ("We will not feel secure until Islam puts away its sword"), and the long list of direct Western actions against the Islamic world that culminate in the strong, not to say aggressive, Israel–United States partnership.

The point about accounts such as Haddad's is not whether in the end they are totally correct, or whether one should accept or reject them unconditionally, but the sense they give of a real interlocutor, with real arguments and real interests that have been ignored in most of the remorseless media coverage of Islam that dominates the picture today. No one, of course, expects journalists or media personalities to spend a great deal of time being scholarly, reading books, looking for alternative views, or trying to inform themselves in ways that do not presume that Islam is both monolithic and hostile. But why the slavish and uncritical adoption of views that stress the unvaryingly reductive arguments about Islam, and why the extraordinary willingness to accept the official rhetoric emanating from the government in its irresponsible characterizations of Islam: by that I mean the loose application of the word "terrorism" to "Islam," and the attitude that elevates Israeli views of Islam's "dangers" to the level of United States policy?

The answer is in how prevalent age-old views of Islam as an acceptable competitor to the Christian West still are. Japan-bashing, for example, exists precisely because Japan is rightly perceived as showing aggressive resistance to Euro-American economic hegemony. The tendency to consider the whole world as one country's *imperium* is very much in the ascendancy in today's United States, the last remaining superpower. But whereas most other great cultural groupings appear to have accepted the United States' role, it is only from within the Islamic world that signs of determined resistance are still strong. Therefore we have an efflorescence of cultural and religious attacks on Islam from individuals and groups whose interests are informed with the idea of the West (and the United States, as its leader) as the standard for enlightened modernity. Yet far from being an accurate description of "the West," such an idea of rightful Western dominance is in reality an uncritical idolization of Western *power*.

One of the worst offenders in the cultural war against Islam has been the senior British Orientalist—now a United States resident, and retired Princeton Professor—Bernard Lewis, whose essays appear regularly in *The New York Review of Books*, *Commentary*, *Atlantic Monthly*, and *Foreign Affairs*. Over many decades his views, which have remained unchanged and indeed have become more strident and reductionist over time, have seeped into the discourse of the "think" pieces and books undertaken by ambitious journalists and a few political scientists. Why Lewis's views, utterly conventional in their derivation from nineteenth-century Orientalists of the British and French school, who saw in Islam a danger to Christianity and liberal values, should acquire so great a currency is easy to explain. All of Lewis's emphases in his work are to portray the whole of Islam as basically *outside* the known, familiar, acceptable world that "we" inhabit, and in addition that contemporary Islam has inherited European anti-Semitism for use in an alleged war against modernity. As I pointed out about Lewis in my book *Orientalism*, his methods are the snide observation, the fraudulent use of etymology to make huge cultural points about an entire set of peoples, and, no less reprehensible, his total inability to grant that the Islamic peoples are entitled to their own cultural, political, and historical practices, free from Lewis's calculated attempt to show that because they are not Western (a notion of which he has an extremely tenuous grasp) they can't be good.

Take as a case in point his essay on the word *watan*, which in Arabic means homeland, or nation. Lewis's tendentious account of this word is an attempt to strip it of any real territorial, or affiliative, connotations; he alleges, with no contextual evidence whatever, that the word does not mean *patria*, or *patrie*, or *patris*, and cannot be compared with them since *watan* for Islam is a neutral place of residence. This demonstration makes up one of the essays in *Islam and the West* (Oxford, 1993), and like its companion pieces in the book its purpose is to display Lewis's erudition in the first place, and in the second, it shows by the Westerner's "superior" authority what Muslims *really* feel, but are somehow unable to express. Everything in the essay, however, reveals a shocking ignorance of the lived actuality of Arab Muslims, for whom in fact the word *watan* certainly *does* have the existential associations of *patria*, and *patrie*. Lewis simply finds two or three examples in medieval Arabic literature to bolster his specious point, thus completely ignoring literary sources from the eighteenth century through the present, as well as common daily usage, in which *watan* is precisely the word real (as opposed to textual) Arabs use to denote home, belonging, and loyalty. Since Arabic for him is only a language of texts, not of spoken or everyday intercourse, he seems totally oblivious to related words like *bilad* and *ard* that connote a strong sense of specific habitation and attachment.

Lewis's extraordinary methods are based in the, once again, profoundly anti-human literalism with which he decrees what it is that Muslims feel, are, and aspire to. Islam, he says, "is not merely a system of belief and worship, a compartment of life, so to speak. . . . It is rather the *whole* of life" [italics added]. Such a statement demonstrates not only bias, but also a ludicrous misunderstanding of how human life actually operates. Lewis's methods suggest that all Muslims—all one billion of them—have read, absorbed, and totally accepted "the rules" he refers to that govern "civil, criminal, and what we call constitutional law," and then slavishly follow those precepts in every significant action of their daily lives. If there was ever an occasion to apply the word preposterous, it is here. Lewis simply cannot deal with the diversity of Muslim, much less human, life because it is closed to him as something foreign, radically different, and other.

Nowhere is this more evident than in the essay on "The Return of Islam," a piece that first appeared in the ultra-right-wing Jewish magazine *Commentary* and is collected in *Islam and the West*. Despite the pretentious ceremonies of scholarship he goes through, Lewis actually uses bogus philology to allege that most of the major political phenomena of the contemporary Arab world that he and his constituency disapprove of are throwbacks to seventh-century Islam. As the perceptive scholar As'ad Abu Khalil notes: "While he [Lewis] has the right to believe in a fundamental—and apparently genetic—difference between 'the modern Western mind' and the Muslim mind—which for Lewis does not change over the ages (a fact that allows him to quote medieval Muslim jurists to explain present-day developments), his analysis of current events is uninformed at best" (*JPS*, Winter 1995). And that is the point, since Lewis's Orientalist procedures are paraded before the reader in order to make sense of what today's "Muslim mind" is up to. This naturally disallows historical change, or human agency, or the possibility that not all Muslims think exactly alike since the seventh century; it also excludes him from concretely discussing the present. But Lewis's intention is to persuade readers that Muslims have always been unregenerately all about Islam and only that, a tautology that simply defies human understanding.

Lewis is at his worst in the ominously entitled "The Roots of Muslim Rage," which appeared in the September 1990 issue of *The Atlantic*. Whoever designed the magazine's cover for that issue got Lewis's point all too well: a glowering, turbaned, obviously Islamic, head stares out at the reader, its pupils showing American flags, its demeanor announcing hate and anger. To call what Lewis does in this extremely influential essay either scholarship or interpretation is to travesty the meaning of both. "The Roots of Muslim Rage" is a crude polemic devoid of historical truth, rational argument, or human wisdom. It attempts to characterize Muslims as one terrifyingly collective person enraged at an outside world that has disturbed his almost primeval calm and unchallenged rule. For example:

> . . . the last straw was the challenge to his [the putative Muslim] mastery in his own house, from emancipated women and rebellious children. It was too much to endure, and the outbreak of rage against these alien, infidel, and incomprehensible forces that had subverted his (*sic*) dominance, disrupted his society, and finally violated the sanctuary of his home was inevitable. It was also natural that this rage should be directed primarily against the millennial enemy and should draw its strength from ancient beliefs and loyalties.

Later Lewis contradicts himself by saying that Muslims had once welcomed the West, responding to it "with admiration and emulation." But this he alleges dissolves into pure hatred and rage "when the deeper passions are stirred," seemingly with only those inner feelings to blame for such unseemly outbursts. By the end of his essay Lewis makes the startling claim that what "we" are discussing is a phenomenon of the purest, most gratuitous anger at modernity itself:

> It should by now be clear that we are facing a mood and a movement far transcending the level of issues and policies and the governments that pursue them. This is no less than a clash of civilizations—the perhaps irrational but surely historic reaction of an ancient rival against our "Judeo-Christian" heritage, our secular present, and the worldwide expansion of both. It is crucially important that we on our side should not be provoked into an equally historic but also equally irrational reaction against that rival.

In other words, Muslims today react only because it is historically, and perhaps genetically, determined that they should do so; what they react to are not policies or actions, or anything so mundane as that. What they are fighting on behalf of is an irrational hatred of the secular present which, Lewis grandly proclaims, is "ours" and ours alone.

The arrogance of these claims is breathtaking. For not only are Muslims and "we" shut off from each other, despite literally centuries of borrowings and crossing over which Lewis totally denies, but "they" are as doomed to rage and irrationalism as "we" are to the enjoyment of our rationalism and cultural supremacy. We represent the real, that is, secular, world; they rail and cry and froth in a world that is scarcely more than a puerile fantasy. Finally, "our" world is the world of Israel and the West; theirs is that of Islam and the rest. "We" must defend against them not by policy or the debate of issues, but by unconditional hostility. No wonder that Samuel P. Huntington's essay on the clash of civilizations borrows its title and its main thesis from Lewis's essay.

To call such ideas hostile and irrational is not to overstate the case, particularly since these same ideas have come to a kind of apotheosis in the work of journalists like Judith Miller of the *New York Times*, whose book *God Has Ninety-Nine Names: A Reporter's Journey Through a Militant Middle East* (Simon and Schuster, 1996) is like a textbook of the inadequacies and distortions of media coverage of Islam. Much in evidence on talk shows and seminars on the Middle East, Miller trades in "The Islamic Threat," as a *Foreign Affairs* symposium to which she contributed had it in 1993; her particular mission has been to advance the millennial thesis that militant Islam is a danger to the West, the very idea that is at the core of Samuel Huntington's clash of civilizations diatribe. So in the supposed intellectual vacuum created by the Soviet Union's dismemberment, the search for a new foreign devil has come to rest, as it did beginning in the eighth century for European Christianity, on Islam, a religion whose physical proximity and unstilled challenge to the West (a vague term used by Lewis and Huntington that denotes "our" civilization as opposed to "theirs") seem as diabolical and violent now as it did then. Miller does not mention that most Islamic countries today are poverty stricken, tyrannical, and hopelessly inept militarily as well as scientifically to be much of a threat to anyone except their own citizens; and she doesn't dwell on the fact that the most powerful of them—Saudi Arabia, Egypt, Jordan, and Pakistan—are totally within the United States' orbit. What matters to "experts" like Miller, Huntington, Martin Kramer, Daniel Pipes, and Barry Rubin, plus a whole battery of Israeli academics, is to make sure that the "threat" is kept before our eyes, the better to excoriate Islam for its terror, despotism, and violence, while assuring themselves profitable consultancies, frequent television appearances, and book contracts. To a basically indifferent and already poorly informed American clientele the Islamic threat is made to seem disproportionately fearsome, lending support to the thesis (which is an interesting parallel to anti-Semitic paranoia) that there is a worldwide conspiracy behind every explosion.

Political Islam has generally not done well wherever it has tried through Islamist parties to take state power. Iran may be an exception, but neither Sudan, which is in fact an Islamic state, nor Algeria, riven by the contest between Islamic groups and a brutal soldiery, nor Afghanistan, a turbulent and now ultrareactionary country, has done anything but make itself poorer and more marginal on the world stage. Lurking beneath the discourse of Islamic peril in the West is, however, some measure of truth, which is that appeals to Islam among Muslims have fueled resistance (in the style of what Eric Hobsbawm has called primitive, preindustrial rebellion) here and there to the *pax Americana-Israelica* throughout the Middle East. Yet neither Hizbollah nor Hamas has presented a serious obstacle to the ongoing steamroller of the anything-but-peace process. I would say that most Arab Muslims today are too discouraged and humiliated, and also too anesthetized by uncertainty and their incompetent and crude dictatorships, to support anything like a vast Islamic campaign against the West. Besides, the elites are for the most part in league with the regimes, supporting martial law which, in Egypt, has endured since 1946, plus various other effective extralegal measures against "extremists." So why then the accents of alarm and fear in most discussions of Islam? Of course there have been suicide bombings and outrageous acts of terrorism, but have these accomplished anything except to strengthen the hand of Israel and the United States as well as their client regimes in the Muslim world?

The answer, I think, is that books like Miller's are symptomatic in that they furnish an additional weapon in the contest to subordinate, beat down, compel, and defeat any Arab or Muslim resistance to United States-Israeli dominance. Moreover, by surreptitiously justifying a policy of single-minded obduracy that links Islamism, however lamentable it is, to a strategically important, oil-rich part of the world, the anti-Islam campaign virtually eliminates the possibility of any sort of equal dialogue between Islam and the Arabs, and the West or Israel. To demonize and dehumanize a whole culture on the grounds that it is "enraged" at modernity is to turn Muslims into the objects of a therapeutic, punitive attention. I do not want to be misunderstood here: the manipulation of Islam, or for that matter Christianity and Judaism, for retrograde political purposes is catastrophically bad, and must be opposed, not just in Saudi Arabia, the West Bank and Gaza, Pakistan, Sudan, Algeria, and Tunisia, but also in Israel, among the right-wing Christians in Lebanon (for whom Miller shows an unseemly sympathy), and wherever theocratic tendencies appear. And I do not at all believe that all the ills of Arab Muslim countries are due to Zionism and imperialism. But this is very far from saying that Israel and the United States, and their intellectual flacks, have not played a combative, even incendiary role in stigmatizing and heaping invidious abuse on an abstraction called "Islam," in order to deliberately stir up feelings of anger and fear about Islam in Americans and Europeans who are also enjoined to see in Israel a secular, liberal democracy. Miller says at the end of her book that right-wing Judaism in Israel is "the subject of another book." It ought actually to be very much a part of the book that she has written, except that she has suppressed it in order to go after "Islam."

Writing about any other religion or part of the world Miller would be considered woefully unqualified. She tells us on numerous occasions that she has been involved with the Middle East as a professional for twenty-five years, yet she has no knowledge of either Arabic or Persian; she admits that wherever she goes she needs a translator whose accuracy or reliability she has no way of assessing. It would be impossible to be taken seriously as a reporter or expert on Russia, France, Germany, Latin America, perhaps even China and Japan, without knowing the requisite languages, but for "Islam" no linguistic knowledge seems to be necessary since what one is dealing with is considered to be a psychological deformation, not a "real" culture or religion.

Most sources Miller cites in her pages of footnotes are affected by her ignorance, whether because she can only cite the things she already knows she wants in English, or because she quotes authorities whose views correspond to hers. An entire library by Muslims, Arabs, and non-Orientalist scholars is therefore closed to her and, of course, to her readers. Nearly every time she tries to impress us with her ability to say a phrase or two in Arabic she unerringly gets it wrong. These are fairly common, by no means recondite, phrases; and her mistakes are not just errors of transliteration, which she laboriously forgives herself for in advance at the book's start. They are crude mistakes committed by a foreigner who neither has the care nor the respect for her subject that after twenty-five years earning a living out of it she might have taken the trouble to acquire. On page 211 she quotes Sadat's description of Qaddafi as *al walid majnoon*, and translates it "that crazy boy." In fact the phrase is *el walad el magnoon*; what she thinks she is quoting is in fact a caricature of "the boy is crazy." Shadia, the popular Egyptian actress, is rendered pretentiously as Sha'adia, indicating that Miller does not even know the difference between letters of the Arabic alphabet. She has a habit of making English plurals out of Arabic words (e.g., thobe/thobes, or hanif/hanifs) and has the effrontery on page 315 to tell us that "a beautiful poem in Arabic . . . suffers greatly, as does most Arabic poetry, in translation."

If her attempts to understand the detail of Arab Islamic life are so unsuccessful, what then of her political and historical information? Each of the ten country chapters (Egypt, Saudi Arabia, Sudan, etc.) begins with an anecdote and moves immediately to a potted history of the place on an undergraduate level. Cobbled together out of various, not always reliable authorities, these histories are meant principally to display command of the material, but actually expose lamentable prejudices and failures of analyses and comprehension. In the Saudi Arabia chapter, for instance, she informs us in a note that her "favorite" source on the Prophet Mohammed is the French Orientalist Maxime Rodinson, a redoubtable Marxist scholar whose biography of the Prophet is written with a bracing combination of anticlerical irony and enormous erudition. What Miller gets from this in her four- or five-page summary of Mohammed's life and ideas is that there is something inherently risible, if not contemptible about the man whom Rodinson says was a combination of Charlemagne and Jesus Christ; for whereas Rodinson understands what that means, Miller tells us (irrelevantly) that she is not convinced. For her, Mohammed is the begetter of an anti-Jewish religion, one that is laced with violence and paranoia. She does not quote one Muslim source on Mohammed and relies completely on the dyspeptic debunkings of Western Orientalists; just imagine a book published in Europe or the United States on Jesus or Moses that makes no use of a single Judaic or Christian authority. "After he conquered Mecca, Muhammad reportedly only killed ten people for their affronts to him and Islam," she says with a pathetic effort at sarcasm. She justifies her attention to Mohammed by reminding us that he founded a religion and a state (the observation is not original) but then jumps from the seventh century to roughly the present, as if the founders of states in the distant past are the best sources for present-day history. This tactic is very much Lewis's.

One is never allowed to forget then that Miller is basically a tendentious, politically motivated reporter, and neither a scholar nor an expert, nor even a coherent writer, since most of her book is made up not of argument and ideas but of interminable interviews with what seems to be a slew of pathetic, unconvincing, self-serving Muslims and their occasional critics. Once we are past her little histories we are soon adrift in the most boring, unstructured meanderings, which testify to an over-filled Rolodex rather than to her genuine knowledge of the place. Here's a typical sentence of resoundingly insubstantial generalization: "And Syrians, mindful of their country's chaotic history [incidentally, of what country on earth is this not also true?] found the prospect of a return to anarchy or yet another prolonged, bloody power struggle [is this uniquely true of Syria as a post–World War Two post-colonial state, or is it true of a hundred others like Syria in Asia, Africa, and Latin America?]—and perhaps even the triumph of militant Islam in the most

secular [with what thermometer did she get that reading?] state —
alarming." Leave aside the abominable diction and jaw-shattering
jargon of the writing. What you have is not an idea at all, but a series of clichés mixed with unverifiable assertions that reflect the
"thought" of "Syrians" much less than they do Miller's.

Miller gilds her paper-thin descriptions with the phrase "my
friend," which she uses to convince her reader that she really knows
the people and consequently what she is talking about. It is as if she
believes that her "friends" tell her intimate things that only she has
been able to pry out of them. But this technique produces extraordinary distortions in the form of long digressions that testify to an Islamic mind-set, even as they obscure or ignore more, or at least
equally, relevant material such as local politics, the functioning of
secular institutions, or the active intellectual contest taking place
between Islamists and nationalist opponents. She seems never to
have heard of Mohammed Arkoun, or Mohammed el-Jabri, or
George Tarabishi, or Adonis, or Hasan Hanafi, or Hisham Djait,
whose theses are hotly debated all over the Islamic world.

This appalling failure of knowledge and analysis is especially
true in the chapter on Israel (mistitled, since it is all about Palestine), where she ignores completely the changes caused by the *intifada*, and the prolonged detailed effect of the three-decade Israeli
occupation, and conveys no sense of the abominations wrought on
the lives of ordinary Palestinians by Oslo and Yasir Arafat's one-man
rule. It is no coincidence that, as a supporter of United States policy, Miller is more obsessed with Hamas than anyone else is, and
she is clearly unable to connect Hamas with the sorry state of affairs
in territories run brutally by Israel for all these years. She neglects to
mention, for instance, that the only Palestinian university not established with Palestinian funds is Gaza's Islamic (Hamas) University, started by Israel to undermine the PLO during the *intifada*.
She records Mohammed's depredations against the Jews but has
virtually nothing at all to say about Israeli beliefs, statements, and
laws against "non-Jews," often rabbinically sanctioned practices of

deportation, killing, house demolition, land confiscation, outright annexation, and what the most credible authority on Gaza, Sara Roy, has called systematic economic de-development. Miller sprinkles around a few of these facts, but nowhere does she accord them the weight and influence as causes of Islamist passion that they undoubtedly have.

Her other tic is to inform her readers of everyone's religion— such and so is Christian, or Muslim Sunni, Muslim Shi'i, and so forth. For someone who is so concerned with this particular aspect of life, she is not always accurate, managing even to produce some rather amusing howlers. She speaks of Hisham Sharabi as a "friend" but misidentifies him as a Christian; he is Sunni Muslim. Badr el Haj is described as Muslim, whereas he is Maronite Christian. These lapses wouldn't be so bad were she not so bent on impressing us with her knowingness and her intimacy with so many people. But the most noteworthy feature of all this is her spectacular bad faith in never identifying her own religious background or political predilections. For a topic as totally charged with religious and ideological passion as she claims hers is, I find it odd that she can assume that her religion (which I don't think is Islam or Hinduism) is irrelevant. One wonders how many of the people from whom she pried information knew *who* exactly they were talking to, and how many have any idea now what she has said of them.

She is embarrassingly forthcoming, however, about her reactions to people in power and certain events. She is "grief-stricken" when King Hussein of Jordan is diagnosed with cancer, although she scarcely seems to mind that he runs a security state whose many victims have been tortured, unfairly imprisoned, or done away with. Her eyes "fill with tears of rage" as she espies evidence of desecration in a Lebanese Christian church, but she doesn't bother to mention other desecrations in Israel, for example, of Muslim graveyards, and hundreds of exterminated villages in Syria, Lebanon, Palestine. Her real feelings of contempt and disdain come out in passages like the following, in which she imputes thoughts and wishes to a middle-class Syrian woman whose daughter has just become an Islamist and who has misguidedly invited Miller to be her guest:

> She would never have any of the things a middle-class Syrian mother yearned for: no grand wedding party and traditional white dress with diamond tiara for her daughter, no silver-framed photos of the happy wedding couple in tuxedo and bridal gown on the coffee table and fireplace mantel, no belly dancers wriggling on a stage and champagne that flowed till dawn. Perhaps Nadine's friends, too, had daughters or sons who had rejected them, who secretly despise them for the compromises they had made to win the favor of Assad's cruel and soulless regime. For if the daughter of such pillars of the Damascene bourgeoisie could succumb to the power of Islam, who was immune?

The most interesting question about Miller's book is why she wrote it at all. Certainly not out of affection. Consider, for instance, that she admits she fears and dislikes Lebanon, hates Syria, laughs at Libya, dismisses Sudan, feels sorry for and a little alarmed by Egypt, and is repulsed by Saudi Arabia. She hasn't bothered to learn the language and is relentlessly only concerned with the dangers of organized Islamic militancy, which, I would hazard a guess, accounts for less than 5 percent of the billion-strong Islamic world. She is totally in favor of the violent suppression of Islamists (but not torture and other "illegal means" used in that suppression: the contradiction in her position seems to have escaped her notice), has no qualms at all about the absence of democratic practices or legal procedures in countries backed by the United States, such as Egypt, Jordan, Syria, and Saudi Arabia, so long as Islamists are the target. In one scene related in the book, she actually participates in the prison interrogation of an alleged Muslim terrorist by Israeli policemen, whose systematic use of torture and other questionable procedures (undercover assassinations, middle-of-the-night arrests, house de-molitions) she politely overlooks as she gets to ask the handcuffed man a few questions of her own.

Perhaps her greatest, most consistent failing as a journalist is that she is willing only to make connections and offer analyses of matters that suit her prevailing thesis about the militant, hateful quality of the Islamic world. Now I have little quarrel with the general view that the Arab Islamic world in particular is in a dreadful state, and have said so in print for the past three decades. But Miller doesn't even give a minimally accurate picture of the role played in this sit-uation by Israel and the United States, and in fact scarcely registers the existence of a determined anti-Arab and anti-Islamic United States policy (barring the Afghanistan episode that she mentions rather gently in passing). Take Lebanon, for example. She refers to Bashir Gemayel's assassination in 1982 and gives one the impression that he was elected by a popular landslide. She does not even allude to the fact that he was brought to power while the Israeli army was in West Beirut, just before the Sabra and Shatila camp massacres, and that for years, according to Israeli sources such as Uri Lubrani, he was the Mosad's man in Lebanon. That he was a killer and a self-proclaimed thug is also elided, as is the fact that Lebanon's current power structure is filled with people like Elie Hobeika, who was charged directly for the camp massacres. In citing instances of Arab anti-Semitism she might also note the existence of a racial discourse inside Israel directed against Arabs and Muslims. As for the facts of Israel's wars against civilians—the protracted, consistent, and sys-tematic campaign against prisoners of war and refugee camp dwellers, village destructions, bombings of hospitals and schools, deliberate creation of hundreds of thousands of refugees—all these are buried (if they are present at all) in gushing prattle. Miller's problem at bottom is that she has a disdain for facts worthy of the airiest deconstructionist, but that she should prefer the inter-minable talk that she quotes as a way of turning Muslims into de-serving victims of Israeli terror and United States support of it says a lot about her as a perfect exemplification of the mainstream media's current Middle East coverage.

One would not know from Miller's book that there is a simmering inter-Islamic conflict in interpretations and representations of the Middle East and Islam, and that, given her choice of sources, she is deeply partisan, an enemy of Arab nationalism, which she declares dead numerous times in the book, a supporter of United States policy which has a lot to answer for, and a committed foe of any Palestinian nationalism that doesn't conform to the sanitized and harmless version foreseen, indeed programmatically planned for, in the Bantustans being set up according to the Oslo accords. Miller in short is a shallow, opinionated journalist whose gigantic book is five hundred pages too long for what it ends up saying, even though it is a perfect compendium of what is wrong with the unthinking, unexamined assumptions taken up and circulated by the media.

How these can actually affect daily reporting is dramatically evident in a radio exchange between Serge Schmemann, the *New York Times* Jerusalem bureau chief, and Robert Fisk, who writes from Lebanon for London's *Independent*. On different sides of the border, both men covered the April 1996 Israeli invasion of Lebanon, yet what emerged in their reports and in their radio debate ("Democracy Now," May 5, 1996, Pacifica Radio) is a radically opposed journalistic practice, in which the American journalist operates according to (perhaps unconscious) guidelines that confirm Miller's. Remark first of all that since 1982, Israel has occupied a strip of South Lebanon as a so-called security zone, and has assembled and continues to maintain a mercenary Lebanese army in the occupied area; resistance to the occupation as well as the South Lebanese Army has come from Hizbollah, the so-called Party of God, whose *raison d'être* has been Israel's occupation. These guerrillas reside and fight in the south, so that by most standards they would be considered basically a guerrilla group fighting an illegal military occupation in their country. But remark, second, that in the United States press Hizbollah's religion is emphasized, as well as the supposition that because it fights Israel it is a terrorist organization.

On April 1, 1996, the *Times* reported that Israel had shelled South Lebanon and killed two civilians. "The militant Party of God threatened to retaliate," the anonymous report stated, and continued, "tension has run high on both sides of the border since the guerrillas killed six Israeli soldiers over the past month in the southern Lebanon border strip occupied by Israel." Normally of course guerrillas are entitled to fight against the soldiers of an occupying army, though here the principle is initially vitiated by references to a "militant" Islamic party, which calls up associations with fundamentalism, the threat of Islam, and so forth, in the reader's mind. By the 10th of April (in a report by the *Times*'s Israeli stringer, Joel Greenberg) the phrase "backed by the Shiite-run Government of Iran" enters the reports, and never leaves any *Times* story until the invasion ended two weeks later. It is as if where Israel is concerned the *Times* wishes it known that that country's enemies are militant Muslims (and soon to become "terrorists") rather than guerrillas resisting occupation. On April 12, Schmemann speaks of Hizbollah as a "militant Shiite Moslem organization backed by Iran," as if to say watch out, the mad Muslims are at it again, killing Jews as usual. References to "frightened Israeli residents of Qiryat Shemona" make their appearance in the same story, although Israel at the same time was bombing Beirut, a city that was full of frightened residents who are not mentioned.

In a clear victory of ideology over facts, the *Times*'s editorial on the same day was called "Israeli's Answer to Terror," and alleged that "Israel's air strikes against terrorist targets in Lebanon were justified and limited. . . . Responsibility for yesterday's raids in Lebanon and the week's senseless casualties on both sides of the border lies squarely with Hizbollah's terrorists and the governments in Beirut and Damascus. Mr. Peres, in this case, only exercised Israel's right to self-defense." These statements were made when the Israeli army was also in the process of displacing 200,000 residents of South Lebanon, having already bombed the area from the air, land, and sea, and—it needs to be recalled—remained in military occupation, which the laws of war allow the inhabitants to resist. The tables were turned first because Israel was in question and second because it was "Islam" that posed a "threat." By April 18, the day that Israel bombed and killed over a hundred people at a United Nations post in Qana that had been a well-marked shelter for civilian Lebanese refugees from the war, the *Times* was reporting that both the United States and Shimon Peres regretted the loss of life but still considered Hizbollah to be responsible "for breaking the 1993 agreement without provocation" (April 21). Moreover, during the entire period of Israel's Lebanese campaign the *Times* published not one op-ed or editorial that conveyed a viewpoint different from Israel's or the United States government's. Above all, it was Syria and Iran who mattered more than the hapless Lebanese or Hizbollah, as if what was going on in South Lebanon was something grander and more impressive than a mere occupation and responses to it. It was Islam versus the West all over again.

The resulting deformations in coverage and reporting were pointed out by Robert Fisk, who remained concentrated on what *in fact* happened, rather than what Israeli or United States officials wanted the world to believe was happening. Fisk did not reverse the principle that guerrillas resisting occupation were justified in doing so, nor did he succumb to the temptation to consider the battle of South Lebanon as one between the West and terrorist Muslims, backed by Iran. Thus he was convincingly able to show in his description of the Qana incident that there was a deliberate Israeli policy since the 1993 cease-fire of initiating twenty incidents as a way of drawing out Hizbollah, and thereby "retaliating" with great force so as to put pressure on Lebanon and Syria. This is what he told Schmemann, whose fidelity, or perhaps prudence, in hewing to the *Times*'s editorial line stands out dramatically by comparison with Fisk's independence. The interviewer on the radio broadcast says to him, "You write that Israel applied precise and selective force in Lebanon. You say without critical comments that 'Israel's officers insisted that their gunners were unaware of the refugees at the Qana camp.' You are deliberately conveying an impression that Israel is not targeting civilians, that is very different from what Robert Fisk is describing."

At this point Fisk presents three pieces of evidence to dispute the absence of Israeli intentionality; these form the basis of his accounts of the massacre in reports to the *Independent* on April 19 and 22; before that (April 15), writing from South Lebanon, Fisk adduces Israel's intentions in a major story entitled "this is not just a military operation. It is an attempt to smash a country." The evidence Fisk puts on the table is 1) that nineteen hours before the Qana attack United Nations officials told the Israeli military command that civilians were sheltered in every United Nations location; 2) an Israeli pilotless drone stood overhead as the bombing was taking place; 3) given all the boasts of Israeli super accuracy and cutting-edge technology why did the shelling go on long after the United Nations, from offices in Naqura (in South Lebanon), "were pleading for it to stop." Schmemann responds that he "could not understand why Israel would deliberately hit civilians," a view which, while he obviously holds it with genuine conviction, also reflects the general United States media view that whereas Muslim terrorists are fully capable of acts of deliberate violence against innocents, Israel, which is like us, is not. Fisk agrees with Schmemann that, reporting from Israel rather than South Lebanon, he was covering what went on there, and quite consciously kept his opinions out of his reports: "there is a distinction between what a reporter does and what a columnist does." Fair enough of course, but the question remains, however, as to what the framework is for the reporter, and what events he connects with what statements. For Fisk the operative context is set by a remark made by Foreign Affairs Minister Ehud Barak when he said (January 3, 1996) that if there were further attacks against Hizbollah then "if Israeli attacks militarily it will be against Lebanon and the victims will be Lebanese."

In short, when the assumption about Hizbollah is that it is primarily a terrorist, militant Shi'a group backed by Iran, a whole set of other, not explicitly stated views about Islam as enraged against modernity, as addicted to gratuitous violence, and the like, comes into play, and these confirm the carefully engineered Israeli view during the invasion of Lebanon (reiterated by Judith Miller on CNN and the *New York Times* in its editorial opinion that Hizbollah is a terrorist organization) that the Lebanese guerrillas more or less deserve what they got. Miller once even said that the guerrillas were not from South Lebanon but from the Bekaa ("I know and I was there"), and were therefore cold-bloodedly putting women and children in the line of fire so as to prove Israeli murderousness. Alexander Cockburn in his column "Israel's Blitzkrieg" in the May 20, 1996 issue of *The Nation*, gives a further analysis of media coverage during the Lebanon crisis.

Stripped of any existential or historical context, these views of Islam as a violent and irrational religion that compels people to commit aggression against Israel in effect vitiate anything like the reporting of what takes place on the ground and deny it from inhabiting a more humane and more understandable context. By calling guerrillas "Iran backed Shi'ite militants" resistance is both dehumanized and rendered illegitimate. In his April 28 column Schmemann fails to find an adequate explanation for the last phases of the invasion as "a baffling endgame in the Mideast," except that "Because this is the Middle East—a phrase used as an old punch line to a long series of anecdotes that purport to explain situations that defy common logic. If there was any need to illustrate the genius of the format, last week had it all."

The misrepresentations and distortions committed in the portrayal of Islam today argue neither a genuine desire to understand nor a willingness to listen and see what there is to see and listen to.

Far from being naive or pragmatic accounts of Islam, the images and processes by which the media has delivered Islam for consideration to the Western consumer of news perpetuate hostility and ignorance for reasons very well analyzed by Noam Chomsky in a long series of books (*Manufacturing Consent* with Edward S. Herman, *The Culture of Terrorism*, and *Deterring Democracy* in particular). Yet, whatever motives we attribute to this situation, which, as I said at the outset, has become a good deal worse since *Covering Islam* first appeared in 1980, the fact is that precious little in the way of dialogue and exchange — both of which occur in scholarly debate, in artistic production, in the encounters between ordinary human beings who do business, interact, and generally talk *to*, as opposed to *at*, each other — makes it into the public domain so dominated by the mass media. Sensationalism, crude xenophobia, and insensitive belligerence are the order of the day, with results on both sides of the imaginary line between "us" and "them" that are extremely unedifying. My hope is that modest efforts such as this book will serve as an antidote in pointing up both what is wrong and what in the way of awareness and exploration might be done to mitigate so enormous an accumulation of negative effects.

In the revisions and updatings required for this new edition I was very ably assisted by my old friend Noubar Hovsepian; Mario Ortiz Robles and Andrew Rubin were especially helpful in bibliographic matters. Zaineb Istrabadi's assistance was crucial. And Shelley Wanger gave me the benefit of her superb editorial skills.

E. W. S.
October 31, 1996
New York

INTRODUCTION

This is the third and last in a series of books in which I have attempted to treat the modern relationship between the world of Islam, the Arabs, and the Orient on the one hand, and on the other the West: France, Britain, and in particular the United States. *Orientalism* is the most general; it traces the various phases of the relationship from the Napoleonic invasion of Egypt, through the main colonial period and the rise of modern Orientalist scholarship in Europe during the nineteenth century, up to the end of British and French imperial hegemony in the Orient after World War II and the emergence then and there of American dominance. The underlying theme of *Orientalism* is the affiliation of knowledge with power.[1] The second book, *The Question of Palestine*, provides a case history of the struggle between the native Arab, largely Muslim inhabitants of Palestine and the Zionist movement (later Israel), whose provenance and method of coming to grips with the "Oriental" realities of Palestine are largely Western. More explicitly than in *Orientalism*, my study of Palestine attempts also to describe what has been hidden beneath the surface of Western views of the Orient—in this case, the Palestinian national struggle for self-determination.[2]

In *Covering Islam* my subject is immediately contemporary: Western and specifically American responses to an Islamic world perceived, since the early seventies, as being immensely relevant and yet antipathetically troubled and problematic. Among the causes of this perception has been the acutely felt shortage of energy supply, with its focus on Arab and Persian Gulf oil, OPEC, and the dislocating effects on Western societies of inflation and dramatically expensive fuel bills. In addition, the Iranian revolution and the hostage crisis have furnished alarming evidence of what has come to be called "the return of Islam." Finally, there has been the resurgence of radical nationalism in the Islamic world and, as a peculiarly unfortunate adjunct to it, the return of intense superpower rivalry there. An example of the former is the Iran-Iraq war; the Soviet intervention in Afghanistan and American preparations for Rapid Deployment Forces in the Gulf region make up an example of the latter.

Even though the pun in "covering Islam" will be obvious to any reader proceeding through this book, a simple explanation is worth having at the outset. One of the points I make here and in *Orientalism* is that the term "Islam" as it is used today seems to mean one simple thing but in fact is part fiction, part ideological label, part minimal designation of a religion called Islam. In no really significant way is there a direct correspondence between the "Islam" in common Western usage and the enormously varied life that goes on within the world of Islam, with its more than 800,000,000 people, its millions of square miles of territory principally in Africa and Asia, its dozens of societies, states, histories, geographies, cultures. On the other hand, "Islam" is peculiarly traumatic news today in the West, for reasons that I discuss in the course of this book. During the past few years, especially since events in Iran caught European and

American attention so strongly, the media have therefore covered Islam: they have portrayed it, characterized it, analyzed it, given instant courses on it, and consequently they have made it "known."

But, as I have implied, this coverage—and with it the work of academic experts on Islam, geopolitical strategists who speak of "the crescent of crisis," cultural thinkers who deplore "the decline of the West"—is misleadingly full. It has given consumers of news the sense that they have understood Islam without at the same time intimating to them that a great deal in this energetic coverage is based on far from objective material. In many instances "Islam" has licensed not only patent inaccuracy but also expressions of unrestrained ethnocentrism, cultural and even racial hatred, deep yet paradoxically free-floating hostility. All this has taken place as part of what is presumed to be fair, balanced, responsible coverage of Islam. Aside from the fact that neither Christianity nor Judaism, both of them going through quite remarkable revivals (or "returns"), is treated in so emotional a way, there is an unquestioned assumption that Islam can be characterized limitlessly by means of a handful of recklessly general and repeatedly deployed clichés. And always it is supposed that the "Islam" being talked about is some real and stable object out there where "our" oil supplies happen to be found.

With this sort of coverage has gone a great deal of covering up. When the *New York Times* explains a surprisingly strong Iranian resistance to Iraq's incursion, it resorts to a formula about the "Shi'a penchant for martyrdom." Superficially, phrases like that have a certain plausibility, but in fact I think they are used to cover a great deal of what the reporter knows nothing about. Not knowing the language is only part of a much greater ignorance, for often enough the reporter is sent to a strange country with no preparation or experience, just because he or she is canny at picking up things quickly or happens already to be in the general vicinity of where front-page news is happening. So instead of trying to find out more about the country, the reporter takes hold of what is nearest at hand, usually a cliché or some bit of journalistic wisdom that readers at home are unlikely to challenge. With approximately three hundred reporters in Teheran during the first days of the hostage crisis, and without a Persian-speaker among them, it was no wonder that all the media reports coming out of Iran repeated essentially the same threadbare accounts of what was taking place; in the meantime, of course, other events and political processes in Iran that could not easily be characterized as instances of "the Islamic mentality" or of "anti-Americanism" went unnoticed.

Between them, the activities of *covering* and *covering up* Islam have almost eliminated consideration of the predicament of which they are symptoms: the general problem of knowing and living in a world that has become far too complex and various for easy and instant generalizations. Islam is both a typical case and, because its history in the West is so old and well defined, a special one. By this I mean that like so much of the postcolonial world, Islam belongs neither to Europe nor, like Japan, to the advanced industrial group of nations. It has been regarded as falling within the purview of "development perspectives," which is another mode of saying that Islamic societies were considered for at least three decades to be in need of "*modernization.*" The ideology of modernization produced a way of seeing Islam whose apex and culmination was the image of the shah of Iran, both at his zenith, as a "modern" ruler, and when his regime collapsed, as a casualty to what was looked upon as medieval fanatacism and religiosity.

On the other hand, "Islam" has always represented a particular menace to the West, for reasons I discussed in *Orientalism* and reexamine in this book. Of no other religion or cultural grouping can it be said so assertively as it is now said of Islam that it represents a threat to Western civilization. It is no accident that the turbulence and the upheavals which are now taking place in the Muslim world (and which have more to do with social, economic, and historical factors than they do unilaterally with Islam) have exposed the limitations of simple-minded Orientalist clichés about "fatalistic" Muslims *without* at the same time generating anything to put in their

place except nostalgia for the old days, when European armies
ruled almost the entire Muslim world, from the Indian subconti-
nent right across to North Africa. The recent success of books, journals, and public figures that argue for a reoccupation of the Gulf
region and justify the argument by referring to Islamic barbarism is
part of this phenomenon. It is no less remarkable that the times
have seen the emergence into American fame of "experts" like New
Zealand's J. B. Kelly, former professor of imperial history at Wisconsin, one-time adviser to Sheikh Zayid of Abu Dhabi,[3] now critical of Muslims and soft Westerners who, unlike Kelly, have sold out
to the oil Arabs. Not a single one of the occasionally critical reviews
of his book had anything to say about the astonishingly frank
atavism of his concluding paragraph, which for its sheer desire of
imperial conquest and its barely concealed racial attitudes deserves
quotation here:

> How much time may be left to Western Europe in which to
> preserve or recover its strategic inheritance east of Suez it is
> impossible to foretell. While the *pax Britannica* endured, that
> is to say, from the fourth or fifth decade of the nineteenth cen-
> tury to the middle years of this century, tranquility reigned in
> the Eastern Seas and around the shores of the Western Indian
> Ocean. An ephemeral calm still lingers there, the vestigial
> shadow of the old imperial order. If the history of the past four
> or five hundred years indicates anything, however, it is that
> this fragile peace cannot last much longer. Most of Asia is fast
> lapsing back into despotism, most of Africa into barbarism —
> into the condition, in short, they were in when Vasco da
> Gama first doubled the Cape to lay the foundations of Por-
> tuguese dominion in the East. . . . Oman is still the key to
> command of the Gulf and its seaward approaches, just as
> Aden remains the key to the passage of the Red Sea. The
> Western powers have already thrown away one of these keys;
> the other, however, is still within their reach. Whether, like

the captains-general of Portugal long ago, they have the bold-
ness to grasp it has yet to be seen.[4]

Although Kelly's suggestion that fifteenth- and sixteenth-century
Portuguese colonialism is the most appropriate guide for contemporary Western politicians may strike some readers as a little quaint,
it is his simplifications of history that are most representative of the
current mood. Colonialism brought tranquillity, he says, as if the
subjugation of millions of people amounted to no more than an
idyll and as if those were their best days; their abused feelings, their
distorted history, their unhappy destiny do not matter, so long as
"we" can continue to get what is useful to "us"—valuable resources,
geographically and politically strategic regions, a vast pool of cheap
native labor. The independence of countries in Africa and Asia after centuries of colonial dominion is dismissed as lapsing into barbarism or despotism. The only course left open, after what he
characterizes as the craven demise of the old imperial order, is a
new invasion according to Kelly. And underlying this invitation to
the West to take what is rightfully "ours" is a profound contempt for
the native Islamic culture of the Asia Kelly wishes "us" to rule.

Let us charitably leave aside the retrograde logic of Kelly's writing, which has brought him the respectful accolades of the American intellectual right wing from William F. Buckley to the *New
Republic*. What is more interesting about the outlook he presents is
how blanket solutions to messy, detailed problems are immediately
preferred to anything else, especially when they recommend force-
ful action against "Islam." No one says what might be taking place
inside Yemen, for example, or in Turkey, or across the Red Sea in
Sudan, Mauritania, Morocco, or even Egypt. Silence in the press,
which is busy covering the hostage crisis; silence in the academy,
which is busy advising the oil industry and the government on how
to forecast trends in the Gulf; silence in the government, which
looks for information only where "our" friends (such as the shah or

Anwar Sadat) direct us to look for it. "Islam" is only what holds the West's oil reserves; little else counts, little else deserves attention.

Given the current state of academic studies of Islam, there is not too much to be found there by way of rectification. In some ways the field as a whole is marginal to the general culture, while in others it is easily co-opted by the government and the corporations. Generally, this has disqualified it to cover Islam in ways that might tell us more than we are otherwise aware of beneath the surface of Islamic societies. Then, too, there are numerous methodological and intellectual problems that still need settling: Is there such a thing as Islamic behavior? What connects Islam at the level of everyday life to Islam at the level of doctrine in the various Islamic societies? How really useful is "Islam" as a concept for understanding Morocco *and* Saudi Arabia *and* Syria *and* Indonesia? If we come to realize that, as many scholars have recently noted, Islamic doctrine can be seen as justifying capitalism as well as socialism, militancy as well as fatalism, ecumenism as well as exclusivism, we begin to sense the tremendous lag between academic descriptions of Islam (that are inevitably caricatured in the media) and the particular realities to be found within the Islamic world.

Yet there is a consensus on "Islam" as a kind of scapegoat for everything we do not happen to like about the world's new political, social, and economic patterns. For the right, Islam represents barbarism; for the left, medieval theocracy; for the center, a kind of distasteful exoticism. In all camps, however, there is agreement that even though little enough is known about the Islamic world there is not much to be approved of there. What there is of value in Islam is principally its anticommunism, with the additional irony that almost invariably anticommunism in the Islamic world has been synonymous with repressive pro-American regimes. Pakistan's Zia al-Haq is a perfect case in point.

Far from being a defense of Islam—a project as unlikely as it is futile for my purposes—this book describes the uses of "Islam" for the West and, though I spend less time doing it, for many Islamic societies. Thus to criticize the abuses of Islam in the West does not by any means entail condoning them within Islamic societies. The fact is that in many—too many—Islamic societies repression, the abrogation of personal freedoms, unrepresentative and often minority regimes, are either falsely legitimated or casuistically explained with reference to Islam, which is doctrinally as blameless in this regard as any other of the great universal religions. The abuses of Islam also happen to correspond in many instances with the inordinate power and authority of the central state.

Nevertheless I believe that even if we do not blame everything that is unhealthy about the Islamic world on the West, we must be able to see the connection between what the West has been saying about Islam and what, reactively, various Muslim societies have done. The dialectic between the two—given that for many parts of the Islamic world the West, whether as former colonizing power or as present trading partner, is a very important interlocutor—has produced a species of what Thomas Franck and Edward Weisband have called "word politics,"[5] which it is the purpose of this book to analyze and explain. The back-and-forth between the West and Islam, the challenging and the answering, the opening of certain rhetorical spaces and the closing of others: all this makes up the "word politics" by which each side sets up situations, justifies actions, forecloses options, and presses alternatives on the other. Thus, when Iranians seized the United States Embassy in Teheran they were responding, not just to the former shah's entry into the United States, but to what they perceived as a long history of humiliation inflicted on them by superior American power: past American actions "spoke" to them of constant intervention in their lives, and therefore as Muslims who, they felt, had been held prisoner in their own country, they took American prisoners and held them as hostages on United States territory, the Teheran embassy. Although the actions themselves made the point, it was the words, and the movements of power they adumbrated, that prepared the way and, to a very great extent, made the actions possible.

This pattern is, I think, of very great importance because it underscores the close affiliation between language and political reality, at least so far as discussions of Islam are concerned. The hardest thing to get most academic experts on Islam to admit is that what they say and do as scholars is set in a profoundly and in some ways an offensively political context. Everything about the study of Islam in the contemporary West is saturated with political importance, but hardly any writers on Islam, whether expert or general, admit the fact in what they say. Objectivity is assumed to inhere in learned discourse about other societies, despite the long history of political, moral, and religious concern felt in all societies, Western or Islamic, about the alien, the strange and different. In Europe, for example, the Orientalist has traditionally been affiliated directly with colonial offices: What we have just begun to learn about the extent of close cooperation between scholarship and direct military colonial conquest (as in the case of the revered Dutch Orientalist C. Snouck Hurgronje, who used the confidence he had won from Muslims to plan and execute the brutal Dutch war against the Atjehnese people of Sumatra[6]) is both edifying and depressing. Yet books and articles continue to pour forth extolling the nonpolitical nature of Western scholarship, the fruits of Orientalist learning, and the value of "objective" expertise. At the very same time there is scarcely an expert on "Islam" who has not been a consultant or even an employee of the government, the various corporations, the media. My point is that the cooperation must be admitted and taken into account, not just for moral reasons, but for intellectual reasons as well.

Let us say that discourse on Islam is, if not absolutely vitiated, then certainly colored by the political, economic, and intellectual situation in which it arises: this is as true of East as it is of West. For many evident reasons, it is not too much of an exaggeration to say that *all* discourse on Islam has an interest in some authority or power. On the other hand, I do not mean to say that all scholarship or writing about Islam is therefore useless. Quite the contrary; I think it is often more useful than not, and very revealing as an index of what interest is being served. I cannot say for sure whether in matters having to do with human society there is such a thing as absolute truth or perfectly true knowledge; perhaps such things exist in the abstract—a proposition I do not find hard to accept—but in present reality truth about such matters as "Islam" is relative to who produces it. It will be noted that such a position does not rule out gradations of knowledge (good, bad, indifferent), nor the possibility of saying things accurately. It simply asks that anyone speaking about "Islam" remember what any beginning student of literature knows: that the writing or reading of texts about human reality brings into play many more factors than can be accounted for (or protected) by labels like "objective."

This is why I take pains to identify the situation out of which statements arise, and why it seems important to note the various groups in society that have an interest in "Islam." For the West generally and the United States in particular, the confluence of power bearing upon "Islam" is notable, as much for its component groups (the academy, the corporations, the media, the government) as for the relative absence of dissent from the orthodoxy it has created. The result has been a gross simplification of "Islam," so that numerous manipulative aims can be realized, from the stirring up of a new Cold War, to the instigation of racial antipathy, to mobilization for a possible invasion, to the continued denigration of Muslims and Arabs.[7] Little of this is, I believe, in the interest of truth; certainly the truth of these manipulative aims is always denied. Instead we have the statements made and the aims served with a shroud of scholarly, even scientific expertise draped over them. An amusing consequence is that when Muslim countries donate money to American universities for Arab or Islamic studies, a great liberal outcry arises about foreign interference in the American university, but when Japan or Germany donates money no such complaint can be heard.

As for the impact of corporate pressures on the university, that, too, is generally regarded as being in the salutary nature of things.[8]

Lest I seem to conform too closely to Oscar Wilde's definition of a cynic—that he knows the price of everything and the value of nothing—I should say finally that I recognize the need for informed expert opinion; that the United States as a great power is likely to have attitudes toward and therefore policies for the outside world that smaller powers do not; that there is great hope for improvement in the dismal situation now prevailing. Nevertheless, I do not believe as strongly and as firmly in the notion of "Islam" as many experts, policymakers, and general intellectuals do; on the contrary, I often think it has been more of a hindrance than a help in understanding what moves people and societies. But what I really believe in is the existence of a critical sense and of citizens able and willing to use it to get beyond the special interests of experts and their *idées reçues*. By using the skills of a good critical reader to disentangle sense from nonsense, by asking the right questions and expecting pertinent answers, anyone can learn about either "Islam" or the world of Islam and about the men, women, and cultures that live within it, speak its languages, breathe its air, produce its histories and societies. At that point, humanistic knowledge begins and communal responsibility for that knowledge begins to be shouldered. I wrote this book to advance that goal.

Parts of Chapter One and Chapter Two have appeared in *The Nation* and the *Columbia Journalism Review*. I am particularly grateful to Robert Manoff, who during his all-too-brief tenure as editor of the *Columbia Journalism Review* made it an exciting publication.

In the course of gathering material for sections of this book I was ably assisted by Douglas Baldwin and Philip Shehadé. Paul Lipari prepared the manuscript in its final form with his usual literate skill and efficiency. To Albert Said I am grateful for assistance given generously.

I owe a special debt to my dear comrade Eqbal Ahmad, whose encyclopedic knowledge and constant solicitude have sustained so

many of us during confusing and trying times. James Peck read the
manuscript in one of its earlier versions and gave me brilliantly detailed suggestions for revision, although of course he is in no way responsible for its still remaining faults. I am pleased to acknowledge
his indispensable help. Jeanne Morton of Pantheon Books copy-
edited the manuscript with tact and vigilance, and to her I am most
grateful. I should also like to thank André Schiffrin.

Mariam Said, to whom this book is dedicated, virtually kept its
author alive during its writing. For her love, her companionship,
and her animating presence, my heartfelt thanks.

E.W.S.
October 1980
New York

POSTSCRIPT

On January 20, 1981, the fifty-two Americans held prisoner in the
United States Embassy for 444 days finally left Iran. A few days later
they arrived in the United States to be greeted by the country's genuine happiness in seeing them back. The "hostage return," as it
came to be called, became a week-long media event. There were
many frequently intrusive and maudlin hours of live television coverage as the "returnees" were transported to Algeria, then to Germany, then to West Point, to Washington, and at last to their various
home towns. Most newspapers and national weeklies ran supple-
ments on the return, ranging from learned analyses of how the final
agreement between Iran and the United States was arrived at, and
what it involved, to celebrations of American heroism and Iranian
barbarism. Interspersed were personal stories of the hostage ordeal,
often embroidered by enterprising journalists and what seemed an
alarmingly available number of psychiatrists eager to explain what
the hostages were *really* going through. Insofar as there was serious
discussion of the past and of the future that went beyond the level of
the yellow ribbons designated as symbolic of Iranian captivity, the

new administration set the tone and determined the limits. Analysis of the past was focused on whether the United States should have made (and whether it ought to honor) the agreement with Iran. On January 31, 1981, the *New Republic* predictably attacked "the ransom," and the Carter administration for giving in to terrorists; then it condemned the whole "legally controvertible proposition" of dealing with Iranian demands, as well as the use as intermediary of Algeria, a country "well practiced at giving refuge to terrorists and laundering the ransoms they bring." Discussion of the future was constrained by the Reagan administration's declared war on terrorism; this, not human rights, was to be the new priority of United States policy, even to the extent of supporting "moderately repressive regimes" if they happen to be allies.

Accordingly, Peter C. Stuart reported in the *Christian Science Monitor* of January 29, 1981, that congressional hearings were likely to be scheduled on "the terms of the hostage release agreement . . . treatment of the hostages . . . embassy security . . . [and as a kind of afterthought] future U.S.-Iran relations." Very much in keeping with the narrowly focused range of problems explored by the media during the crisis (with few exceptions), there was no careful scrutiny of what the Iranian trauma has meant, what it suggests about the future, what might be learned from it. The London *Sunday Times* reported on January 26 that before he left office President Carter allegedly advised the State Department to "focus all public attention on building up a wave of resentment against the Iranians." Whether or not this was in fact true, it appeared to be plausible at least, since no public official and few columnists and journalists were interested in reevaluating the long American history of intervention in Iran and other parts of the Islamic world. There was much talk of stationing forces in the Middle East; conversely, when the Islamic summit was held in Taif during the last week in January, the United States media all but ignored it.

Ideas about retribution and loud assertions of American force were accompanied by a symphonic elaboration of the hostages'

ordeal and triumphant return. The victims were directly transmuted into heroes (understandably upsetting various veterans' and
former-POW groups) and symbols of freedom, their captors into
subhuman beasts. To this end the *New York Times* said editorially on
January 22, "let there be rage and revulsion in those first hours of release," and then, having reflected for a while, came up with the following questions on January 28: "What should have been done?
Mining harbors, or landing marines, or dropping a few bombs
might frighten rational foes. But was Iran—*is* Iran—rational?" Certainly, as Fred Halliday wrote in the *Los Angeles Times* on January
25, there was much to be critical of in Iran, religion and unceasing
revolutionary turmoil having proved incapable of providing a modern state with the kind of day-to-day decisions likely to benefit the
population at large. Internationally Iran was isolated and vulnerable. And certainly it was just as clear that the students at the embassy had not been gentle with their prisoners. Yet not even the
fifty-two themselves went so far as to say that they had been tortured
or systematically brutalized: this emerges in the transcript of their
news conference at West Point (see the *New York Times*, January
28), where Elizabeth Swift says quite explicitly that *Newsweek* lied
about what she said, inventing a story about torture (much ampli-
fied by the media) that had nothing to do with the facts.

It was the leap from a specific experience—unpleasant, anguished,
miserably long in duration—to huge generalizations about Iran and
Islam that the hostage return licensed in the media and in the culture at large. Once again, in other words, the political dynamics of a
complex historical experience were simply effaced in the service of an
extraordinary amnesia. We were back to the old basics. Iranians were
reduced to "fundamentalist screwballs" by Bob Ingle in the *Atlanta
Constitution* on January 23; Claire Sterling in the *Washington Post* on
January 23 argued that the Iran story was an aspect of "Fright Decade
I," the war against civilization by terrorists. To Bill Green on the
same page of the *Post*, "the Iranian obscenity" raised the possibility
that "freedom of the press," which presented news about Iran, might

be "perverted into a weapon aimed directly at the heart of American nationalism and self-esteem." This remarkable combination of confidence and insecurity is somewhat deflated by Green when he asks a little later whether the press helped "us" to understand "the Iranians' revolution," a question easily answered by Martin Kondracke in the *Wall Street Journal*, January 29, who wrote that "American television [with scant exceptions] treated the Iran crisis either as a freak show, featuring self-flagellants and fist-wavers, or as a soap opera."

There were some journalists, however, who were genuinely reflective. H. D. S. Greenway acknowledged in the *Boston Globe* on January 21 that "there was damage done to U.S. interests by the American obsession with the hostage crisis to the exclusion of other, pressing issues," but he was able to arrive at one clear conclusion: "The realities of a pluralistic world will not change and the new Administration will be bound by the practical limits of power in the late 20th century." Writing in the *Globe* on the same day, Steven Erlanger praised Carter for having defused the crisis and thereby succeeding in making the debate conducive to "less passion and more reason." For its part, the *New Republic* (January 31) censured "the ever-accommodating *Globe*," which is to say that Iran is best treated as an aberration in the process of rebuilding American power and of fighting communism. Indeed, this essentially militant line was elevated to the rank of quasi-official American ideology. In "The Purposes of American Power" (*Foreign Affairs*, Winter 1980–81) Robert W. Tucker claims to be steering a new course between proponents of "resurgent America" and "isolationism." Yet, for the Persian Gulf and Central America he proposes a policy of frank interventionism since, he says, the United States can "allow" neither changes in internal order there nor the spread of Soviet influence. In either event, it would be up to the United States to decide what constitutes allowable and nonallowable changes. Thus a like-minded colleague, Richard Pipes of Harvard, suggested that the new administration reclassify the world into two simple camps: procommunist nations and anticommunist nations.

If the return to the Cold War seems on one level to entail a new assertiveness, it has also encouraged a renaissance of self-delusion. Enemies include anyone who asks the West to consider its past, not so much out of guilt as out of self-awareness: such people are simply to be ignored. A symbolically powerful instance of this took place during the West Point press conference. A person in the audience declared that it was "the height of hypocrisy for the United States government to talk about torture" when the United States had abetted the mutilation of Iranians during the Pahlevi era. Bruce Laingen, the Teheran embassy's *chargé d'affaires* and the United States' senior diplomat in Iran, said twice that he had not heard the question, then moved rapidly to the more congenial subject of Iranian brutality and American innocence.

No expert, media personality, or government official seemed to wonder what might have happened if a small fraction of the time spent on isolating, dramatizing, and covering the unlawful embassy seizure and the hostage return had been spent exposing oppression and brutality during the ex-shah's regime. Was there no limit to the idea of using the vast information-gathering apparatus to inform the justifiably anxious public about what was really taking place in Iran? Did the alternatives have to be limited either to stirring up patriotic feelings or to fueling a kind of mass anger at crazy Iran?

These are not idle questions, now that this lamentably exaggerated episode is over. It will be beneficial as well as practical for Americans in particular, Westerners in general, to puzzle out the changing configurations in world politics. Is "Islam" going to be confined to the role of terroristic oil-supplier? Are journals and investigations to focus on "who lost Iran," or will debate and reflection be better employed around topics more suited to world community and peaceful development?

Hints of how the media, for example, might responsibly use their enormous capability for public information were to be found in the three-hour special broadcast by ABC, "The Secret Negotiations," on January 22 and 28, 1981. In exposing the various methods used to free the hostages, the broadcasts put forth an impressive amount of unknown material, little of it more telling than those moments when unconscious and deep-seated attitudes were suddenly illuminated.

One such moment occurs when Christian Bourguet describes his late March 1980 meeting with Jimmy Carter at the White House. Bourguet, a French lawyer with ties to the Iranians, acted as an intermediary between the United States and Iran; he had come to Washington because, despite an arrangement worked out with the Panamanians to arrest the ex-shah, the deposed ruler had left suddenly for Egypt. So they were back to square one:

BOURGUET: At a given moment [Carter] spoke of the hostages, saying, you understand that these are Americans. These are innocents. I said to him, yes, Mr. President, I understand that you say they are innocent. But I believe you have to understand that for the Iranians they aren't innocent. Even if personally none of them has committed an act, they are not innocent because they are diplomats who represent a country that has done a number of things in Iran.

You must understand that it is not against their person that the action is being taken. Of course, you can see that. They have not been harmed. They have not been hurt. No attempt has been made to kill them. You must understand that it is a symbol, that it is on the plane of symbols that we have to think about this matter.*

In fact Carter does seem to have viewed the embassy seizure in symbolic terms, but unlike the Frenchman, he had his own frame of reference. To him Americans were by definition innocent and in a sense outside history: Iran's grievances against the United States, he would say on another occasion, were ancient history. What mattered now was that Iranians were terrorists, and perhaps had always

*Transcript provided courtesy of Veronica Pollard, ABC, New York.

been potentially a terrorist nation. Indeed, anyone who disliked America and held Americans captive was dangerous and sick, beyond rationality, beyond humanity, beyond common decency.

Carter's inability to connect what some foreigners felt about the United States' longstanding support for local dictators with what was happening to the Americans held unlawfully in Teheran is extraordinarily symptomatic. Even if one completely opposes the hostage-taking, and even if one has only positive feelings about the hostages' return, there are alarming lessons to be learned from what seems like the official national tendency to be oblivious to certain realities. All relationships between people and nations involve two sides. Nothing at all enjoins "us" to like or approve of "them," but we must at least recognize (a) that "they" are there, and (b) that so far as "they" are concerned "we" are what we are, plus what they have experienced and known of us. This is not a matter of innocence or guilt, nor of patriotism and treason. Neither side commands reality so totally as to disregard the other. Unless, of course, we believe as Americans that whereas the other side is ontologically guilty, we are innocent.

Consider now, as another item usefully presented by the media, the confidential cable sent from Teheran by Bruce Laingen to Secretary of State Vance on August 13, 1979, a document entirely consistent with Carter's attitude in his conversations with Bourguet. It was published on the *New York Times* op-ed page January 27, 1981, perhaps to help focus the nation on what Iranians are really like, perhaps only as an ironic footnote to the recently ended crisis. Yet Laingen's message is not a scientific account of "the Persian psyche" he discusses, despite the author's pretense to calm objectivity and to expert knowledge of the culture. The text is rather an ideological statement designed, I think, to turn "Persia" into a timeless, acutely disturbing essence, thereby enhancing the superior morality and national sanity of the American half of the negotiations. Thus each assertion about "Persia" *adds* damaging evidence to the profile while shielding "America" from scrutiny and analysis.

This self-blinding is accomplished rhetorically in two ways that are worth looking at closely. First, history is eliminated unilaterally: "the effects of the Iranian revolution" are set aside in the interests of the "relatively constant . . . cultural and psychological qualities" underlying "the Persian psyche." Hence modern Iran becomes ageless Persia. The unscientific version of this operation has Italians becoming dagoes, Jews yids, blacks niggers, and so on. (How refreshingly honest is the street fighter as compared with the polite diplomat!) Second, the "Persian" national character is portrayed with reference only to the Iranians' imagined (i.e., paranoid) sense of reality. Laingen neither credits the Iranians' experience of real treachery and suffering nor grants them the right to have arrived at a view of the United States based on what, as they see it, the United States actually did in Iran. This is not to say that the United States did *not* do anything in Iran; it only means that the United States is entitled to do what it pleases, without irrelevant complaints or reactions from Iranians. The only thing that counts for Laingen in Iran is the *constant* "Persian psyche" that overrides all other realities.

Most readers of the Laingen message will concede, as doubtless he does too, that one should not reduce other people or societies to such a simple and stereotypical core. We do not today allow that public discourse should treat blacks and Jews that way, just as we would (and do) laugh off Iranian portrayals of America as the Great Satan. Too simple, too ideological, too racist. But for this particular enemy, Persia, the reduction serves, as it did when the *New Republic*'s Martin Peretz reproduced a page of manifestly racist prose (February 7, 1981) by a seventeenth-century Englishman on "The Turk," called it a "classic" for students of Middle Eastern culture, and then said it tells us how Muslims behave. One wonders how Peretz would react if a page of seventeenth-century prose on "The Jew" were printed today as a guide for understanding "Jewish" behavior. The question is what exactly such documents as Laingen's or Peretz's serve if, as I shall argue, they neither teach one anything about Islam or Iran nor, given the existing tension between the

United States and Iran after the revolution, have helped to guide Western actions there.

Laingen's argument is that no matter what happens, there is a "Persian proclivity" to resist "the very concept of a rational (from the Western point of view) negotiating process." We can be rational: Persians cannot. Why? Because, he says, they are overridingly ego-istical; reality for them is malevolent; the "bazaar mentality" urges immediate advantage over long-term gain; the omnipotent god of Islam makes it impossible for them to understand causality; for them words and reality are not connected. In sum, according to the five lessons he abstracts from his analysis, Laingen's "Persian" is an unreliable negotiator, having neither a sense of "the other side," nor a capacity for trust nor for good will, nor character enough to carry out what his words promise.

The elegance of this modest proposal is that literally everything imputed to the Persian or Muslim, without any evidence at all, can be applied to "the American," that quasi-fictional, unnamed author behind the message. Who but "the American" denies history and re-ality in saying unilaterally that these mean nothing to "the Persian"? Now play the following parlor game: find a major Judeo-Christian cultural and social equivalent for the traits that Laingen ascribes to "the Persian." Overriding egoism? Rousseau. Malevolence of real-ity? Kafka. Omnipotence of God? Old and New Testaments. Lack of causal sense? Beckett. Bazaar mentality? The New York Stock Ex-change. Confusion between words and reality? Austin and Searle. But few people would construct a portrait of the essential West using only Christopher Lasch on narcissism, the words of a fundamental-ist preacher, Plato's *Cratylus*, an advertising jingle or two, and (as a case of the West's inability to believe in a stable or beneficent real-ity) Ovid's *Metamorphoses* laced with choice verses from Leviticus.

Laingen's message is a functional equivalent of such a portrait. In a different context it would appear a caricature at best, a crude and not particularly damaging attack at worst. It is not even effective as a bit of psy-war, since it reveals the writer's weaknesses more than his opponent's. It shows, for example, that the author is extremely nervous about his opposite number, and that he cannot see others except as a mirror image of himself. Where is his capacity for understanding the *Iranian* point of view or for that matter the Islamic Revolution itself, which one would suppose had been the direct result of intolerable *Persian* tyranny and the need for overthrowing it?

And as for good will and trust in the rationality of the negotiating process, even if the events of 1953 were not mentioned, much could be said about the attempted army coup against the revolution, directly encouraged by the United States' General Huyser in late January 1979. Then, too, there was the action of various United States banks (unusually compliant in bending the rules to suit the shah) who during 1979 were prepared to cancel Iranian loans contracted in 1977 on the grounds that Iran had not paid the interest on time; *Le Monde*'s Eric Rouleau reported on November 25–26, 1979, that he had seen proof that Iran had actually paid the interest *ahead* of time. No wonder "the Persian" assumes his opposite number is an adversary. He *is* an adversary, and an insecure one at that: Laingen says it plainly.

But let us concede that the issue is not fairness but accuracy. The United States' man-on-the-spot is advising Washington. What does he rely on? A handful of Orientalist clichés that could have been taken verbatim from Sir Alfred Lyall's description of the Eastern mind, or from Lord Cromer's account of dealing with the natives in Egypt. If according to Laingen, Ibrahim Yazdi, then foreign minister of Iran, resists the idea that "Iranian behavior has consequences on the perception of Iran in the United States," which American decision-maker was prepared to accept in advance that American behavior had consequences on the perception of the United States in Iran? Why then was the shah admitted here? Or do we, like the Persians, have an "aversion to accepting responsibility for one's own action"?

Laingen's message is the product of uninformed, unintelligent power and certainly adds little to one's understanding of other societies. As an instance of how we might confront the world, it does not inspire confidence. As an inadvertent *American* self-portrait it is frankly insulting. What use is it, then? It tells us how United States representatives, and with them a good part of the Orientalist establishment, have created a reality that corresponds neither to our world nor to Iran's. But if it does not also demonstrate how such misrepresentations had better be thrown away forever, then Americans are in for more international troubles and, alas, their innocence will again be uselessly offended.

Granted that Iran and the United States have undergone wrenching unpleasantness, and granted too that the embassy seizure turned out to be an index of an overall Iranian lapse into unproductive, retrogressive chaos. Still, there is no need complacently to glean insufficient wisdom from recent history. The fact is that change is taking place in "Islam" much as it is taking place in "the West." The modes and paces are different, but some dangers and some uncertainties are similar. As rallying cries for their constituencies, "Islam" and "the West" (or "America") provide incitement more than insight. As equal and opposite reactions to the disorientations of new actualities, "Islam" and "the West" can turn analysis into simple polemic, experience into fantasy. Respect for the concrete detail of human experience, understanding that arises from viewing the Other compassionately, knowledge gained and diffused through moral and intellectual honesty: surely these are better, if not easier, goals at present than confrontation and reductive hostility. And if in the process we can dispose finally of both the residual hatred and the offensive generality of labels like "the Muslim," "the Persian," "the Turk," "the Arab," or "the Westerner," then so much the better.

E.W.S.
February 9, 1981
New York

COVERING ISLAM

CHAPTER
ONE

ISLAM AS NEWS

I. ISLAM AND THE WEST

In order to make a point about alternative energy sources for Americans, Consolidated Edison of New York (Con Ed) ran a striking television advertisement in the summer of 1980. Film clips of various immediately recognizable OPEC personalities—Yamani, Qaddafi, lesser-known robed Arab figures—alternated with stills as well as clips of other people associated with oil and Islam: Khomeini, Arafat, Hafez al-Assad. None of these figures was mentioned by name, but we were told ominously that "these men" control America's sources of oil. The solemn voice-over in the background made no reference to who "these men" actually are or where they come from, leaving it to be felt that this all-male cast of villains has placed Americans in the grip of an unrestrained sadism. It was enough for "these men" to appear as they have appeared in newspapers and on television for American viewers to feel a combination of anger, resentment, and fear. And it is this combination of feelings that Con

Ed instantly aroused and exploited for domestic commercial reasons, just as a year earlier Stuart Eizenstat, President Carter's domestic policy adviser and now a senior official in the Clinton administration, had urged the president that "with strong steps we [should] mobilize the nation around a real crisis and with a clear enemy—OPEC."

There are two things about the Con Ed commercial that, taken together, form the subject of this book. One, of course, is Islam, or rather the image of Islam in the West generally and in the United States in particular. The other is the use of that image in the West and especially in the United States. As we shall see, these are connected in ways that ultimately reveal as much about the West and the United States as they do, in a less concrete and interesting way, about Islam. But let us first consider the history of relationships between Islam and the Christian West before we go on to examine the current phase.

From at least the end of the eighteenth century until our own day, modern Occidental reactions to Islam have been dominated by a radically simplified type of thinking that may still be called Orientalist. The general basis of Orientalist thought is an imaginative and yet drastically polarized geography dividing the world into two unequal parts, the larger, "different" one called the Orient, the other, also known as "our" world, called the Occident or the West.[1] Such divisions always come about when one society or culture thinks about another one, different from it; but it is interesting that even when the Orient has uniformly been considered an inferior part of the world, it has always been endowed both with greater size and with a greater potential for power (usually destructive) than the West. Insofar as Islam has always been seen as belonging to the Orient, its particular fate within the general structure of Orientalism has been to be looked at first of all as if it were one monolithic thing, and then with a very special hostility and fear. There are, of course, many religious, psychological, and political reasons for this, but all of these reasons derive from a sense that so far as the West is concerned, Islam represents not only a formidable competitor but also a latecoming challenge to Christianity.

For most of the Middle Ages and during the early part of the Renaissance in Europe, Islam was believed to be a demonic religion of apostasy, blasphemy, and obscurity.[2] It did not seem to matter that Muslims considered Mohammed a prophet and not a god; what mattered to Christians was that Mohammed was a false prophet, a sower of discord, a sensualist, a hypocrite, an agent of the devil. Nor was this view of Mohammed strictly a doctrinal one. Real events in the real world made of Islam a considerable political force. For hundreds of years great Islamic armies and navies threatened Europe, destroyed its outposts, colonized its domains. It was as if a younger, more virile and energetic version of Christianity had arisen in the East, equipped itself with the learning of the ancient Greeks, invigorated itself with a simple, fearless, and warlike creed, and set about destroying Christianity. Even when the world of Islam entered a period of decline and Europe a period of ascendancy, fear of "Mohammedanism" persisted. Closer to Europe than any of the other non-Christian religions, the Islamic world by its very adjacency evoked memories of its encroachments on Europe, and always, of its latent power again and again to disturb the West. Other great civilizations of the East—India and China among them—could be thought of as defeated and distant and hence not a constant worry. Only Islam seemed never to have submitted completely to the West; and when, after the dramatic oil-price rises of the early 1970s, the Muslim world seemed once more on the verge of repeating its early conquests, the whole West seemed to shudder. The onset of "Islamic terrorism" in the 1980s and 1990s has deepened and intensified the shock.

Then in 1978 Iran occupied center stage, causing Americans to feel increasing anxiety and passion. Few nations so distant and different from the United States have so intensely engaged Americans. Never have Americans seemed so paralyzed, so seemingly powerless to stop one dramatic event after another from happening. And never in all this could they put Iran out of mind, since on so many levels the country impinged on their lives with a defiant obtrusiveness. Iran was a major oil supplier during a period of energy scarcity. It lies in a region of the world that is commonly regarded as volatile and strategically vital. An important ally, it lost its imperial regime, its army, its value in American global calculations during a year of tumultuous revolutionary upheaval virtually unprecedented on so huge a scale since October 1917. A new order which called itself Islamic, and appeared to be popular and anti-imperialist, was struggling to be born. Ayatollah Khomeini's image and presence took over the media, which failed to make much of him except that he was obdurate, powerful, and deeply angry at the United States. Finally, as a result of the ex-shah's entry into the United States on October 22, 1979, the United States Embassy in Teheran was captured by a group of students on November 4; many American hostages were held, and then released several months later.

Reactions to what took place in Iran did not occur in a vacuum. Further back in the public's subliminal cultural consciousness, there was the longstanding attitude to Islam, the Arabs, and the Orient in general that I have been calling Orientalism. For whether one looked at such recent, critically acclaimed fiction as V. S. Naipaul's A Bend in the River and John Updike's The Coup, or at grade-school history textbooks, comic strips, television serials, films, and cartoons, the iconography of Islam was uniform, was uniformly ubiquitous, and drew its material from the same time-honored view of Islam: hence the frequent caricatures of Muslims as oil suppliers, as terrorists, and more recently, as bloodthirsty mobs. Conversely, there has been very little place either in the culture generally or in discourse about non-Westerners in particular to speak or even to think about, much less to portray, Islam or anything Islamic sympathetically. Most people, if asked to name a modern Islamic writer, would probably be able to pick only Khalil Gibran (who wasn't Islamic). The academic experts whose specialty is Islam have generally treated the religion and its various cultures within an invented or culturally determined ideological framework filled with passion, defensive prejudice, sometimes even revulsion; because of this framework, *understanding* of Islam has been a very difficult thing to achieve. And to judge from the various in-depth media studies and interviews on the Iranian revolution during the spring of 1979, there has been little inclination to accept the revolution itself as much more than a defeat for the United States (which in a very specific sense, of course, it was), or a victory of dark over light.

The preoccupation with Iran continues into the 1990s. With the end of the Cold War it, and along with it "Islam," has come to represent America's major foreign devil. It is considered to be a terrorist state because it backs groups like Hizbollah in South Lebanon—an organization founded after the Israeli invasion of Lebanon specifically to fight Israeli occupation of a sizable strip of South Lebanon—and is seen as an exporter of fundamentalism, and is especially feared for its unbowed opposition to United States hegemony in the Middle East, the Gulf in particular. Robin Wright, the *Los Angeles Times*'s main expert on Islam, wrote in a column dated January 26, 1991, that United States and Western government officials were still looking for a strategy to deal with the "Islamic challenge," and she quotes an unnamed "senior" Bush administration official as conceding that "we have to be smarter in dealing with Islam than in dealing with communism 30 or 40 years ago." The danger of simplifying a "myriad of countries" was noted, but the only picture in the five column piece was of Ayatollah Khomeini. He, and Iran, embodied all that was objectionable about Islam, from terrorism and anti-Westernism to being "the only major monotheistic nation offering a set of rules by which to govern society as well as a set of spiritual beliefs." That even in Iran there was a major, on-going dispute about what those rules were, and even what "Islam" was, plus a vociferous debate that contested Khomeini's legacy, were not mentioned. It was enough to use the word "Islam" to cover what "we" were worried about on a world scale. To aggravate matters, the Clinton administration introduced legislation penalizing

other countries for doing business with Iran (and Libya, as well
as Cuba).

V. S. Naipaul's role in helping to clarify this general hostility
toward Islam is an interesting one. In an interview published in
Newsweek International (August 18, 1980) he spoke about a book he
was writing on "Islam," and then volunteered that "Muslim fundamentalism has no intellectual substance to it, therefore it must col-
lapse." What Muslim fundamentalism he was referring to specifically,
and what sort of intellectual substance he had in mind, he did not
say: Iran was undoubtedly meant, but so too—in equally vague
terms—was the whole postwar wave of Islamic anti-imperialism in
the Third World, for which Naipaul has developed a particularly intense antipathy, as demonstrated in his *Among the Believers: An Islamic Journey.* In *Guerrillas* and *A Bend in the River,* among Naipaul's
most recent novels, Islam is in question, and it is part of Naipaul's
general (and with liberal Western readers, popular) indictment of
the Third World that he lumps together the corrupt viciousness of a
few grotesque rulers, the end of European colonialism, and post-
colonial efforts at rebuilding native societies as instances of an over-
all intellectual failure in Africa and Asia. "Islam" plays a major part
according to Naipaul, whether it is in the use of Islamic surnames
by pathetic West Indian guerrillas, or in the vestiges of the African
slave trade. For Naipaul and his readers, "Islam" somehow is made
to cover everything that one most disapproves of from the standpoint of civilized, and Western, rationality.[3]

It is as if discriminations between religious passion, a struggle for
a just cause, ordinary human weakness, political competition, and
the history of men, women, and societies seen *as* the history of men,
women, and societies cannot be made when "Islam," or the Islam
now at work in Iran and in other parts of the Muslim world, is dealt
with by novelists, reporters, policy-makers, "experts." "Islam" seems
to engulf all aspects of the diverse Muslim world, reducing them all
to a special malevolent and unthinking essence. Instead of analysis
and understanding as a result, there can be for the most part only

the crudest form of us-versus-them. Whatever Iranians or Muslims say about their sense of justice, their history of oppression, their vision of their own societies, seems irrelevant; what counts for the United States instead is what the "Islamic revolution" is doing right now, how many people have been executed by the Komitehs, how many bizarre outrages the Ayatollah, in the name of Islam, used to order. Of course no one has equated the Jonestown massacre or the destructive horror of the Oklahoma bombing or the devastation of Indochina with Christianity, or with Western or American culture at large; that sort of equation has been reserved for "Islam."

old examples

Why is it that a whole range of political, cultural, social, and even economic events has often seemed reducible in so Pavlovian a way to "Islam"? What is it about "Islam" that provokes so quick and unrestrained a response? In what way do "Islam" and the Islamic world differ for Westerners from, say, the rest of the Third World and, during the Cold War, the Soviet Union? These are far from simple questions, and they must therefore be answered piecemeal, with many qualifications and much differentiation.

Labels purporting to name very large and complex realities are notoriously vague and at the same time unavoidable. If it is true that "Islam" is an imprecise and ideologically loaded label, it is also true that "the West" and "Christianity" are just as problematic. Yet there is no easy way of avoiding these labels, since Muslims speak of Islam, Christians of Christianity, Westerners of the West, Jews of Judaism, and all of them about all the others in ways that seem to be both convincing and exact. Instead of trying to propose ways of going around the labels, I think it is more immediately useful to admit at the outset that they exist and have long been in use as an integral part of cultural history rather than as objective classifications: A little later in this chapter I shall speak about them as interpretations produced for and by what I shall call communities of interpretation. We must therefore remember that "Islam," "the West," and even "Christianity" function in at least two different ways, and produce at least two meanings, each time they are used. First, they perform a simple identifying function, as when we say Khomeini is a Muslim, or Pope John Paul II is a Christian. Such statements tell us as a bare minimum what something is, as opposed to all other things. On this level we can distinguish between an orange and an apple (as we might distinguish between a Muslim and a Christian) only to the extent that we know they are different fruits, growing on different trees, and so forth.

The second function of these several labels is to produce a much more complex meaning. To speak of "Islam" in the West today is to mean a lot of the unpleasant things I have been mentioning. Moreover, "Islam" is unlikely to mean anything one knows either directly or objectively. The same is true of our use of "the West." How many people who use the labels angrily or assertively have a solid grip on all aspects of the Western tradition, or on Islamic jurisprudence, or on the actual languages of the Islamic world? Very few, obviously, but this does not prevent people from confidently characterizing "Islam" and "the West," or from believing they know exactly what it is they are talking about.

For that reason, we must take the labels seriously. To a Muslim who talks about "the West" or to an American who talks about "Islam," these enormous generalizations have behind them a whole history, enabling and disabling at the same time. Ideological and shot through with powerful emotions, the labels have survived many experiences and have been capable of adapting to new events, information, and realities. At present, "Islam," and "the West" have taken on a powerful new urgency everywhere. And we must note immediately that it is always the West, and not Christianity, that seems pitted against Islam. Why? Because the assumption is that whereas "the West" is greater than and has surpassed the stage of Christianity, its principal religion, the world of Islam—its varied societies, histories, and languages notwithstanding—is still mired in religion, primitivity, and backwardness. Therefore, the West is modern, greater than the sum of its parts, full of enriching contradictions and yet always "Western" in its cultural identity; the world of

Islam, on the other hand, is no more than "Islam," reducible to a small number of unchanging characteristics despite the appearance of contradictions and experiences of variety that seem on the surface to be as plentiful as those of the West.

An example of what I mean is to be found in an article for the "News of the Week in Review" section of the Sunday *New York Times*, September 14, 1980. The piece in question is by John Kifner, the able *Times* correspondent in Beirut, and its subject is the extent of Soviet penetration of the Muslim world. Kifner's notion is evident enough from his article's title ("Marx and Mosque Are less Compatible Than Ever"), but what is noteworthy is his use of Islam to make what in any other instance would be an unacceptably direct and unqualified connection between an abstraction and a vastly complex reality. Even if it is allowed that, unlike all other religions, Islam is totalistic and makes no separation between church and state or between religion and everyday life, there is something uniquely—and perhaps deliberately—uninformed and uninforming, albeit conventional enough, about such statements as the following:

> The reason for Moscow's receding influence is disarmingly simple: Marx and mosque are incompatible. [Are we to assume, then, that Marx and church, or Marx and temple, are more compatible?]
>
> For the Western mind [this is the point, obviously enough], conditioned since the Reformation to historical and intellectual developments which have steadily diminished the role of religion, it is difficult to grasp the power exerted by Islam [which, presumably, has been conditioned neither by history nor by intellect]. Yet, for centuries it has been the central force in the life of this region and, for the moment at least, its power seems on the upsurge.
>
> In Islam, there is no separation between church and state. It is a total system not only of belief but of action, with fixed

rules for everyday life and a messianic drive to combat or con-
vert the infidel. To the deeply religious, particularly to the
scholars and clergy but also to the masses [in other words, no
one is excluded], Marxism, with its purely secular view of
man, is not only alien but heretical.

Not only does Kifner simply ignore history and such complications
as the admittedly limited but interesting series of parallels between
Marxism and Islam (studied by Maxime Rodinson in a book that attempts to explain why Marxism seems to have made some inroads
in Islamic societies over the years[4]) but he also rests his argument on
a hidden comparison between "Islam" and the West, so much more
various and uncharacterizable than simple, monolithic, totalitarian
Islam. The interesting thing is that Kifner can say what he says without any danger of appearing either wrong or absurd. The main
problem is that commentators like Kifner make the leap from Islam
as an abstraction to a hugely complex reality without a second
thought.

Islam versus the West: this is the ground bass for a staggeringly
fertile set of variations. Europe versus Islam, no less than America
versus Islam, is a thesis that it subsumes.[5] But quite different concrete experiences with the West as a whole play a significant role
too. For there is an extremely important distinction to be made between American and European awareness of Islam. France and England, for example, until very recently possessed large Muslim
empires; in both countries, and to a lesser degree in Italy and Hol-
land, both of which had Muslim colonies too, there is a long tradition of direct experience with the Islamic world.[6] In addition,
millions of Muslims from Africa and Asia now live in metropolitan
France and Britain. This is reflected in a distinguished European
academic discipline of Orientalism, which of course existed in
those countries with colonies as well as those (Germany, Spain, prerevolutionary Russia) that either wanted them, or were close to
Muslim territories, or were once Muslim states. Today Russia and

its republics have a Muslim population of over 50 million, and between 1979 and 1988 the Soviet Union was in military occupation of Muslim Afghanistan. None of these things is comparably true of the United States, despite a growing number of Muslims here, and never before have so many Americans written, thought, or spoken about Islam.

The absence in America either of a colonial past or of a long-standing cultural attention to Islam makes the current obsession all the more peculiar, more abstract, more secondhand. Very few Americans, comparatively speaking, have actually had much to do with real Muslims; by comparison, in France the country's second religion in point of numbers is Islam, which may not be more popular as a result, but is certainly more known. The modern European burst of interest in Islam was part of what was called "the Oriental renaissance," a period in the late eighteenth and early nineteenth centuries when French and British scholars discovered "the East" anew—India, China, Japan, Egypt, Mesopotamia, the Holy Land. Islam was seen, for better or for worse, as part of the East, sharing in its mystery, exoticism, corruption, and latent power. True, Islam had been a direct military threat to Europe for centuries before; and true also that during the Middle Ages and early Renaissance, Islam was a problem for Christian thinkers, who continued for hundreds of years to see it and its prophet Mohammed as the rankest variety of apostasy. But at least Islam existed for many Europeans as a kind of standing religiocultural challenge, which did not prevent European imperialism from building its institutions on Islamic territory. And however much hostility there was between Europe and Islam, there was also direct experience, and in the case of poets, novelists, and scholars like Goethe, Gérard de Nerval, Richard Burton, Flaubert, and Louis Massignon, there was imagination and refinement.

Yet in spite of these figures and others like them, Islam has never been welcome in Europe. Most of the great philosophers of history from Hegel to Spengler have regarded Islam without much enthusiasm. In a dispassionately lucid essay, "Islam and the Philosophy of History," Albert Hourani has discussed this strikingly constant derogation of Islam as a system of faith.[7] Apart from some occasional interest in the odd Sufi writer or saint, European vogues for "the wisdom of the East" rarely included Islamic sages or poets. Omar Khayyám, Harun al-Rashid, Sindbad, Aladdin, Hajji Baba, Scheherazade, Saladin, more or less make up the entire list of Islamic figures known to modern educated Europeans. Not even Carlyle could make the Prophet widely acceptable, and as for the substance of the faith Mohammed propagated, this has long seemed to Europeans basically unacceptable on Christian grounds, although precisely for that reason not uninteresting. Toward the end of the nineteenth century, as Islamic nationalism in Asia and Africa increased, there was a widely shared view that Muslim colonies were meant to remain under European tutelage, as much because they were profitable as because they were underdeveloped and in need of Western discipline.[8] Be that as it may, and despite the frequent racism and aggression directed at the Muslim world, Europeans *did* express a fairly energetic sense of what Islam meant to them. Hence the representations of Islam — in scholarship, art, literature, music, and public discourse — all across European culture, from the end of the eighteenth century until our own day.

In addition, many European governments have had a policy of cultural and spiritual dialogue with the Muslim and Arab worlds. This has produced a whole series of seminars, conferences, and translations of books that have no equivalent in the United States, where Islam is mainly a policy question for the Council on Foreign Relations, a "threat" or military and security challenge without parallel in the numerous cultures and nations with which the United States has relations.

Little of this European concreteness is therefore to be found in America's experience of Islam. Nineteenth-century American contacts with Islam were very restricted; one thinks of occasional travelers like Mark Twain and Herman Melville, or of missionaries here and there, or of short-lived military expeditions to North Africa. Culturally there was no distinct place in America for Islam before World War II. Academic experts did their work on Islam usually in quiet corners of schools of divinity, not in the glamorous limelight of Orientalism nor in the pages of leading journals. For about a century there has existed a fascinating although quiet symbiosis between American missionary families to Islamic countries and cadres of the foreign service and the oil companies; periodically this has surfaced in the form of hostile comments about State Department and oil-company "Arabists," who are considered to harbor an especially virulent and anti-Semitic form of philo-Islamism. On the other hand, all the great figures known until about twenty years ago in the United States as important academic experts and the founders of university departments and programs on Islam have been foreign-born: Lebanese Philip Hitti at Princeton, Austrian Gustave von Grunebaum at Chicago and UCLA, British H. A. R. Gibb at Harvard, German Joseph Schacht at Columbia. Yet none of these men has had the relative cultural prestige enjoyed by Jacques Berque in France and Albert Hourani in England.

But even men like Hitti, Gibb, von Grunebaum, and Schacht have disappeared from the American scene, as indeed it is unlikely that scholars such as Berque and Hourani, both of whom died in 1993, will have successors in France and England. No one today has their breadth of culture, nor anything like their range of authority. Academic experts on Islam in the West today tend to know about jurisprudential schools in tenth-century Baghdad or nineteenth-century Moroccan urban patterns, but never (or almost never) about the whole civilization of Islam—literature, law, politics, history, sociology, and so on. This has not prevented experts from generalizing from time to time about the "Islamic mind-set" or the "Shi'a penchant for martyrdom," but such pronouncements have been confined to popular journals or to the media, which solicited these opinions in the first place. More significantly, the occasions for public discussions of Islam, by experts or by nonexperts, have

almost always been provided by political crises. It is extremely rare
to see informative articles on Islamic culture in the *New York Review of Books*, say, or in *Harper's*. Only when there is a bomb in
Saudi Arabia or the threat of violence against the United States in
Iran has "Islam" seemed worthy of general comment. Then, as has
occurred with some regularity since the World Trade Center bombing in 1993, newspapers, magazines, and an occasional film have
tried to inform the public about "the world of Islam" with considered surveys, tables, and human interest stories (the Pakistani water-
seller, the Egyptian peasant family, etc.). Against a lowering and
much more impressive background of militancy and *jihad* these efforts have proved ineffective.

Consider therefore that Islam has entered the consciousness of
most Americans—even of academic and general intellectuals who
know a great deal about Europe and Latin America—principally if
not exclusively because it has been connected to newsworthy issues
like oil, Iran and Afghanistan, or terrorism.⁹ And all of this by the
middle of 1979 had come to be called either the Islamic revolution,
or "the crescent of crisis," or "the arc of instability," or "the return of
Islam." A particularly telling example was the Atlantic Council's
Special Working Group on the Middle East (which included Brent
Scowcroft, George Ball, Richard Helms, Lyman Lemnitzer, Walter
Levy, Eugene Rostow, Kermit Roosevelt, and Joseph Sisco, among
others): when this group issued its report in the fall of 1979, the title
given it was "Oil and Turmoil: Western Choices in the Middle
East."¹⁰ When *Time* magazine devoted its major story to Islam on
April 16, 1979, the cover was adorned with a Gérôme painting of a
bearded muezzin standing in a minaret, calmly summoning the
faithful to prayer; it was as florid and overstated a nineteenth-century
period piece of Orientalist art as one could imagine. Anachronisti-
cally, however, this quiet scene was emblazoned with a caption that
had nothing to do with it: "The Militant Revival." There could be
no better way of symbolizing the difference between Europe and
America on the subject of Islam. A placid and decorative painting

done almost routinely in Europe as an aspect of the general culture had been transformed by three words into a general American obsession.

But surely I am exaggerating? Wasn't *Time*'s cover story on Islam simply a piece of vulgarization, catering to a supposed taste for the sensational? Does it *really* reveal anything more serious than that? And since when have the media mattered a great deal on questions of substance, or of policy, or of culture? Besides, was it *not* the case that Islam had indeed thrust itself upon the world's attention? And what had happened to the experts on Islam, and why were their contributions either bypassed entirely or submerged in the "Islam" discussed and diffused by the media?

A few simple explanations are in order first. As I said above, there has never been any American expert on the Islamic world whose audience was a wide one; moreover, with the exception of the late Marshall Hodgson's three-volume *The Venture of Islam*, posthumously published in 1975, no general work on Islam has ever been put squarely before the literate reading public.[11] Either the experts were so specialized that they only addressed other specialists, or their work was not distinguished enough intellectually to command the kind of audience that came to books on Japan, Western Europe, or India. But these things work both ways. While it is true that one could not name an American "Orientalist" with a reputation outside Orientalism, as compared with Berque or Rodinson in France, it is also true that the study of Islam is neither truly encouraged in the American university nor sustained in the culture at large by personalities whose fame and intrinsic merit might make their experiences of Islam important on their own.[12] Who are the American equivalents of Rebecca West, Freya Stark, T. E. Lawrence, Wilfred Thesiger, Gertrude Bell, P. H. Newby, or more recently, Jonathan Raban? At best, they might be former CIA people like Miles Copeland or Kermit Roosevelt, very rarely writers or thinkers of any cultural distinction. Gifted younger writers and translators like Peter Theroux have not yet made a very strong impression.

A second reason for the critical absence of expert opinion on Islam is the experts' marginality to what seemed to be happening in the world of Islam when it first became "news" in the mid-1970s. The brutally impressive facts are, of course, that the Gulf oil-producing states suddenly appeared to be very powerful; there was an extraordinarily ferocious and seemingly unending civil war in Lebanon; Ethiopia and Somalia were involved in a long war; the Kurdish problem unexpectedly became pivotal and then, after 1975, just as unexpectedly subsided; Iran deposed its monarch in the wake of a massive, wholly surprising "Islamic" revolution; Afghanistan was gripped by a Marxist coup in 1978, then invaded by Soviet troops in late 1979; Algeria and Morocco were drawn into protracted conflict over the Southern Sahara issue; a Pakistani president was executed and a new military dictatorship set up. There were other things taking place too, most recently a war between Iran and Iraq, the rise of Hamas and Hizbollah, a series of bomb outrages in Israel and elsewhere, a bloody civil war in Algeria between Islamists and a discredited government, but let us be satisfied with these. On the whole I think it is fair to say that few of these happenings might have been illuminated by expert writing on Islam in the West; for not only had the experts not predicted them nor prepared their readers for them, they had instead provided a mass of literature that seemed, when compared with what was happening, to be about an impossibly distant region of the world, one that bore practically no relation to the turbulent and threatening confusion erupting before one's eyes in the media.

This is a central matter, which has scarcely begun to be discussed rationally even now, and so we should proceed carefully. Academic experts whose province was Islam as it was before the seventeenth century worked in an essentially antiquarian field; moreover, like that of specialists in other fields, their work was very compartmentalized. They neither wanted nor tried in a responsible way to concern themselves with the modern consequences of Islamic history. To some extent their work was tied to notions of a "classical" Islam, or to supposedly unchanging patterns of Islamic life, or to archaic philological questions. In any event, there was no way of using it to understand the modern Islamic world, which to all intents and purposes, and depending on what part of it was of interest, had been developing along very different lines from those adumbrated in Islam's earliest centuries (that is, from the seventh to the ninth century).

The experts whose field was modern Islam—or to be more precise, whose field was made up of societies, people, and institutions within the Islamic world since the eighteenth century—worked within an agreed-upon framework for research formed according to notions decidedly *not* set in the Islamic world. This fact, in all its complexity and variety, cannot be overestimated. There is no denying that a scholar sitting in Oxford or Boston writes and researches principally, though not exclusively, according to standards, conventions, and expectations shaped by his or her peers, not by the Muslims being studied. This is a truism, perhaps, but it needs emphasis just the same. Modern Islamic studies in the academy belong to "area programs" generally—Western Europe, the Soviet Union, Southeast Asia, and so on. They are therefore affiliated to the mechanism by which national policy is set. This is not a matter of choice for the individual scholar. If someone at Princeton happened to be studying contemporary Afghan religious schools, it would be obvious (especially during times like these) that such a study *could* have "policy implications," and whether or not the scholar wanted it he or she would be drawn into the network of government, corporate, and foreign policy associations; funding would be affected, the kind of people met would also be affected, and in general, certain rewards and types of interaction would be offered. Willy-nilly, the scholar would be transmuted into an "area expert" or, as is the case with mediocre and unqualified journalists like Judith Miller on Israel and publicists like Martin Peretz, would be listened to in reverential silence.

For scholars whose interests are directly connected to policy issues (political scientists, principally, but also modern historians, economists, sociologists, and anthropologists), there are sensitive, not to say dangerous, questions to be addressed. For example, how is one's status as a scholar reconciled with the demands made on one by governments? Iran is a perfect case in point. During the shah's regime, there were funds available to Iranologists from the Pahlevi Foundation, and of course from American institutions. These funds were disbursed for studies that took as their point of departure the status quo (in this case, the presence of a Pahlevi regime tied militarily and economically to the United States), which in a sense became the research paradigm for students of the country. Late in the crisis a House Permanent Select Committee on Intelligence staff study said that the United States' assessments of the regime were influenced by existing policy "not directly, through the conscious suppression of unfavorable news, but indirectly . . . policymakers were not asking whether the shah's autocracy would survive indefinitely; policy was premised on that assumption."[13] This in turn produced only a tiny handful of studies seriously assessing the shah's regime and identifying the sources of popular opposition to him. To my knowledge only one scholar, Hamid Algar of Berkeley, was correct in estimating the contemporary political force of Iranian religious feelings, and only Algar went so far as to predict that Ayatollah Khomeini was likely to bring down the regime. Other scholars—Richard Cottam and Ervand Abrahamian among them—also departed from the status quo in what they wrote, but they were a small band indeed.[14] (In fairness we must note that European scholars on the left, who were less sanguine about the shah's survival, did not do very well either in identifying the religious sources of Iranian opposition.[15])

Even if we leave aside Iran, there were plenty of no less important intellectual failures elsewhere, all of them the result of relying uncritically on what a combination of government policy and cliché dictated. Here, the Lebanese and Palestinian cases are instructive. For years Lebanon had been regarded as a model of what a pluralistic or mosaic culture was supposed to be. Yet so reified and static had the models been which were used for the study of Lebanon that no inkling was possible of the ferocity and violence of the civil war (which ran from 1975 to 1980 at least). Expert eyes seem in the past to have been extraordinarily transfixed by images of Lebanese "stability": traditional leaders, elites, parties, national character, and successful modernization were what was studied.

Even when Lebanon's polity was described as precarious, or when its insufficient "civility" was analyzed, there was a uniform assumption that its problems were on the whole manageable and far from being radically disruptive.[16] During the sixties, Lebanon was portrayed as "stable" because, one expert tells us, the "inter-Arab" situation was stable; so long as that equation was kept up, he argued, Lebanon would be secure.[17] It was never even supposed that there could be inter-Arab stability and Lebanese *instability*, mainly because—as with most subjects in this consensus-ridden field—the conventional wisdom assigned perpetual "pluralism" and harmonious continuity to Lebanon, its internal cleavages and its Arab neighbors' irrelevance notwithstanding. Any trouble for Lebanon therefore had to come from the surrounding *Arab* environment, never from Israel or from the United States, both of which had specific but never-analyzed designs on Lebanon.[18] Then, too, there was the Lebanon that embodied the modernization myth. Reading a classic of this sort of ostrich-wisdom today, one is struck by how serenely the fable could be advanced as recently as 1973, when the civil war was in fact already beginning. Lebanon might undergo revolutionary change, we were told, but that was a "remote" likelihood; what was much more likely was "future modernization involving the public [a sadly ironic euphemism for what was to be the bloodiest civil war in recent Arab history] within the prevailing political structure."[19] Or as a distinguished anthropologist put it, "The Lebanese 'nice piece of mosaic' remains intact. Indeed . . . Lebanon has continued to be the most effective in containing its deep primordial cleavages."[20]

As a result, in Lebanon and in other places, experts failed to understand that much of what truly mattered about postcolonial states could not easily be herded under the rubric of "stability." In Lebanon it was precisely those devastatingly mobile forces the experts had never documented or had consistently underestimated—social dislocations, demographic shifts such as the emergence of the Shi'a population, confessional loyalties, ideological currents—that tore the country apart so savagely.[21] Similarly, it has been conventional wisdom for years to regard the Palestinians merely as resettlable refugees, not as a political force having estimable consequences for any reasonably accurate assessment of the Near East. Yet by the mid-seventies the Palestinians were one of the major acknowledged problems for United States policy, and still they had not received the scholarly and intellectual attention their importance deserved;[22] instead, the persisting attitude was to treat them as adjuncts to United States policy toward Egypt and Israel and quite literally to ignore them in the Lebanese conflagration. When the *intifada* broke out in late 1987, it came as a surprise to officials and commentators alike. There has been no important *scholarly* or expert counterweight to the blindness of this policy, and the results for American national interests in the long run are likely to be disastrous, especially since the Iran-Iraq war seems, once again, to have caught the intelligence community off guard and very wrong in estimates of both countries' military capacities. Besides, the main point is that the United States and its battery of willing "experts" cannot expect Muslims who have seen their fellows killed in Bosnia, Chechnya, and Palestine, who have seen their unpopular rulers praised as friends of the United States, and who endure endless characterization of their religion and culture as "enraged" and "violent," to embrace the "West" wholeheartedly.

Add to this conformity between a docilely plodding scholarship and unfocused government interests the sorry truth that too many expert writers on the Islamic world did not command the relevant languages and hence had to depend on the press or other Western writers for their information. This reinforced dependence on the official or the conventional picture of things was a trap into which, in their over-all performance on prerevolutionary Iran, the media fell. They did exactly the same before the *intifada* and during the hysteria about Islamic "fundamentalism" and "terrorism." There was a tendency to study and restudy, to focus resolutely on the same things: elites, modernization programs, the role of the military, greatly visible leaders, sensational crises, *jihad* networks, geopolitical strategy (from the American point of view), "Islamic" inroads.[23] Those things may at the time have seemed interesting to the United States as a nation, yet the fact is that in Iran they were all literally swept away by the revolution in a matter of days. The whole imperial court crumbled; the army, into which billions of dollars had been poured, disintegrated; the so-called elites either disappeared or found their way into the new state of affairs, though in neither case could it be asserted, as it had been, that they determined Iranian political behavior. One of the experts given credit for predicting what the "crisis of '78" might lead to, James Bill of the University of Texas, nevertheless recommended to American policymakers as late as December 1978 that the United States government should encourage "the shah . . . to open the system up."[24] In other words, even a supposedly dissenting expert voice was still committed to maintaining a regime against which, at the very moment he spoke, literally millions of its people had risen in one of the most massive insurrections in modern history.

Yet Bill made important points about general United States ignorance on Iran. He was right to say that media coverage was superficial, that official information had been geared to what the Pahlevis wanted, and that the United States made no effort either to get to know the country in depth or to make contact with the opposition. Although Bill did not go on to say it, these failures were and are symptomatic of the general United States and to a lesser degree of the European attitude toward the Islamic world and, as we shall see, toward most of the Third World; indeed, the fact that Bill did not connect what he was justly saying about Iran to the rest of the Islamic world was part of the attitude too. There has been no responsible grappling first of all with the central methodological question, namely, What is the value (if any) of speaking about "Islam" and the Islamic resurgence? What, secondly, is or ought to be the relationship between government policy and scholarly research? Is the expert supposed to be above politics or a political adjunct to governments? Bill and William Beeman of Brown University argued on separate occasions that a major cause of the United States–Iran crisis in 1979 was the failure to consult those academic experts who had been given expensive educations precisely to learn to know the Islamic world.[25] Yet what went unexamined by Bill and Beeman was the possibility that it was *because* scholars sought out such a role, at the same time calling themselves scholars, that they seemed ambiguous and hence not credible figures to the government as well as to the intellectual community.[26]

Besides, is there any way for an independent intellectual (which is, after all, what an academic scholar is meant to be) to maintain his or her independence and also to work directly for the state? What is the connection between frank political partisanship and good insight? Does one preclude the other, or is that true only in some cases? Why was it that the whole (but admittedly small) cadre of Islamic scholars in the country could not get a larger hearing? Why was this the case at a time, like now, when the United States seemed to be most in need of instruction? All of these questions, of course, can be answered only within the actual and largely political framework governing relationships historically between the West and the Islamic world. Let us look at this framework and see what role there is in it for the expert.

I have not been able to discover any period in European or American history since the Middle Ages in which Islam was generally discussed or thought about *outside* a framework created by passion, prejudice, and political interests. This may not seem a surprising discovery, but included in it is the entire gamut of scholarly and scientific disciplines which, since the early nineteenth century, have either called themselves collectively the discipline of Orientalism or have tried systematically to deal with the Orient. No one would disagree with the statement that early commentators on Islam like Peter the Venerable and Barthélemy d'Herbelot were passionate Christian polemicists in what they said. But it has been an unexamined assumption that since Europe and the West advanced into the modern scientific age and freed themselves of superstition and ignorance, the march must have included Orientalism. Wasn't it true that Silvestre de Sacy, Edward Lane, Ernest Renan, Hamilton Gibb, and Louis Massignon were learned, objective scholars, and isn't it true that following upon all sorts of advances in twentieth-century sociology, anthropology, linguistics, and history, American scholars who teach the Middle East and Islam in places like Princeton, Harvard, and Chicago are therefore unbiased and free of special pleading in what they do? The answer is no. Not that Orientalism is more biased than other social and humanistic sciences; it is simply as ideological and as contaminated by the world as other disciplines. The main difference is that Orientalist scholars have tended to use their standing as experts to deny—and sometimes even to cover—their deep-seated feelings about Islam with a language of authority whose purpose is to certify their "objectivity" and "scientific impartiality."

That is one point. The other distinguishes a historical pattern in what would otherwise be an undifferentiated characterization of Orientalism. Whenever in modern times an acutely political tension has been felt between the Occident and *its* Orient (or between the West and *its* Islam), there has been a tendency in the West to resort not to direct violence but first to the cool, relatively detached instruments of scientific, quasi-objective representation. In this way "Islam" is made more clear, the "true nature" of its threat appears, an implicit course of action against it is proposed. In such a context both science and direct violence come to be viewed by many Muslims, living in widely varied circumstances, as forms of aggression against Islam.

Two strikingly similar examples illustrate my thesis. We can now see retrospectively that during the nineteenth century both France and England preceded their occupations of portions of the Islamic East with a period in which the various scholarly means of characterizing and understanding the Orient underwent remarkable technical modernization and development.[27] The French occupation of Algeria in 1830 followed a period of about two decades during which French scholars literally transformed the study of the Orient from an antiquarian into a rational discipline. Of course, there had been Napoleon Bonaparte's occupation of Egypt in 1798, and of course one should remark the fact that he had prepared for his expedition by marshaling a sophisticated group of scientists to make his enterprise more efficient. My point, however, is that Napoleon's short-lived occupation of Egypt closed a chapter. A new one began with the long period during which, under Silvestre de Sacy's stewardship at French institutions of Oriental study, France became the world leader in Orientalism; this chapter climaxed a little later when French armies occupied Algiers in 1830.

I do not at all want to suggest a causal relationship between one thing and the other, nor to adopt the anti-intellectual view that all scientific learning necessarily leads to violence and suffering. All I want to say is that empires are not born instantaneously, nor during the modern period have they been run by improvisation. If the development of learning involves the redefinition and reconstitution of fields of human experience by scientists who stand above the material they study, it is not impertinent to see the same development occurring among politicans whose realm of authority is redefined to include "inferior" regions of the world where new "national" interests can be discovered—and later seen to be in need of close supervision.[28] I very much doubt that England would have occupied Egypt in so long and massively institutionalized a way had it not been for the durable investment in Oriental learning first cultivated by scholars like Edward William Lane and William Jones. Familiarity, accessibility, representability: these were what Orientalists demonstrated about the Orient. The Orient could be seen, it could be studied, it could be managed. It need not remain a distant, marvelous, incomprehensible, and yet very rich place. It could be brought home—or more simply, Europe could make itself at home there, as it subsequently did.

My second example is a contemporary one. The Islamic Orient today is clearly important for its resources or for its geopolitical location. Neither of these, however, is interchangeable with the interests, needs, or aspirations of the native Orientals. Ever since the end of World War II, the United States has been taking positions of dominance and hegemony once held in the Islamic world by Britain and France. It went to war in 1991 in order to safeguard its economic interests in the Persian Gulf, it armed Afghan militias against the Soviet Union, it coordinates research and intelligence with Israel against Islamic militancy on the occupied West Bank and Gaza strip. With this replacement of one imperial system by another have gone two things: first, the moderate burgeoning of crisis-oriented academic and expert interest in Islam, and second, an extraordinary revolution in the techniques available to the largely private-sector press and electronic journalism industries. Never before has an international trouble spot like Iran, or Bosnia, been covered so instantaneously and so regularly as it has by the media: Iran therefore seemed to be *in* American lives, and yet deeply alien from them, with an unprecedented intensity, much as during the 1990s did Bosnia. Together these two phenomena—the second much more than the first—by which a sizable apparatus of university, government, and business experts study Islam and the Middle East and by which Islam has become a subject familiar to every consumer of news in the West, have almost entirely domesticated the Islamic world, or at least those aspects of it that are considered newsworthy. Not only has that world become the subject of the most profound cultural and economic Western saturation in history—for no non-Western realm has been so dominated by the United States as the Arabic-Islamic world is today—but the interchange between Islam and the West, in this case the United States, is profoundly one-sided and, so far as other, less newsworthy parts of the Islamic world are concerned, profoundly skewed.

It is only a slight overstatement to say that Muslims and Arabs are essentially covered, discussed, and apprehended either as oil suppliers or as potential terrorists. Very little of the detail, the human density, the passion of Arab-Muslim life has entered the awareness of even those people whose profession it is to report the Islamic world. What we have instead is a limited series of crude, essentialized caricatures of the Islamic world presented in such a way as, among other things, to make that world vulnerable to military aggression.[29] I do not think it is an accident that talk during the 1970s of United States military intervention in the Arabian Gulf, or the Carter Doctrine, or discussions of Rapid Deployment Forces, or the military and economic "containment" of "political Islam," has often been preceded by a period of "Islam's" rational presentation through the cool medium of television and through "objective" Orientalist study (which, paradoxically, either in its "irrelevance" to modern actualities or in its propagandistic "objective" variety, has a uniformly alienating effect): In many ways our actual situation today bears a chilling resemblance to the nineteenth-century British and French examples cited previously.

There are other political and cultural reasons for this. After World War II, when the United States took over the imperial role played by France and Britain, a set of policies was devised for dealing with the world that suited the peculiarities and the problems of each region that affected (and was affected by) United States interests. Europe was designated for postwar recovery, for which the Marshall Plan, among other similar American policies, was suited. The Soviet Union of course emerged as the United States' most formidable competitor, and, as no one needs to be told, the Cold War produced policies, studies, even a mentality, which still dominate relationships between one superpower and the other. After the end of the Cold War, that left what used to be called the Third World, an arena of competition between the United States and various native powers only recently in possession of their independence from European colonizers.

Almost without exception, the Third World first seemed to American policymakers to be "underdeveloped," in the grip of unnecessarily archaic and static "traditional" modes of life, dangerously prone to communist subversion and internal stagnation. For the Third World "modernization" became the order of the day, so far as the United States was concerned. And, as has been suggested by James Peck, "modernization theory was the ideological answer to a world of increasing revolutionary upheaval and continued reaction among traditional political elites."[30] Huge sums were poured into Africa and Asia with the aim of stopping communism, promoting United States trade, and, above all, developing a cadre of native allies whose express *raison d'être* seemed to be the transformation of backward countries into mini-Americas. In time the initial investments required additional sums and increased military support to keep them going. And this in turn produced the interventions all over Asia and Latin America which regularly pitted the United States against almost every brand of native nationalism.

The history of United States efforts on behalf of modernization and development in the Third World can never be completely understood unless it is also noted how the policy itself produced a style of thought and a habit of seeing the Third World which increased the political, emotional, and strategic investment in the very idea of modernization. Vietnam was a perfect instance of this. Once it was decided that the country was to be saved from communism and indeed from itself, a whole science of modernization for Vietnam (whose latest and most costly phase came to be known as "Vietnamization") came into being. Not only government specialists but university experts were involved. In time, the survival of pro-American and anticommunist regimes in Saigon dominated everything, even when it became clear that a huge majority of the population viewed those regimes as alien and oppressive, and even

when the cost of fighting unsuccessful wars on behalf of those
regimes had devastated the whole region and cost Lyndon Johnson
the presidency. Still, a very great amount of writing on the virtues of
modernizing traditional society had acquired an almost unquestioned social, and certainly cultural, authority in the United States,
at the same time that in many parts of the Third World "modernization" was connected in the popular mind with foolish spending,
unnecessary gadgetry and armaments, corrupt rulers, and brutal
United States intervention in the affairs of small, weak countries.

Among the many illusions that persisted in modernization theory was one that seemed to have a special pertinence to the Islamic
world: namely, that before the advent of the United States, Islam existed in a kind of timeless childhood, shielded from true development by an archaic set of superstitions, prevented by its strange
priests and scribes from moving out of the Middle Ages into the
modern world. At this point, Orientalism and modernization theory
dovetail nicely. If, as Orientalist scholarship had traditionally
taught, Muslims were no more than fatalistic children tyrannized
by their mind-set, their 'ulama, and their wild-eyed political leaders
into resisting the West and progress, could not every political scientist, anthropologist, and sociologist worthy of trust show that, given
a reasonable chance, something resembling the American way of
life might be introduced into Islam via consumer goods, and "good"
leaders? The main difficulty with Islam, however, was that unlike
India and China, it had never really been pacified or defeated. For
reasons which seemed always to defy the understanding of scholars,
Islam (or some version of it) continued its sway over its adherents,
who, it came regularly to be argued, were unwilling to accept reality, or at least that part of reality in which the West's superiority was
demonstrable.

Efforts at modernization persisted all through the two decades
that followed World War II. Iran became in effect the modernization success story and its ruler the "modernized" leader *par excel-
lence*. As for the rest of the Islamic world, whether it was Arab

nationalists, Egypt's Gamal Abdel Nasser, Indonesia's Sukarno, the Palestinian nationalists, Iranian opposition groups, or thousands of unknown Islamic teachers, brotherhoods, and orders, it was all either opposed or not covered by Western scholars with a heavy investment in modernization theory and American strategic and economic interests in the Islamic world.

During the explosive decade of the seventies, Islam gave further proof of its fundamental intransigence. There was, for example, the Iranian revolution: neither procommunist nor promodernization, the people who overthrew the shah were simply not explainable according to the canons of behavior presupposed by modernization theory. They did not seem grateful for the quotidian benefits of modernization (cars, an enormous military and security apparatus, a stable regime) and appeared indifferent to the blandishments of "Western" ideas altogether.[31] What was especially troubling about their attitude—Khomeini's in particular—was their fierce unwillingness to accept any style of politics (or for that matter, of rationality) that was not deliberately their own. Above all, it was their attachment to an Islam that was Iranian, fiercely contested, and idiosyncratically defended that seemed especially defiant. Ironically, only a few commentators on "Islamic" atavism and medieval modes of logic in the West noted that a few miles to the west of Iran, in Begin's Israel, there was a regime fully willing to mandate its actions by religious authority and by a very backward-looking theological doctrine.[32] An even smaller number of commentators decrying the apparent upsurge in Islamic religiosity connected it to the upsurge in the United States of television religions numbering many millions of adherents, or to the fact that two of the three major presidential candidates in 1980 were enthusiastic born-again Christians.

It became a commonplace to use one or two Orientalist generalizations (many of them circulated by aging Orientalists like Bernard Lewis) to slap against the whole of the Islamic world without bothering to inquire whether such vast platitudes always accounted for the behavior of every Muslim. This was never more evident than in

discussions that purported to show the inevitable connection between Islam and terrorism. Consider Conor Cruise O'Brien, a former leftist intellectual, who slowly became part of the reactionary
right during the 1980s; he somehow retained his credentials as a serious progressive intellectual despite his breaking of the cultural
boycott against apartheid in South Africa and his endless justifica-
tions of right-wing Zionism in Israel. Here is a typical paragraph of
lazy historical judgment, over-generalization, and incredible stereotyping of the kind no one who has anything seriously to do with Islam would recognize except as near-nonsense:

Certain cultures and subcultures, homes of frustrated causes,
are destined breeding grounds for terrorism. The Islamic culture [O'Brien does not inform us how he makes the jump
from religion to culture in this instance, nor does he specify
where the limits of each lie] is the most notable example.
That culture's view of its own rightful position in the world
[O'Brien does not tell us how or where he managed to glean
this particularly privileged bit of information] is profoundly at
variance with the actual order of the contemporary world [this
can certainly be said of almost any culture's "view of itself"].
It is God's will that the House of Islam should triumph over
the House of War (the non-Moslem) world, and not just by
spiritual means. "Islam Means Victory" is a slogan of the Iranian fundamentalists in the Gulf [i.e., Iran–Iraq war, 1980–88].
To strike a blow against the House of War is meritorious; consequently, there is widespread support for activities condemned in the West as terrorist. [Note that O'Brien has not
vouchsafed his reader one fact, source, quotation, or context,
and he does not seem concerned at all by this rather peculiar
procedure or method of argument.] Israel is one main target
for these activities [what Israel has done or continues to do is
never the issue: it is just pure Islamic terror], but the activities

would not be likely to cease even if Israel came to an end ("Thinking about Terrorism," *The Atlantic,* June 1986, p. 65).

Religious intensity of a particularly violent kind was thus ascribed solely to Islam even when religious feeling was spreading remarkably everywhere: One need only remember the effusive treatment by the liberal press of patently illiberal religious figures like Solzhenitsyn or Pope John Paul II, and the way the massacres of Muslims in Bosnia was *not* ascribed to Christianity, to see how one-sidedly hostile the attitude to Islam was.[33] A retreat into religion became the way most Islamic states could be explained, from Saudi Arabia—which, with what was supposed to be a peculiarly Islamic logic, refused to ratify the Camp David Accords—to Pakistan, Afghanistan, and Algeria. In this way, we can see how the Islamic world was differentiated, in the Western mind generally, in the United States in particular, from regions of the world to which a cold-war analysis could be applied, even though the Cold War did in fact play a role, as well as the corruptions and tyrannies of certain Islamic countries. There seemed to be no way, for example, in which one could speak of Saudi Arabia and Kuwait as parts of "the free world"; even Iran during the shah's regime, despite its overwhelming anti-Soviet commitment, never really belonged to "our" side the way France and Britain do. Nevertheless policymakers in the United States persisted in speaking of the "loss" of Iran as, during the past three decades, they spoke of the "loss" of China, Vietnam, and Angola. Moreover it has been the singularly unhappy lot of the Persian Gulf's Islamic states to be considered by American crisis managers as places ready for American military occupation. Thus George Ball in the *New York Times Magazine* of June 28, 1970, warned that "the tragedy of Vietnam" might lead to "pacifism and isolation" at home, whereas United States interests in the Middle East were so great that the president ought to "educate" Americans about the possibility of military intervention there.[34] One of the themes of the 1991 Gulf War was to lay the ghost of Vietnam finally to rest.

One more thing needs mention here: the role of Israel in mediating Western and particularly American views of the Islamic world since World War II. In the first place, Israel's avowedly religious character is rarely mentioned in the Western press: Only recently have there been overt references to Israeli religious fanaticism, and many of these have been to the zealots of Gush Emunim, whose principal activity has been the violent setting up of illegal settlements on the West Bank. Yet most accounts of militant Israeli settlers in the West simply leave out the inconvenient fact that it was "secular" labor governments that first instituted illegal settlements in occupied Arab territory, not just the religious fanatics now stirring things up. This kind of one-sided reporting is, I think, an indication of how Israel—the Middle East's "only democracy" and "our staunch ally"—has been used as a foil for Islam.[35] Thus Israel has appeared as a bastion of Western civilization hewn (with much approbation and self-congratulation) out of the Islamic wilderness. Secondly, Israel's security in American eyes has become conveniently interchangeable with fending off Islam, perpetuating Western hegemony, and demonstrating the virtues of modernization. In these ways, three sets of illusions economically buttress and reproduce one another in the interests of shoring up the Western self-image and promoting Western power over the Orient: the view of Islam, the ideology of modernization, and the affirmations of Israel's general value to the West.

In addition, and to make "our" attitudes to Islam very clear, a whole information and policymaking apparatus in the United States depends on these illusions and diffuses them widely. Large segments of the intelligentsia allied to the community of geopolitical strategists together deliver themselves of expansive ideas about Islam, oil, the future of Western civilization, and the fight for democracy against turmoil and terrorism. For reasons that I have already discussed, the Islamic specialists feed into this great stream, despite the undeniable fact that only a relative fraction of what goes on in academic Islamic studies is directly infected with the cultural and political visions to be found in geopolitics and cold-war ideology. A little lower down come the mass media, which take from the other two units of the apparatus what is most easily compressed into images: hence the caricatures, the frightening mobs, the concentration on "Islamic" punishment, and so on. Never was their prejudice and ignorance more in evidence than when in the immediate aftermath of the Oklahoma City bombing (April 1995) they leaped collectively to the conclusion—led by instant "experts" like Steven Emerson—that Islamic terrorists were to blame, and they repeated their allegations, albeit on a smaller, quieter scale after the TWA Flight 800 disaster in July 1996. All of this is presided over by the great power establishments—the oil companies, the mammoth corporations and multinationals, the defense and intelligence communities, the executive branch of the government. When President Carter spent his first New Year in office with the shah in 1978 and said that Iran was "an island of stability," he was speaking with the mobilized force of this formidable apparatus, representing United States interests and covering Islam at the same time. And when eighteen years later the United States Secretary of Defense, visiting Saudi Arabia after the Khobar bombing, said there on August 2 that Iran was "the leading candidate" for culprit, he threatened that country with "strong action"; even though he reversed himself a few days later, the same forces were at work.

II. COMMUNITIES OF INTERPRETATION

How geopolitical strategists and the liberal intellectuals have made use of Islam in the United States is worth some attention here. It is not too much of an exaggeration to say that before the sudden OPEC price rises in early 1974, "Islam" as such scarcely figured either in the culture or in the media. One saw and heard of Arabs and Iranians, of Pakistanis and Turks, rarely of Muslims. But the dramatically higher cost of imported oil soon became associated in the public mind with a cluster of unpleasant things: American dependence on imported oil (which was usually referred to as "being at the mercy of foreign oil producers"); the apprehension that intransigence was being communicated from the Middle East and Persian Gulf regions to individual Americans; above all a signal — as if from a new, hitherto unidentified force — saying that energy was no longer "ours" for the taking. Words like "monopoly," "cartel," and "block" thereafter achieved a remarkably sudden if selective currency, although very rarely did anyone speak of the small group of American multinationals as a cartel, a designation reserved for the OPEC members. Mainly, though, it now seemed that with the new pressure on the economy, an equally new cultural and political situation was at hand. From being the world's dominant power, the United States was dramatically embattled. This was now the end of the postwar period, Fritz Stern said in *Commentary*.[36]

The most significant early statement of the change came in a series of articles published in *Commentary* during the early part of 1975. First there was Robert W. Tucker's "Oil: The Issue of American Intervention" (January), then there was Daniel Patrick Moynihan's "The United States in Opposition" (March), both in their titles making their arguments absolutely unmistakable. Moynihan went on to represent the United States at the United Nations, and there he made many speeches putting the world on notice that the "Western democracies" could not idly stand by and let themselves be bullied by a mere automatic majority of former colonies. But the terms were set in what he and Tucker had put forth previously in their *Commentary* essays.

Neither man had anything to say about Islam: however, "Islam," as it appeared a year later, was to play a role already prepared for it by the sudden and unacceptable changes described by Tucker and Moynihan. And they in turn gave shape, rhetoric, and dramatic structure to what many in the country were actually experiencing. For the first time in United States history it seemed that, as Tucker put it, egalitarianism was being applied from abroad to the United States itself. Here were foreign nations, according to Moynihan, essentially the creatures of British imperialism, whose ideas and identities were borrowed from British socialism. Their philosophies were based on the expropriation or, failing that, the distribution of wealth; they were interested in mere equality, not in production nor, it seemed, in liberty. "We *are* of the liberty party," he said, and then went on to add with a military flourish, "it might surprise us what energies might be released were we to unfurl those banners."[37]

These new nations, among them the oil producers, were interested in evening out the disparities between "us" and "them," something Tucker thought would introduce an ominous "interdependence," which we had better be prepared to resist—by invading them, if necessary.[38]

A number of strategies in these two articles are particularly worth mentioning. Neither Tucker's oil producers nor Moynihan's new Third World countries have identities, histories, or national trajectories of their own. They are simply mentioned, briefly characterized as a collective unit, then dropped. Former colonies are former colonies; oil producers are oil producers. Otherwise they appear to be both anonymous and strangely, even threateningly, obdurate. Their very *thereness* is something of an implied risk to "us." Secondly, these countries are abstractions against which the formerly established world powers are now arrayed. "Suddenly," Tucker says in a later essay on oil and force, "we are confronted with the prospect of an international society in which it may no longer be possible to insure an orderly distribution of what has been termed 'the world product' and this because the principal holders of power among the developed and capitalist states may no longer be the principal creators and generators of order."[39] If these new nations are not creators and generators of order, they can only be disruptors of it. And thirdly, they disrupt because all they are and can be as a group is inversely equal and opposite to "us."

What Tucker and Moynihan were saying followed in part the logic of a canonical hymn to the beleaguered Western ethos, which appears and reappears periodically in the modern history of the West. We see it, for example, in Henri Massis's *La Défense de l'Occident* (1927), and more recently in Anthony Hartley's article "The Barbarian Connection: On the 'Destructive Element' in Civilized History."[40] For Tucker and Moynihan, however, what opposes the West is not something "we" know, in the way that a European imperialist might speak of Orientals as "people we know" because in fact "we" have actually ruled them. At best, according to Moynihan, the new states of the Third World are imitations, known only through what they are imitating, not by virtue of what they are. There seems to be no point of reference on the new "international society" that Tucker refers to, except that it violates the old order. Who are the people, what are their actual desires, where did they come from, why do they behave as they do? These are unasked and consequently unanswerable questions.

At almost the very same time, the United States was retreating from Indochina. Much has recently been written about the "post-Vietnam syndrome" in American politics, although few people have also noted how the claim that very distant American interests need military defense against instability and insurrection seems to have been transferred whole from out of Vietnam and into a nearer place, the Muslim world. This has been accompanied by a progressive liberal disenchantment with Third World causes in general, particularly those whose promise seems to have been betrayed. One thinks, for example, of Gerard Chaliand's *Revolution in the Third World*, an anguished *cri de coeur* by a well-known supporter of the Vietnamese, Cuban, Angolan, Algerian, and Palestine liberation movements; writing in 1977, he concluded that most anticolonial efforts had resulted in mediocre, repressive states, hardly worth Western enthusiasm.[41] Or there is the case of *Dissent* magazine, which sponsored a symposium in its fall 1978 issue based on the question "Do the recent events in Cambodia [the Khmer Rouge victory there and subsequent reported horrors] warrant a reconsideration of our opposition to the Vietnam war?" The question, if not the answers, indicates the mood of withdrawal from 1960s enthusiasm and its replacement by a troubling discomfort with new international realities, all of them suggesting impending catastrophe. The general failure of the international economic system was justifiably adduced by the argument.

What the consumer of news and of oil sensed, in short, was an unprecedented potential for loss and disruption with no face or visible identity to it. All we knew was that what we took for granted was about to be taken from us. We could no longer drive our cars the way we used to; oil was much more expensive; our comforts and habits seemed to be undergoing a radical and most unwelcome change. Even the oil—that is, the actual material in question—remained vague in comparison with the threat of losing it: no one seemed to know whether there was a real shortage, or whether the long gas lines were induced by panic, or whether the oil companies' inexorably rising margins of profit had anything to do with the crisis.[42] Other things seemed more relevant. Robed Arabs, fantastically monied and well armed, obtrusively appeared everywhere in the West. The new Islamic assertiveness then could easily be traced back to what some called the Ramadan War in October 1973. On that occasion the Egyptian army crossed the formidable Bar-Lev line, but Arab soldiers did not run away as in 1967; they fought surprisingly well. Then the Palestine Liberation Organization appeared at the United Nations in 1974. Sheikh Yamani became a figure of authority for no ascertainable reason, except that he was Muslim and came from oil-rich Saudi Arabia. The shah of Iran also became a world leader. Indonesia, the Philippines, Nigeria, Pakistan, Turkey, various Gulf states, Algeria, Morocco: the suddenness of their capacity to trouble the United States in the mid-1970s was a disturbing concomitant of how little of their past and of their identity was known. A large number of Islamic states, personalities, and presences thereby passed imperceptibly in the general consciousness from the status of barely acknowledged existence to the status of "news."

There was no real transition from one to the other. Neither was there any significant segment of the population ready to explain or identify what appeared to be a new phenomenon, except for those who, like Moynihan and Tucker, were drawing world-historical conclusions in a framework that simply accommodated but made no specific allowances for Islam. As a result the image of Islam today, in every place that one encounters it, is an *unrestrained* and *immediate* one. There is an unstated assumption, first of all, that the proper name "Islam" denotes a simple thing to which one can refer immediately, as one refers to "democracy," or to a person, or to an institution like the Catholic Church. This immediacy is at work, for example, in the *Time* cover story referred to above. More disturbingly, however, it is regularly apparent in higher forms of general cultural argument, most often as a subject reflected on with gravity and seriousness in important liberal journals. In this respect, because of the changes in intellectual-geopolitical thinking that I have described, there is little difference between them and the mass media.

A noteworthy instance is an essay by Michael Walzer in the December 8, 1979 issue of the *New Republic*. Walzer's title is "The Islam Explosion," and he deals as a self-confessed layman with the vast number of important if (according to him) largely violent and unpleasant twentieth-century events—in the Philippines, in Iran, in Palestine, and elsewhere—which, he argues, can be interpreted as instances of the same thing: Islam. What all these events have in common, says Walzer, is first of all that they show a persistent pattern of political power encroaching on the West; second, that they are all generated from a frightening moral fervor (for instance, when Palestinians resist Israeli colonialism it is Walzer's firm assertion that such resistance is *religious*, not political or civil or human); and third, that these events shatter "the thin colonialist façade of liberalism, secularism, socialism, or democracy." In all three of these common characteristics it is "Islam" that can be discerned, and this "Islam" is a force overriding the distances in time and space that otherwise separate all these events. One could also notice how— again according to Walzer—if you speak of Islam you more or less automatically eliminate space and time, you eliminate political complications like democracy, socialism, and secularism, and you eliminate moral restraint. By the end of his essay Walzer has convinced himself (at least) that when *he* says the word "Islam" he is talking about a real object called Islam, an object so immediate as to make any mediation or qualifications applied to it seem mere supererogatory fussiness. With this immediacy, as its inevitable adjunct, goes the tendency to treat Islam as something without a history of its own; or if a history is conceded to it, that history will either seem irrelevant or it will essentially replicate itself—violence, fanaticism, despotism—over and over across the centuries. Thus it is that the arguments of conservatives like Moynihan and Tucker are confirmed and fleshed out by left-liberals.

Another aspect of the public image of Islam in the new geopolitical-intellectual setting is that it is invariably found in a confrontational relationship with whatever is normal, Western, everyday, "ours." This is certainly the impression one gets from reading Walzer, or from reading the scholars on whom Walzer relies. The very concept of a world of Islam—which was the subject of a four-part series by Flora Lewis in the *New York Times* on December 28, 29, 30, and 31, 1979 (about which I shall have something to say in Chapter Two)—implies its antagonism towards "our" world. Indeed, the very reason for the series was that Islam (that is, those Iranians holding American hostages) was "against" us. This feeling was intensified when Islam's apparent aberrations from normalcy were catalogued by Lewis: the peculiarities of the Arabic language, the oddities of its beliefs, the illiberal totalitarianism of its domination over its faithful, and so forth. If Islam's immediacy makes it seem directly available, then its divergence from our familiar reality and norms sets it against us directly, threateningly, drastically. The net result is that Islam has acquired the polymorphous status of a tangible, recognizable reality about which many statements and logical strategies—most of them anthropomorphic—become possible without restraint.

The literal apex of this trend was formulated in Samuel P. Huntington's celebrated summer 1993 *Foreign Affairs* article, "The Clash of Civilizations?" in which the former cold warrior articulates his view of the new, post–Cold War form of conflict. This, he says portentously, is nothing less than a clash of civilizations, nine or ten of them, the most dangerous of which to the West is Islam (or rather when it occurs, the alliance between Islam and Confucianism, for which he gives no evidence). Interestingly enough, the title of Huntington's amateurish foray into history and culture is taken from one of Bernard Lewis's essays, "The Roots of Muslim Rage," in which Lewis advances the daring, not to say sweeping, thesis that "Islam"—he is not very specific—is angry at modernity itself. From this tendentious nonsense Huntington, and no doubt many of his impressionable readers, draws such alarming conclusions as "the crescent-shaped Islamic bloc, from the bulge of Africa to central Asia, has bloody borders" (p. 34), thereby engendering more fear and less knowledge about Islam. It is the irreconcilability between certain civilizations and the West that Huntington is trying to promote, despite millenia of peaceful exchange and the possibility of future dialogue. Islam is the number one enemy of any Westerner, as if every Muslim and every Westerner were watertight little containers of civilizational identity, doomed to endless self-replication.

Thus you can readily equate Islam with almost any Muslim: Ayatollah Khomeini is the readiest candidate for this but so too are the railing Muslim mobs of Karachi, or Cairo, or Tripoli that are featured on television whenever instant examples of fundamentalism are required. Then you can go on to compare Islam to everything you dislike, regardless of whether what you say is factually accurate. As an example there is the Manor Books paperback publication of Khomeini's *Islamic Government* under the title *Ayatollah Kohmeini's Mein Kampf*. Accompanying this text is an analysis of it by one George Carpozi, Jr. (a senior *New York Post* reporter), who for reasons of his own claims that Khomeini is an Arab and that Islam began in the fifth century B.C. Carpozi's analysis begins euphoniously as follows:

Like Adolph Hitler in another time, Ayatollah Ruhollah Khomeini is a tyrant, a hater, a baiter, a threat to world order

and peace. The principal difference between the author of
Mein Kampf and the compiler of the vapid *Islamic Government* is that one was an atheist while the other pretends to be
a man of God.[43]

Such representations of Islam have regularly testified to a penchant for dividing the world into pro- and anti-American (or pro-
and anticommunist), an unwillingness to report political processes,
an imposition of patterns and values that are ethnocentric or irrelevant or both, pure misinformation, repetition, an avoidance of detail, an absence of genuine perspective. All of this can be traced, not
to Islam, but to aspects of society in the West and to the media
which this idea of "Islam" reflects and serves. The result is that we
have redivided the world into Orient and Occident—the old Orientalist thesis pretty much unchanged—the better to blind ourselves not only to the world but to ourselves and to what our
relationship to the so-called Third World has really been.

A number of rather important consequences have followed. One
is that a specific picture—for it is that—of Islam has been supplied.
Another is that its meaning or message has on the whole continued
to be circumscribed and stereotyped. A third is that a confrontational political situation has been created, pitting "us" against "Islam." A fourth is that this reductive image of Islam has had
ascertainable results in the world of Islam itself. A fifth is that both
the media's Islam and the cultural attitude to it can tell us a great
deal not only about "Islam" but about institutions in the culture,
the politics of information and knowledge, and national policy.

Yet in listing all these things about the general image of Islam
now current, I do not mean to suggest that a "real" Islam exists
somewhere out there that the media, acting out of base motives,
have perverted. Not at all. For Muslims as for non-Muslims, Islam
is an objective and also a subjective fact, because people create that
fact in their faith, in their societies, histories, and traditions, or, in
the case of non-Muslim outsiders, because they must in a sense fix,

personify, stamp the identity of that which they feel confronts them collectively or individually. This is to say that the media's Islam, the Western scholar's Islam, the Western reporter's Islam, and the Muslim's Islam are all acts of will and interpretation that take place in history, and can only be dealt with in history as acts of will and interpretation. I myself am neither religious nor of an Islamic background, although I think I can understand someone who declares himself or herself to be convinced of a particular faith. But insofar as I feel it is possible to discuss faith at all, it is in the form of *interpretations* of faith manifesting themselves in human acts that take place in human history and society. When, for example, we discuss the "Islamic" revolution that brought down the Pahlevi regime, or the Algerian Islamic Salvation Front (FIS) that defeated the government in municipal elections in 1990, we ought to say nothing about whether or not the revolutionaries were *really* Muslims in their faith; but we can say something about their conception of Islam as it pitted them self-consciously—Islamically, so to speak— against a regime they viewed as anti-Islamic, oppressive, tyrannical. We can then compare their interpretation of Islam with what *Time* and *Le Monde* have said about Islam, the Iranian revolution, and the Algerian Islamists.

In other words, what we are dealing with here are in the very widest sense communities of interpretation, many of them at odds with one another, prepared in many instances literally to go to war with one another, all of them creating and revealing themselves and their interpretations as very central features of their existence. No one lives in direct contact either with truth or with reality. Each of us lives in a world actually made by human beings, in which such things as "the nation" or "Christianity" or "Islam" are the result of agreed-upon convention, of historical processes, and, above all, of willed human labor expended to give those things an identity we can recognize. Not that truth and reality do not in fact exist. They do, as we know when we see the trees and the houses in our neighborhoods, or break a bone, or feel the anguish of a loved one's death. But on the whole, we tend to disregard or minimize the extent to which we depend for our sense of reality not just on the interpretations and meanings we form individually for ourselves but also on those we *receive*. For these received interpretations are an integral part of living in society. This has been clearly put by C. Wright Mills:

> The first rule for understanding the human condition is that men live in second-hand worlds. They are aware of much more than they have personally experienced; and their own experience is always indirect. The quality of their lives is determined by meanings they have received from others. Everyone lives in a world of such meanings. No man stands alone directly confronting a world of solid fact. No such world is available. The closest men come to it is when they are infants or when they become insane: then, in a terrifying scene of meaningless events and senseless confusion, they are often seized with the panic of near-total insecurity. But in their everyday life they do not experience a world of solid fact; their experience itself is selected by stereotyped meanings and shaped by ready-made interpretations. Their images of the world, and of themselves, are given to them by crowds of witnesses they have never met and never shall meet. Yet for every man these images—provided by strangers and dead men—are the very basis of his life as a human being.
>
> The consciousness of men does not determine their material existence; nor does their material existence determine their consciousness. Between consciousness and existence stand meanings and designs and communications which other men have passed on—first, in human speech itself, and later, by the management of symbols. These received and manipulated interpretations decisively influence such consciousness as men have of their existence. They provide the clues to what men see, to how they respond to it, to how they feel

about it, and to how they respond to these feelings. Symbols focus experience; meanings organize knowledge, guiding the surface perceptions of an instant no less than the aspirations of a lifetime.

Every man, to be sure, *observes* nature, social events, and his own self: but he does not, he has never, observed most of what he takes to be fact, about nature, society, or self. Every man interprets what he observes—as well as much that he has not observed: but his terms of interpretation are not his own; he has not personally formulated or even tested them. Every man talks about observations and interpretations to others: but the terms of his *reports* are much more likely than not the phrases and images of other people which he has taken over as his own. For most of what he calls solid fact, sound interpretation, suitable presentations, every man is increasingly dependent upon the observation posts, the interpretation centers, the presentation depots, which in contemporary society are established by means of what I am going to call the cultural apparatus.[44]

For most Americans (the same is generally true for Europeans) the branch of the cultural apparatus that has been delivering Islam to them for the most part includes the television and radio networks, the daily newspapers, and the mass-circulation news magazines; films play a role, of course, if only because to the extent that a visual sense of history and distant lands informs our own, it often comes by way of the cinema. Together, this powerful concentration of mass media can be said to constitute a communal core of interpretations providing a certain picture of Islam and, of course, reflecting powerful interests in the society served by the media. Along with this picture, which is not merely a picture but also a communicable set of feelings about the picture, goes what we may call its over-all context. By context I mean the picture's setting, its place in reality, the values implicit in it, and, not least, the kind of attitude it promotes in the beholder. Thus, if the Iranian crisis is regularly rendered by television pictures of chanting "Islamic" mobs accompanied by commentary about "anti-Americanism," the distance, unfamiliarity, and threatening quality of the spectacle limit "Islam" to those characteristics; this in turn gives rise to a feeling that something basically unattractive and negative confronts us. Since Islam is "against" us and "out there," the necessity of adopting a confrontational response of our own towards it will not be doubted. And if we see and hear a Walter Cronkite framing his nightly broadcast with the phrase "that's the way it is," we too will go on to conclude, not that the scene before us is what a television company has caused to appear before us in this way, but that it is indeed the way things are: natural, unchanging, "foreign," opposed to "us." No wonder that Jean Daniel of *Le Nouvel Observateur* was able to say on November 26, 1979, "les États-Unis [sont] assiégés par l'Islam." This is no less true in 1996.

Although one depends on them a great deal, television, newspapers, radio, and magazines are not our only source on "Islam." There are books, specialized journals, and lecturers available whose views are more complex than the essentially fragmented and immediate things delivered by the mass media.[45] Also, it is important to say that even in newspapers and on radio and television, there are a host of variations to be observed, as between one editorial line and another, or between different "op-ed" viewpoints, or between alternative or countercultural images and conventional ones. We do not, in short, live at the mercy of a centralized propaganda apparatus, even though a great deal of what is really propaganda is churned out by the media and even by reputable scholars. Yet despite the variety and the differences, and however much we proclaim the contrary, what the media produce is neither spontaneous nor completely "free": "news" does not just happen, pictures and ideas do not merely spring from reality into our eyes and minds, truth is not directly available, we do not have unrestrained variety at our disposal. For like all modes of communication, television, radio, and newspapers observe certain rules and conventions to get things across intelligibly, and it is these, often more than the reality being conveyed, that shape the material delivered by the media. Since these tacitly agreed-upon rules serve efficiently to reduce an unmanageable reality into "news" or "stories," and since the media strive to reach the same audience which they believe is ruled by a uniform set of assumptions about reality, the picture of Islam (and of anything else, for that matter) is likely to be quite uniform, in some ways reductive, and monochromatic. It ought to go without saying that the media are profit-seeking corporations and therefore, quite understandably, have an interest in promoting some images of reality rather than others. They do so within a *political* context made active and effective by an unconscious ideology, which the media disseminate without serious reservations or opposition.

A number of qualifications are now in order. It cannot be said that the Western industrial states are repressive, propaganda-ruled polities; they are not, of course. In the United States, for example, virtually any opinion can be expressed somewhere, and there exists an unparalleled receptivity on the part of citizens and the media to new, unconventional, or unpopular points of view. Moreover, the sheer variety of newspapers, magazines, and television and radio programs available, to say nothing of books and pamphlets, almost defies description or easy characterization. How then can one say, with any sort of fairness and accuracy, that it all expresses *one* general view?

Certainly one cannot say it, nor do I want even to try. But I do think that despite this extraordinary variety there is a qualitative and a quantitative tendency to favor certain views and certain representations of reality over others. Let me quickly recapitulate some things I have already said, and then go on to show how they synchronize with certain aspects of the media. We do not live in a natural world: things like newspapers, news, and opinions do not occur naturally; they are *made*, as the result of human will, history, social circumstances, institutions, and the conventions of one's profession.

Such aims of the press as objectivity, factuality, realistic coverage, and accuracy are highly relative terms; they express intentions, perhaps, and not realizable goals. They are definitely not to be thought of as occurring as a matter of course, just because we have grown accustomed to thinking of our newspapers as reliable and factual, while those in communist and non-Western countries are considered propagandistic and ideological. The actuality is, as Herbert Gans has shown in his important book *Deciding What's News*, that journalists, news agencies, and networks consciously go about deciding what is to be portrayed, how it is to be portrayed, and the like.[46] News, in other words, is less an inert given than the result of a complex process of usually deliberate selection and expression.

We have recently been given ample evidence of the way the major news-gathering and news-disseminating apparatus works in the West. Books by Gay Talese and Harrison Salisbury on the *New York Times*, David Halberstam's *The Powers That Be*, Gaye Tuchman's *Making News*, Herbert Schiller's various studies of the communications industry, Michael Schudson's *Discovering the News*, Armand Mattelart's *Multinational Corporations and the Control of Culture*:[47] these are but a few of the studies done from differing standpoints that affirm the extent to which the formation of news and opinion in the society at large operates according to rules, within frameworks, by means of conventions that give the whole process an unmistakable over-all identity. Like every human being, the reporter assumes that certain things are normal; values are internalized and need not always be tested, just as the habits of one's society are taken for granted; one's education, one's nationality and religion, are not forgotten as foreign societies and cultures are described; the consciousness of a professional code of ethics and a way of doing things are involved in what one says, how one says it, and who one feels it is said *for*. Robert Darnton has described these matters very engagingly in his essay "Writing News and Telling Stories," so much so that he makes us acutely sensitive not only to the reporter's working reality but to such things as "the symbiosis as well as antagonisms that grow up between a reporter and his sources," the pressures of "standardizing and stereotyping," and the way in which reporters "bring more to the events they cover than they take away from them."[48]

The American media differ from the French and British media because the societies differ so much, the audiences differ, the organizations and the interests differ. Every American reporter has to be aware that his or her country is the only superpower with interests and ways of pursuing those interests that other countries do not have. Independence of the press is an admirable thing, whether in practice or in theory; but nearly every American journalist reports the world with a subliminal consciousness that his or her corporation is a participator in American power which, when it is threatened by foreign countries, makes press independence subordinate to what are often only implicit expressions of loyalty and patriotism, of simple national identification. But surely this is not surprising. What is surprising is that the independent press is not normally thought of as taking part in foreign policy, although in many ways it so effectively does. Leaving aside CIA use of journalists working abroad, the American media inevitably collect information on the outside world inside a framework dominated by government policy; when there are conflicts with that policy, as was the case with Vietnam, then the media formulate their independent views, but even then the point is to have those bear upon, if not actually change, government policy, which is what counts for all Americans, members of the press included.

Abroad, the American journalist is understandably thrust back on what he or she knows best. This is always the case when one is transplanted to a foreign culture, and is especially true when the journalist feels he is abroad to translate what happens there into language that compatriots at home (policymakers included) can understand. He seeks out the company of other journalists abroad, but he also keeps in touch with his embassy, other American residents, and people known to have good relations with Americans.

Something not to be underestimated is the journalist's sense while abroad of relying not only on what he knows and learns but also on what as an American media representative abroad he *ought* to know, learn, and say. A *New York Times* correspondent knows exactly what the *Times* is and what in a corporate way it thinks of itself as being: surely there is a crucial, perhaps even a determining, difference between what the *Times*'s Cairo or Teheran correspondent files as a story and what a freelance journalist who hopes to get an article in *The Nation* or *In These Times* writes while in Cairo or Teheran. The medium itself exercises great pressure. Doing a spot on *NBC Nightly News* will cause a Cairo correspondent to put things differently than might *Time* magazine's Cairo bureau chief in an article prepared over a longer period of time. Then, too, there is the way a correspondent's foreign report is recast by the editors at home: another set of unconscious political and ideological constraints comes into play here.

American media coverage of foreign countries not only creates itself but also intensifies interests "we" already have there. Media points of view stress certain things for an American, others for an Italian or Russian. All of this converges around a common center, or consensus, which all the media organizations almost certainly feel themselves to be clarifying, crystallizing, forming. This is the point. The media can do all sorts of things, represent all sorts of points of view, provide many things that are eccentric, unexpectedly original, even aberrant. But in the end, because they are corporations serving and promoting a corporate identity—"America" and even "the West"—they all have the same central consensus in mind. This, as we shall see a little later in the case of Iran, shapes the news, decides *what* is news and *how* it is news. It does not, however, dictate or determine the news involuntarily: it is neither the result of deterministic laws, nor of conspiracy, nor of dictatorship. It is the result of the culture; better, it *is* the culture; and it is, in the case of the United States media, an appreciable component of contemporary history. There would be no point in analyzing and criticizing the phenomenon if it were not true that the media are responsive to what we are and want.[49]

The contents of this consensus are better described as actually occurring than either prescriptively or abstractly. So far as media coverage of Islam and Iran is concerned, I shall let the consensus speak for itself as it emerges in the course of analysis in my next chapter. Here, however, I want to make only two concluding comments on the subject.

First of all, we must remember that because the United States is a complex society made up of many often incompatible subcultures, the need to impart a more or less standardized common culture through the media is felt with particular strength. This is not a feature associated only with the mass media in our era, but one that has a special pedigree going back to the founding of the American republic. Beginning with the Puritan "errand in the wilderness," there has existed in this country an institutionalized ideological rhetoric expressing a peculiarly American consciousness, identity, destiny, and role whose function has always been to incorporate as much of America's (and the world's) diversity as possible, and to reform it in a uniquely American way. This rhetoric and its institutional presence in American life have been convincingly analyzed by numerous scholars, among them Perry Miller and, most recently, Sacvan Bercovitch.[50] One result of this is the illusion, if not always the actuality, of consensus, and it is as part of this essentially nationalist consensus that the media, acting on behalf of the society they serve, believe themselves to be functioning.

The second point concerns how this consensus actually works. The simplest and, I think, the most accurate way of characterizing it is to say that it sets limits and maintains pressures.[51] It does not dictate content, and it does not mechanically reflect a certain class or economic group's interests. We must think of it as drawing invisible lines beyond which a reporter or commentator does not feel it necessary to go. Thus the notion that American military power might be used for malevolent purposes is relatively impossible within the consensus, just as the idea that America is a force for good in the world is routine and normal. Similarly, Americans tend to identify with foreign societies or cultures projecting a pioneering, new spirit (e.g., Israel) of wresting the land from ill use or savages,[52] whereas they often mistrust and do not have much interest in traditional cultures, even those in the throes of revolutionary renewal. Americans assume that communist propaganda is guided by similar cultural and political constraints, but in America's case, the media's setting of limits and maintaining of pressures is done with little apparent admission or awareness that this is what in fact is being done.[53] And this, too, is an aspect of set limits. Let me give another simple example. When the American hostages were seized and held in Teheran, the consensus immediately came into play, decreeing more or less that only what took place concerning the hostages was important about Iran; the rest of the country, its political processes, its daily life, its personalities, its geography and history, were eminently ignorable: Iran and the Iranian people were defined in terms of whether they were for or against the United States.

So much for some general points about what might be considered the qualitative emphases in reporting and distributing. What needs to be said about quantitative aspects of the news as interpretation can be said straightforwardly. The widest distribution and therefore the strongest impact is made by a handful of organizations: two or three wire services, three television networks, CNN, half a dozen daily newspapers, two (or perhaps three) weekly news magazines.[54] It is only necessary to mention a few names for the point to be made: CBS, *Time*, the *New York Times*, AP. Among them they reach more people, make a deeper impression, get more of a certain kind of news across than do other smaller, less wealthy news-distributing agencies. What this means as far as foreign news is concerned is obvious: Such corporations have more on-the-spot reporters than others, and therefore their reporters furnish the basis for what participating newspapers, local television stations, and radio stations distribute to their immediate clientele. This sheer mass

and density of foreign-news reporting usually means greater authority and hence more frequent citation by people using the news, so
that a *New York Times* or CBS report will have credibility by virtue
of its source, its institutional prestige, its frequency (daily, hourly,
etc.), its air of expertise and experience. Together, the small group
of principal news suppliers and the extraordinary array of much
smaller suppliers that are independent of and yet in many ways dependent on the giants furnish an *American* image of reality that
does have a recognizable coherence.

A very serious consequence is that Americans have scant opportunity to view the Islamic world *except* reductively, coercively,
oppositionally. The tragedy of this is that it has spawned a set of
counterreductions here and in the Islamic world itself. "Islam" can
now have only two possible general meanings, both of them unacceptable and impoverishing. To Westerners and Americans, "Islam"
represents a resurgent atavism, which suggests not only the threat of
a return to the Middle Ages but the destruction of what is regularly
referred to as the democratic order in the Western world. For a great
many Muslims, on the other hand, "Islam" stands for a reactive
counterresponse to this first image of Islam as a threat. Anything said
about "Islam" gets more or less forced into the apologetic form of a
statement about Islam's humanism, its contribution to civilization,
development, and moral righteousness. That kind of counterresponse
has occasionally elicited the foolishness of a counter-counterresponse:
trying to equate "Islam" with the immediate situation of one or another Islamic country, or one or another Islamic authority. Then
you have Sadat calling Khomeini a lunatic and a disgrace to Islam,
Khomeini returning the compliment, and various people in the
United States debating the merits of each case. What is any Islamic
apologist to say when confronted with the daily count of people executed by the Islamic Komitehs, or when—as was reported by
Reuter's on September 19, 1979—the Ayatollah Khomeini announces
that enemies of the Islamic revolution will be destroyed out and
out? My point here is that all these relative, reductive meanings of

"Islam" depend on one another and are equally to be rejected for perpetuating the double bind.

How dire the consequences of this double bind are can be seen when we consider that United States support of the shah's modernization came to be regarded by Iranians as a rallying cry for opposing him, which was translated into a political interpretation of the monarchy as an affront to Islam; the Islamic revolution set itself in part the goal of resisting United States imperialism, which in turn appeared to resist the Islamic revolution by reinstating the shah symbolically in New York. Thereafter the drama has unfolded as if according to an Orientalist program: the so-called Orientals acting the part decreed for them by what so-called Westerners expect; Westerners confirming their status in Oriental eyes as devils.[55]

Nor is this all: many parts of the Islamic world are now inundated with United States–produced television shows. Like all other residents of the Third World, Muslims tend to be dependent upon a tiny group of news agencies whose job it is to transmit the news back to the Third World, even in the large number of cases where the news is *about* that world. From being the source of news, the Third World generally and Islamic countries in particular have become consumers of news. For the first time in history (for the first time, that is, on such a scale) the Islamic world may be said to be learning *about itself* by means of images, histories, and information manufactured in the West. This was dramatically in evidence during the Gulf War when CNN was watched by most Arabs (including, it is rumored, Saddam Hussein) as the principal source on the war. If one adds to this the fact that students and scholars in the Islamic world are still dependent upon American and European libraries and institutions of learning for what now passes as Middle East studies (consider that not one really complete and central library of Arabic material exists anywhere in the entire Islamic world), the fact that English is a world language in a way that Arabic, Persian, and Turkish are not, and the fact that for its elite much of the Islamic, economically oil-based world is now producing a managerial class of natives who are indebted for their economies, their defense establishments, and many of their political opportunities to the worldwide consumer-market system dominated by the West, one gets an accurate though extremely depressing picture of what the media revolution, serving a small segment of the societies that produced it, has done to "Islam."[56]

Not that there really is not an Islamic revival independent of the reactive process I have been describing. But it would be more accurate to speak of it in a less undifferentiated way. I for one feel more comfortable *not* using words like "Islam" and "Islamic" except with great restraint and many qualifications, precisely because in many Muslim societies and states (and of course in the West) "Islam" has become a political cover for much that is not at all religious. How then can we begin to discuss Muslim interpretations of Islam, and developments within it, responsibly?

First of all, following Maxime Rodinson, we should isolate the basic teachings of the Muslim religion as contained in the Koran, which is considered to be the word of God.[57] This is the bedrock identity of Islamic faith, which Salman Rushdie's *Satanic Verses* was seen as tampering with, although how it is interpreted and lived immediately moves us away from it. A second level comprises various conflicting interpretations of the Koran that make up the numerous Islamic sects, jurisprudential schools, hermeneutic styles, linguistic theories, and the like. A major tendency within this massive web of derivations from the Koran (most of which have had whole institutions, in some cases societies, built out of them) is what Rodinson has called "a return to the source." This means the impulse radically to get at the pristine spirit of things Islamic, and it is this impulse which Rodinson likens to a "permanent revolution" within Islam. What he does not say, however, is that all of the monotheistic religions and most ideological movements have this impulse within them; whether Islam is more consistently revolutionary in this regard than the others is very difficult to tell. In any event, "a return to the source" initiates movements (e.g., the

Wahhabis or, it is evident, the religious component of the Iranian revolution) whose impact on the society in which they occur varies from place to place and from time to time. Mahdism as an ideology in nineteenth-century Sudan was not the same thing as Mahdism there today. Similarly, the Egyptian Muslim Brotherhood during the late 1940s to the mid-1950s was a considerably more powerful ideological movement than today's Brotherhood; and both of those are different in organization and objectives from what is called the Muslim Brotherhood in Syria, which Hafez al-Assad in 1982 tried brutally to eradicate in Hama: his soldiers massacred several thousand reported members of the Brotherhood.

So far we have been speaking in terms of an Islam that is principally, but not exclusively, doctrinal and ideological, and already we have entered a field of considerable variation and contradiction. Already, in fine, the labels "Islam" and "Islamic" have to be used with some indication of *which* (and, for that matter, *whose*) Islam one is referring to. The matter is further complicated when we add a third level to our analysis, again following Rodinson. But it is best to quote him at length here:

> There is within Islam a third level, which must be carefully distinguished from the other two, comprising the way in which the various ideologies have been lived, the practices to which they have been linked, practices which certainly influenced them if they did not inspire them. The various systems into which Medieval Islam resolved itself were each lived in a different way, transformed from within even where they remained identical in terms of external references and texts. What is at issue here cannot be reduced to a mere contrast between the doctrines and texts of the "heretical" tendencies on the one hand, the Muslim "orthodoxy" recognized by the majority of Muslims on the other. In a conformist setting, here as elsewhere, it is often the case that the reinterpretation of one phrase of a holy text is enough to bring about an existential

change and the adoption of a critical or revolutionary attitude, which may remain an individual attitude or may spread to others. By contrast, it often happens that, as time goes by, a revolutionary or innovatory breakthrough comes to be interpreted in a conservative, conformist and quietist sense. There are many examples of such a process, which could indeed be called a general law of ideologies. The evolution of the Ishmaeli "sect" is particularly striking. In the Middle Ages, the Ishmaelis preached revolutionary subversion of the established order. Today, its leaders are the Aga Khans, millionaire potentates whose main concern is to enjoy the *dolce vita* in the company of film stars and celebrities, as the scandal sheets never tire of telling us.

In conclusion, the holy texts make no explicit pronouncements. The cultural tradition in general, be it in its more explicit formulations, its proclamations, its doctrinal texts or in the attitudes evoked by the former, presents a wide variety of aspects and allows one to justify the most mutually contradictory theses.[58]

This level, then, is the third type of interpretation, but it cannot take place without the other two. There can be no Islam without the Koran; conversely, there can be no Koran without Muslims reading it, interpreting it, attempting to translate it into institutions and social realities. Even when there is a strong orthodoxy of interpretation, as in Sunnite Islam—Sunna itself meaning orthodoxy based on consensus—there can very easily be revolutionary turmoil. The conflict between the Sadat government in Egypt and the various so-called fundamentalist Muslim parties takes place on the very same disputed ground of orthodoxy, Sadat and *his* Muslim authorities claiming to be the party of Sunna, his opponents making a very strong case that *they* are the true followers of Sunna.

If we add to these three levels of Islam the considerable numbers of Muslims past, present, and future, the sheer historical duration of "the venture of Islam" (from the seventh century to the present), the staggeringly varied geographical circumstances of Islamic societies (from China to Nigeria, from Spain to Indonesia, from Russia and Afghanistan to Tunisia), we will, I think, begin to understand the *political* implications of Western media and cultural attempts to call all of this "Islam" *tout court*. And I also think we will begin to sense that various *Islamic* attempts to respond to Islamic as well as Western circumstances, in all their variety and contradiction, are no less political, no less to be analyzed in terms of processes, struggles, and strategies of interpretation.[59] Let me try now rather sketchily to show what a staggeringly complex set of things is involved, although I should say at the outset that *the* greatest problem is that much of what one has to assess essentially escapes documentation.

We are very far from being able to say whether there is something called "an Islamic history," except as a rudimentary way of distinguishing the Islamic world from, say, Europe or Japan. Beyond that, Islamic and Western scholars are not in agreement as to whether Islam has taken root in certain geographical locations because of ecology or socioeconomic structure or the particular relationship between sedentary and nomadic patterns. As for the periods of Islamic history, these too are so complex as to defy a simple "Islamic" characterization. What are the points of similarity between the Alawi, Ottoman, Safavid, Uzbek, and Mogul states (which represent the great state organizations in Islamic history, until the twentieth century, in India, Turkey, and the Near and Middle East) and the modern Islamic nation-states? How do we explain the difference between (and even the origin of) the so-called Turco-Iranian and Turco-Arabian segments of the Islamic regions? In fine, as Albert Hourani clearly shows, the problems of definition, interpretation, and characterization within Islam itself are so great as to give Western scholars pause (to say nothing of Western nonscholars):

It is clear, then, that words like Islamic history do not mean the same things in different contexts, and that in no context are they enough by themselves to explain all that exists. In other words, "Islam" and the terms derived from it are "ideal types," to be used subtly, with infinite reservations and adjustments of meaning, and in conjunction with other ideal types, if they are to serve as principles of historical explanation. The extent to which they can be used varies according to the type of history we are writing. They are least relevant to economic history; as Rodinson has shown in *Islam et capitalisme*, the economic life of societies where Islam is dominant cannot be explained primarily in terms of religious beliefs or laws. In spite of the influence of Islamic law on commercial forms, other kinds of explanation are more relevant; as Cahen and others have suggested, concepts such as "Near Eastern," "Mediterranean," "medieval," "preindustrial" society are more useful than that of Islamic. For sociopolitical history, Islam can furnish some elements of explanation but by no means all that are needed. The institutions and policies of even the most fervently "Islamic" states cannot be explained without taking into account geographical position, economic needs, and the interests of dynasties and rulers. Even the history of those institutions that seem to be based upon Islamic law cannot be wholly explained in these terms: a concept like "Islamic slavery" dissolves if one looks at it closely; as Milliot's examination of the *'amal* literature of Morocco suggests, there were always ways in which local customs were incorporated into Islamic law as it was actually practiced. Only some kinds of intellectual history, at least before the modern period, can be explained in mainly Islamic terms, as a process by which ideas from outside were blended with those generated from within Islam itself to form a self-maintaining and self-developing system; even the *falâsifa* must now be seen, not as Greek philosophers in Arab clothes, but as Muslims using the concepts and methods of Greek philosophy to give their own explanation of the Islamic faith.[60]

Going still further, we will find no answer from anthropologists as to whether there is a *Homo islamicus,* or whether such a type has any analytical or epistemological value at all. We know much less than we need to know about the distribution of power and authority in Islamic societies—given that there are so many different ones scattered throughout history and geography—to say how we should assess the relationship between Islamic jurisprudential codes and their enforcement, or concepts of rule and their application, transformation, or persistence. We cannot with real certainty say, for example, whether some or all or any Islamic societies changed the bases of their authority from concepts of the sacred to concepts of legalistic doctrine. Language, aesthetic structures, sociologies of taste, problems of ritual, urban space, population shifts, revolutions of feelings: these are things in relation to context that have barely begun to be studied, either by Muslim or non-Muslim scholars. Is there such a thing as Muslim political behavior? How do class formations occur in Muslim societies, and how do these differ from those in Europe? What are the concepts, the tools of research, the organizational frameworks, the documents by means of which we can locate the best indications of everyday Muslim life in general? Is "Islam" in the end useful as a notion, or does it hide, distort, deflect, and ideologize more than it actually says? Above all, what bearing does the position of the person asking any or all of these questions have on the answers? In what ways is it different for a Muslim theologian to ask them in Iran, in Egypt, in Saudi Arabia, today as opposed to ten years ago? How do those statements compare with questions asked by a Russian Orientalist, a French Arabist at the Quai d'Orsay, or an American anthropologist at the University of Chicago?

In political terms, what has emerged as a standard Islamic response can be no less reifying, no less unhealthy, no less a cover for a multitude of devastatingly contradictory things than "Islam" is in the West. In nearly every instance, the state in the central Islamic region with the specific exception of Lebanon (from North Africa to

South Asia) expresses itself in consciously Islamic terms. This is a political as well as a cultural fact, and it has only just begun to be recognized in the West.[61] Saudi Arabia, for example, is (as its name indicates) the state of the royal house of Saud, whose victory over the other leading tribes in the region produced the state. What this family says and does in the name of the state and of Islam expresses the family's power, in addition to what has accrued to it as a member of the international community and what it has gathered to itself by way of considerable authority and legitimacy with regard to its people. Similar things can be said of Jordan, Iraq, Kuwait, Syria, prerevolutionary Iran, and Pakistan, except that it is not true in all instances that the ruling oligarchy is a family. But it is true that in numerous cases a relative minority—whether a religious sect, a single party, a family, or a regional grouping—dominates all others in the name of the state and of Islam. Lebanon and Israel are exceptions: both belong *in* the Islamic world, but in one a Christian minority rules (with increasing challenges from the other communities), in the other a Jewish. But they too express some considerable part of their hegemony in religious terms.

To a very large degree all of these states, each in its own way, have felt themselves to be responding to outside threats and have had recourse to religion, tradition, or nationalism reactively. Yet no one of them—and this is the main point—is free from an extraordinarily difficult dilemma. On the one hand, the state structure is not completely sensitive to the plurality of nationalities, religions, and sects contained within it. Thus in Saudi Arabia various tribes or clans feel themselves perhaps constrained by a state calling itself the Arabia of the Saud clan; and in Iran to this day, the state structure effectively stifles Azerbaijanis, Baluchis, Kurds, Arabs, and others, who feel their individual ethnic existence compromised as a result. The same tension on a wider front is repeated in Syria, Jordan, Iraq, Lebanon, and Israel. On the other hand, the dominant power in each of these states has used a national or religious ideology to give an appearance of unity against what are perceived as outside threats.

This is clearly the case in Saudi Arabia, where Islam is the only ideological current wide and legitimate enough to rally people to it. Since the late 1980s the king is referred to as *Khadim al Haramein* (the Custodian of the Two Shrines, i.e., Mecca and Medina), an even more specifically, more Islamically privileged title. In Saudi Arabia and in postrevolutionary Iran "Islam" has consequently come to be identified with many levels of national security; that these polities also fulfill the Western stereotype of Islam brings even more pressure, both external and internal, upon them.

Thus, far from being a uniform or even a coherent movement, "the return to Islam" embodies a number of political actualities. For the United States it represents an image of disruption to be resisted at some times, encouraged at others. We speak of the anticommunist Saudi Muslims, of the valiant Muslim rebels of Afghanistan, of "reasonable" Muslims like Sadat, the Saudi royal family, Mubarak, and King Hussein of Jordan. Yet we also rail at Khomeini's Islamic militants and Qaddafi's Islamic "Third Way," and in our morbid fascination with "Islamic punishment" (as administered by Khalkali) we paradoxically strengthen its power as an authority-maintaining device. In Egypt the Muslim Brotherhood, in Saudi Arabia the Muslim militants who took the Medina mosque, in Syria the Islamic Brotherhoods and Vanguards who once opposed the Baath party regime, in Iran the Islamic Mujahideen, as well as the Fedayeen and the liberals: these make up a small part of what is an adversarial current running through the nation, although we know very little about it. In addition, the various Muslim nationalities whose identities have been blocked in various post-colonial states clamor for *their* Islam. And beneath all this—in madrasas, mosques, clubs, brotherhoods, guilds, parties, universities, movements, villages, and urban centers all through the Islamic world—surge still more varieties of Islam, many of them claiming to guide their members back to "the true Islam."[62]

Only the tiniest fraction of this diverse Muslim energy is available to the Westerner now being asked by the media and by government spokesmen to consider "Islam." The most serious misrepresentations occur when Islamic "resurgence" is solicited.[63] In the minds and hearts of its adherents, surely Islam has always been resurgent, alive, rich in thought, feeling, and human production. And always in the thoughts of the faithful the "Islamic vision" (in W. Montgomery Watt's useful phrase[64]) has involved them in creative dilemmas. What is justice? What is evil? When are orthodoxy and tradition to be relied on? When is *ijtihad* (individual interpretation) in order? The questions multiply, and the work gets done—yet we in the West see or hear little of it. So much of Islamic life is neither bound by texts nor confined to personalities or neat structures as to make the overused word "Islam" an unreliable index of what we try to apprehend.

Nevertheless the conflict between "Islam" and "the West" is very real. One tends to forget that all wars have two sets of trenches, two sets of barricades, two military machines. And just as the war with Islam seems to have unified the West around opposition to Islam's power, so too has the war with the West unified many sectors of the Islamic world. For if Islam is a comparatively recent factor in the United States, for many Muslims the United States has seemed part of the West and has therefore been a phenomenon much deliberated upon for decades in many Islamic circles. Numerous Western scholars of Islamic culture tend, I think, to exaggerate the impact of "the West" upon Islamic thought during the last two hundred years, and they wrongly assume that "the West" and "modernization" have long occupied the center of Islamic awareness, from the Atlantic to the Gulf. That is not true, simply because like all societies Islamic ones focus on some things sometimes, on others at other times. But it is true that "the West" has furnished reams of polemics, treatises, and interpretative feats, as well as providing numerous personalities, parties, and movements in the Islamic world with various projects and tasks.[65] But it would be wrong and condescending to conceive of the whole Islamic world as bothered only by what after all is external to it.

It is also very important to remember that one of the great hall-marks of Islamic culture is its rich and vastly ingenious interpreta-tive energy. While it is perhaps true that Islam has produced no very powerful visual aesthetic tradition, it is more interesting and no less true that few civilizations have encouraged the arts of verbal inter-pretation on so wide a scale as Islam. Whole institutions, whole tra-ditions, whole schools of thought are built out of such things as a system of commentary, a linguistic theory, a hermeneutical perfor-mance. Not that we do not find the same things in other religious traditions; we do, but it needs to be remembered that the oral and verbal experiences in Islam developed with less competition, with more exclusiveness of domain, than elsewhere. No wonder, then, that the new Iranian constitution specified a *faqih* as the nation's guide, a *faqih* being, not a philosopher-king as the media seemed to believe, but literally a master of *fiqh*, of jurisprudential hermeneu-tics—in other words, a great reader.

Both the Islamic community of interpretation and the Western or American community as formed mainly by the mass media have tragically staked much of their energies on the narrow point of con-frontation between them, and in the process have ignored what did not concern this confrontation. Since we have been all too ready to believe this about Muslims opposing "satanic" America, it is worth-while to pay attention to some of what has actually happened. While it is undoubtedly true that control of "news" and "images" in the West is not in Muslim hands, it is no less true that only an over-all Muslim delay in understanding the reasons for Muslim depen-dence prevents their doing something about it. The oil-rich states, for their part, cannot complain that resources are lacking. What is lacking is some concerted political decision to enter the world in earnest, a lack which proves that far from being a united force the Muslim states are not yet politically mobilized or coherent. There are many talents that need to be encouraged first, not least among them the capacity to produce and articulate a conscious and force-ful self-image. But this means a serious assessment of the positive (not merely the reactive and defensive) values for which Muslims, in many different ways, stand. A great debate on this subject, usually in the form of discussions of *turath* (that is, the specifically Islamic heritage) has been going on in the Muslim world:[66] now its findings and its issues need to be communicated to the rest of the world. There is no longer much excuse for bewailing the hostility of "the West" towards the Arabs and Islam and then sitting back in outraged righteousness. When the reasons for this hostility and those aspects of "the West" that encourage it are fearlessly analyzed, an important step has been taken toward changing it, but that is by no means the whole way: something must be put in its place if a new mass of anti-Islamic propaganda is not to result. Certainly there are great dangers today in actually *following*, actually *fulfilling*, the prevailing hostile image of Islam, though that has thus far only been the doing of *some* Muslims and *some* Arabs and *some* black Africans. But such fulfillments underline the importance of what still has to be done.

In the great rush to industrialize, modernize, and develop themselves, many Muslim countries have sometimes been too compliant, I think, about turning themselves into consumer markets. To dispel the myths and stereotypes of Orientalism, the world as a whole has to be given an opportunity, by the media and by Muslims themselves, to see Muslims and Orientals producing and, more important, diffusing a different form of history, a new kind of sociology, a new cultural awareness: in short, Muslims need to emphasize the goal of living a new form of history, investigating what Marshall Hodgson has called the Islamicate world[67] and its many different societies with such seriousness of purpose and urgency as also to communicate the results outside the Muslim world. Surely that is what Ali Shariati had in mind for Iranian Muslims when he universalized Mohammed's migration (*hejira*) from Mecca to Medina into the idea of man as "a choice, a struggle, a constant becoming. He is an infinite migration, a migration within himself, from clay to God; he is a migrant within his own soul."[68]

Ideas like Shariati's informed the Iranian revolution in its early phases, which once and for all dismissed the dogmatically held supposition that Muslims were essentially incapable either of true revolution or of categorically throwing off tyranny and injustice. More important even than that, the Iranian revolution in its early phases demonstrated—as Shariati always argued—that Islam had to be lived as an invigorating existential challenge to man, not as a passive submission to authority, human or divine. In a world without "fixed standards" and with only a divine injunction to "migrate" from human clay to God, the Muslim, according to Shariati, had to carve a path of his own. Human society was itself a migration, or rather a vacillation, between "the pole of Cain" (ruler, king, aristocracy: power concentrated in one individual) and the "pole of Abel" (the class of the people, what the Koran calls *al-nass*: democracy, subjectivity, community).[69] Ayatollah Khomeini's moral teachings at first were just as compelling as this: with less suppleness than Shariati he also understood the Muslim predicament as a constantly lived choice between *hallal* and *haram* (righteousness and evil). Hence his call for an "Islamic" republic, by which he intended to institutionalize righteousness and rescue *al-mostazafin* (the oppressed) from their plight.

Such ideas of course produced an immense upheaval in Iran. In the West, however, the Islamic revolution brought forth no sympathetic attention. Even in Islamic countries, the Iranian experience is still feared for its energy, its fire, its disruptive, almost millenarian enthusiasm, although there has been an enormous post-Khomeini debate inside Iran, which has not been paid much attention. So in the Islamic world there runs a broad cleavage between official, orthodox views of Islamic life and, opposing that in many different forms, a countercultural Islam one of whose vanguard expressions was the Iranian revolution.[70] The irony is that Western views of Islam on the whole prefer to associate "Islam" with what many Muslims themselves are opposed to in the current scene: punishment, autocracy, medieval modes of logic, theocracy.

III. THE <u>PRINCESS</u> EPISODE IN CONTEXT

Still, the Islam before us is attenuated perforce by our power to represent it for our purposes, and reduced for the occasion by a state, a government, a group in response to us: this is a far thing from Islam as such, and at present the encounter between "us" and "them" does neither very much credit. More significantly, in what it covers it hides far more than it explicitly reveals. An analysis of one notorious early episode will illustrate what I mean.

On May 12, 1980, the Public Broadcasting Service ran the film *Death of a Princess*, which had been made by Anthony Thomas, a British filmmaker. A month before, the film had created a diplomatic incident between the United Kingdom and Saudi Arabia, resulting (though none of these measures lasted for very long) in the withdrawal of the Saudi ambassador from London, the boycott of England as a Saudi vacation spot, and the threat of further sanctions. Why? Because, according to the Saudis, the film insulted

Islam and gave an erroneous picture of Arab society in general and Saudi justice in particular. Based on the well-known execution of a young princess and her commoner lover, the film was done in the docudrama form of a search for truth: a British reporter tries to find out exactly what happened to the couple and in so doing travels to Beirut, where he talks to Lebanese and Palestinians, then to Saudi Arabia, where he is, of course, given the official runaround. In the process he learns only that the princess's story was interpreted by the people with whom he spoke as a symbol of their political and moral dilemmas. For the Palestinians she is, like them, an outcast in search of freedom and political self-expression. For some Lebanese she typifies the inter-Arab struggle that tore Lebanon apart. For official Saudis she is no one's business but theirs; they say that Westerners find her case interesting only because it discredits the regime. Finally, for a small handful of insiders, her plight is an indictment of the regime's hypocrisy, in which "Islam" and the Islamic *lex talionis* are used to cover up the royal family's corruption. The film's conclusion is open-ended: all the explanations have some truth to them, although no one of them seems adequate to cover what apparently happened.

In the United States, the Saudi government made known its opposition to the film's showing; two unpopular results were that Warren Christopher of the State Department brought the Saudis' displeasure publicly to PBS's attention, and Exxon took out advertisements in leading newspapers asking PBS to "review" its decision. In several cities the showing was canceled. As a concession to the film's controversial nature, PBS ran a sixty-minute panel discussion immediately following the broadcast. Six individuals plus a moderator talked about the film: one was the Arab League representative, another a Harvard law professor, a third a Boston-area Muslim clergyman, a fourth a young American "Arabist" (an unusual designation for someone who is neither an academic nor a government officer); then there were a young woman with business and journalistic experience in the Middle East, and, finally, a British journalist who was honest in his dislike of the Saudi scene. Together the six individuals delivered a reasonably incoherent hour of talk. Those who knew something about the region were often bound by their positions to stick to an officially apologetic "Muslim" line. Those who knew only a little showed it, of course, and the rest were fairly irrelevant.

Pressures against showing the film correctly raised First Amendment questions, and I believe it should have been shown. The important unstated things about the film (which as a work of cinematic art was, in my opinion, quite banal) were (*a*) that it was *not* made by a Muslim, (*b*) that it was likely to be the only, or if not the only, then certainly the most impressive film about Muslims the average viewer was likely to see, and (*c*) that discussions of the film, both during the panel show and elsewhere, very rarely touched on the question of context, power, and representation. Thomas's undertaking obviously had the ready-made glamour that a film about Yemen, for example, would not have: sex and "Islamic" punishment (particularly of the sort confirming "our" worst suspicions of Muslim barbarity) dressed up as an earnest docudrama could get a very wide audience. As *The Economist* said in April 1980: "Islamic law to most Westerners means Islamic punishment: a simplified myth that this film will have fostered." The audience became still wider once it was known that the Saudi government had been pulling strings (involving Exxon to boot) in the background. And all of this emphasized that *Death of a Princess* was clearly *not* a Muslim film but a film about which Muslims had only very limited, relatively unpopular, and ineffective things to say.

The filmmakers and PBS had to be conscious—as indeed any Muslim or Third World individual would be conscious—that no matter what the film contained, the making of it, the very act of representing scenes in images, was a prerogative deriving from what I have elsewhere called cultural power, in this case the West's cultural power.[71] It was simply irrelevant that the Saudis have more money: the actual production and distribution of news and of

images were more powerful than money because these, more than
mere capital, were the system that counted in the West. As against
this system, official Saudi objections about the film being an insult
to Islam were in their turn an attempt to mobilize another, far
weaker system of representation—the regime's self-image as a de-
fender of Islam—in order to neutralize the so-called Western one.

There was a further victory for the system in PBS's panel discussion. On the one hand, the network could accurately claim to have
responded to Saudi unhappiness by sensitively airing a discussion of
issues; on the other hand, PBS controlled the discussion by making
certain that a "balance" of views, disparate and not very well articu-
lated by relatively unknown "representative" individuals, would
blunt any intense or protracted analysis. The appearance alone of a
discussion served as a substitute for careful analysis. It was part of
the event's success that no one commented on how both the film's
Rashomon-style structure and the "balanced" panel left judgment
on the actual subject—a contemporary Muslim society—misleadingly open-ended. We never know (and perhaps do not really care)
what the princess actually did, just as we had the panel saying "the
film was bad" as well as "it was honest and good." But underlying
both film and discussion is the unacknowledged fact that such a
film *could* be made and shown with far more serious consequences
than a Saudi film that was considered damaging to Christianity, the
United States, or President Carter.

Besides seeking actively to prevent the film from being shown,
the Saudi regime was put in the position of denying something—
the incident itself—it really could not deny and at the same time
being unable to offer anything as a counter-version of Islam. The reductive double bind I spoke about earlier rendered any such objections to the film ineffective. For either one could say, No, that is not
really like that, or it is *this* way, provided of course there was some
way of saying such a thing effectively, as well as some place in
which to stand and say it. For the official Saudi spokesperson there
was no way and no place, except in the culturally discredited mode

of attempting to prevent the film from being shown at all. Saudi officials made some halfhearted efforts to suggest "good" aspects of Islam, but these did not resonate in the debate. Worse, there seemed to be no American constituency strong enough on cultural grounds to point out that the film was too inconsequential either as art or as politics to communicate anything of great moment. Unfortunately there was nothing worse, both in the United States and in England, than for opponents of the film to appear to be lackeys of Saudi financial interests (as was suggested with unconcealed contempt by J. B. Kelly in the *New Republic*, May 17, 1980). In fine, the film's opponents commanded no apparatus of diffusion by means of which to challenge the film critically. How trite the controversy was is quickly made evident when it is compared with the debate over Marcel Ophuls's *The Memory of Justice* or over *Holocaust* or when various Leni Riefenstahl films were revived.

The *Death of a Princess* showing enabled one to note more things than that. Both the American media and the surrounding intellectual and cultural milieu, well before *Princess* was ever heard of, had been literally teeming with overt anti-Islamic and anti-Arab slurs. On at least two occasions in the past, a Saudi Arabian king was directly insulted by New York City's mayor, who refused to greet him or show him even the commonest form of courtesy. Assiduous research has shown that there is hardly a prime-time television show without several episodes of patently racist and insulting caricatures of Muslims, all of whom tend to be represented in unqualified categorical and generic terms: one Muslim is therefore seen to be typical of all Muslims and of Islam in general.[72] High school textbooks, novels, films, advertisements: how many of them are really informative about, much less complimentary to, Islam? How widespread is knowledge of the difference between Shi'a and Sunni Islam? Not at all. Consider the general humanities courses offered by our own universities: most if not all of them in their syllabuses equate "the humanities" with the line of masterpieces that goes from Homer and the Attic tragedians to Dostoevsky and T. S. Eliot via the Bible,

Shakespeare, Dante, and Cervantes. Where does the civilization of
Islam, adjacent to Christian Europe, fit into such an ethnocentric
scheme of things? Barring very recent books with titles like *Militant
Islam* or *The Dagger of Islam* or *Ayatollah Khomeini's Mein Kampf,*
what general work on the civilization of Islam is widely circulated,
or referred to, or sought out? Would it have been possible to identify
a sector of the population as Islamophiles, the way we could name
Anglophiles, Francophiles, and the like? Only because during the
late 1980s an increased number of Muslim immigrants as well as
African-American converts to Islam were more visible (e.g., Louis
Farrakhan) could one speak of an American constituency.

After the *Princess* controversy died down, the Saudis unfortunately forgot to take offense when the *American Spectator* published an article by Eric Hoffer called "Muhammad's Sloth,"
subtitled "Muhammad, Messenger of Plod."[73] Nor did they include
in their list of misperceptions of Islam some reminder that the only
three countries in the world whose territory was under occupation
by a United States ally were Islamic states. Only when the royal
family's reputation was directly tarnished did the Saudi regime
threaten retaliation. How was it that Islam was injured only in the
one instance and not in the others? Why until the present have the
Saudis done relatively little to help promote an understanding of Islam? Hitherto their major educational contribution has been to the
University of Southern California's Middle East Studies Program,
which is run by a former ARAMCO employee.[74]

The full context of the *Death of a Princess* episode is still more
complex, however. United States military intervention in the Gulf
has been a common topic of discussion for at least five years, well
before the Gulf crisis and war of 1990–91. Ever since late 1978,
when the Saudis did not join the Camp David peace process, articles (some of them crammed with authentic-looking disinformation) highlighting the regime's numerous faults and weaknesses
have cropped up regularly. It was acknowledge in late July 1980 that
the CIA was behind some of these stories: see "The Washington

Leak That Went Wrong: A CIA Gaffe That Shocked Saudi Arabia,"
by David Leigh (*Washington Post*, July 30, 1980). For the first sixteen
years of its existence the *New York Review of Books* more or less ignored the Persian Gulf: then during the one year immediately following Camp David it published several articles on the Gulf, all of
them stressing the fragility of the present Saudi ruling arrangement.
At the same time, the daily press discovered Islam's ascendancy and
the medieval attributes of its punishments, jurisprudence, and conception of women; no one remarked at the same time that Israeli
rabbis expressed remarkably similar views on women or on non-
Jews, personal hygiene, and punishment, or that various Lebanese
clerics were just as bloodthirsty and medieval in their outlook. The
selectivity of focus on Saudi Arabia's Islamic regime seemed orchestrated around its vulnerability and its peculiarity, none of
which made it any less vulnerable and peculiar. But the intention
seemed to be that because it had defied the United States, Saudi
Arabia should now endure the benefit of "honest" reporting, as well
as submit to demands for ending cover-ups of Saudi censorship
(whereas no one complained about the fact that every news item
coming out of Israel had to pass the military censor). There was
widespread outrage routinely expressed at the absence of freedom
of the press in Saudi Arabia. (How many feelings of outrage were expressed about Israeli rules against Arab newspapers, schools, and
universities on the West Bank?) Saudi Arabia all of a sudden became a unique case to be upbraided by liberals and Zionists in one
chorus, praised and nearly coddled by conservative financiers and
senior establishment figures in another. This further demoted
Saudi Arabia, made it more unacceptable and intellectually preposterous, which in many ways it is, except that it is made into a
convenient symbol for everything about the "Islamic" world.

One result of all this was that when the *Princess* film episode occurred "we" loudly deplored "their" hypocrisy and corruption,
"they" in turn resented our power and our insensitivity. The confrontation further channeled the range of discussion between "us"

and "them," making true discussion, analysis, and exchange virtually out of the question. Muslim self-identity has consequently tended to be strengthened by losing encounters with a monolithic block representing itself as "Western civilization," and sensing this, the West's own demagogues inveigh against medieval fanaticism and cruel tyranny. For almost every Muslim, the mere assertion of an Islamic identity becomes an act of nearly cosmic defiance and a necessity for survival. War seems an extremely logical outcome; hence the appeal of Huntington's fatalistic prescription for the clash of civilizations.

An index of this is to contrast *Death of a Princess* with another "Islamic" film shown on PBS fifteen years later, *Jihad in America* (1995). Whereas the earlier documentary presents an exotic, distant version of Islam, its more recent counterpart hammers home the point that the United States itself has become the battleground, with all sorts of mad Muslims plotting terror and horrifying warfare against us in our midst. The film's presenter is one Steven Emerson, whose background in Middle Eastern politics, history, culture, or religion is non-existent; his qualification, stated proudly at the film's outset, is that he has been a reporter on Islamic terror. For in the past decade there has arisen a new cadre of such dubious experts, whose appeal to an understandably anxious public—the World Trade Center bombing was indeed a frightening episode, and a tiny handful of extremist Muslims were indeed the culprits, although Emerson does not directly connect their leader, Sheikh Omar Abdel Rahman, a veteran of United States-sponsored Mujahideen in Afghanistan, with a calculated United States policy in that country to breed groups of such extremists as fighters against the Soviet Union—in the name of counter-terrorism, expertise on terrorism, knowledge of the Islamic threat and the like, has given them an easy prominence in the sensationalist media. Although *Jihad in America* makes a gesture toward responsibility and careful discrimination in talk about Islam, and despite a few explicit statements in the film that most Muslims are peace-loving and "like us," the purport of the film is to agitate against Islam as a sinister breeder of cruel, insensate killers, plotters, and lustfully violent men. In scene after scene—all of them isolated from any real context—we are regaled with fulminating, bearded imams, raging against the West and Jews most especially, threatening genocide and unending warfare against the West. By the film's end the viewer is convinced that the United States contains a vast, intricate web of secret bases, conspiratorial plotting centers, and bomb factories, all of them intended for use against innocent, unsuspecting citizens.

It is interesting that Emerson was called on by the media immediately after the April 1995 Oklahoma City bombing; he was remarkably unhesitant in proclaiming that the outrage was the work of Middle Easterners, which fueled the search for swarthy Islamic-looking types in the first few days after the bombing. Emerson was not heard from when it was revealed that home-grown extremists—white and Protestant—were responsible for the bombing, although it is not unreasonable to suppose that he will be called on again. His film makes no effort to compare the size and potential of Islamic *jihad* terrorists with the various local networks of militiamen, una-bombers, and the like, that have bedeviled the country. Nor in its furiously concentrated last half, with its jump cutting from scene to scene, from one unsupported assertion to another that Muslims are trying to destroy the United States, does he give any indication of actual numbers, of actual frequency of occurrences, meetings, and so forth. The impression Emerson finally leaves the viewer with is that Islam equals *jihad* equals terrorism, and this in turn reinforces a feeling of cultural fear and hatred against Islam and Muslims.

The power of Emerson's film, and the cleverness of its strategy, is that of course there is no influential countervailing view of Islam in the media, little sense that the huge majority of Muslims should not really be associated with the marginal and tiny groups that he has blown out of all proportion. A considerable part of the animus fed by Emerson's representation of "Islam" also derives from its putative anti-Semitism and hatred of Israel; several scenes of havoc after suicide bombings in Israel are shown, as well as a brief visual reference to the bombing of the Jewish cultural center in Buenos Aires, for which no Muslim culprits have been arrested. It is clear therefore that these depictions of Islamic terror are meant to arouse feelings of anger and resentment in American supporters of Israel, for whom that country is an innocent victim of gratuitous, anti-Semitic Islamic terror. This of course is the Israeli official line, which obscures anything Israel might have done—with unconditional United States support—in a military occupation of the West Bank, Gaza, East Jerusalem, the Golan Heights, and South Lebanon that has endured for decades, in which Israeli planes have conducted strikes against hospitals, civilian concentrations, schools, orphanages, etc. All this is calculatedly left out of Emerson's film, the better to be able to direct the American viewers' hatred and fear of Islam against all Muslims, with the sense that "we" are innocent of anything except our democracy, love of freedom, etc.

Perhaps it is too much to hope that some people here and in the Islamic world *may* discover the deplorable limits of coercive labels like "the West" and "Islam." Perhaps it is too much to expect that these labels and the frameworks supporting them will over time lose their imprisoning force, but it may be possible that "Islam" will seem less monolithic and frightening and more the result of interpretations that serve our immediate political purposes and characterize our anxieties, whether "we" happen to be Muslims or non-Muslims. Once we finally grasp the sheer power and the subjective components of interpretation, and once we recognize that many of the things we know are *ours* in more ways than we normally admit, we are well on our way to disposing of some naïveté, a great deal of bad faith, and many myths about ourselves and the world we live in. Thus to understand even "the news" is in a certain sense to understand what we are and how a certain sector of the society in which we live works. Only after we have understood those things can we go on to grasp the "Islam" that is ours and the different kinds of Islam that exist for Muslims.

Let us now try to analyze in detail what has been the most troubling episode between "us" and "Islam": the Iranian hostage crisis, whose resonance is felt in the continuing impasse between the United States and Iran in the 1990s. There is much to be seen and much political confusion to dispel in this episode, both because it has been so traumatic and dense for us and because, looked at critically, it says many things about processes now at work elsewhere in the Muslim world. Once we have approached Iran, we can then go on to discuss the broader issues linking Islam and the West in this latest phase.

CHAPTER
TWO

THE IRAN STORY

I. HOLY WAR

Iran continues to arouse seething passions in Americans, not only because of the deeply insulting and unlawful seizure of the Teheran embassy, which was occupied by Iranian students on November 4, 1979, but also as a result of the incredibly detailed, highly focused attention of the media to the event and Iran's demonization for years after it. It is one thing to know that the country's diplomats have been seized and that Americans seem incapable of freeing them; it is quite another thing to watch that taking place night after night on prime-time television. But we have reached a point, I think, where there is some need to evaluate critically the meaning of "the Iran story," as it has been called, to understand its presence in the American consciousness rationally and dispassionately, especially since around ninety percent of what Americans have recently come to know about Iran they know through radio, television, and newspapers. There is no way of mitigating the hurt and outrage caused by the holding of the American hostages, nor the confusion caused by the conflicts within the Islamic world, but in my opinion we should feel grateful that, except on one occasion, the United States did not use military force against Iran. In any event, we must start to take stock of the origins of what Iran has been to Americans in the general context of United States and Western relations with the Islamic world: how it has looked, how it was literally presented and re-presented to Americans by the media day after day.

Iran took up much of the nightly network news immediately after the embassy was seized. For several months ABC scheduled a daily late-evening special, *America Held Hostage*, and PBS's *Mac-Neil/Lehrer Report* ran an unprecedented number of shows on the crisis. For months Walter Cronkite would add to his "that's the way it is" a reminder of how many days the hostages had been in captivity: "the two-hundred and seventh day," and so on. Ted Koppel's ABC program *Nightline*, which achieved longevity and success, began because of the hostage crisis. Hodding Carter, the State Department spokesman during the period, achieved star status within about two weeks; on the other hand, neither then Secretary Cyrus Vance nor Zbigniew Brzezinski was very much in evidence until after the abortive rescue effort in late April 1980. Interviews with Abolhassan Bani-Sadr, with Sadegh Ghotbzadeh, with parents of the hostages, alternated regularly with Iranian demonstrations, three-minute courses on the history of Islam, bulletins from the ex-shah's hospital, solemn-faced commentators and experts analyzing, reflecting, debating, haranguing, and advancing theories, courses of action, speculations about the future interpretations of events, psychologies, Soviet moves, and Muslim reactions: and still the fifty-odd Americans remained incarcerated.

Throughout the period, it became evident that the Iranians were using the media to what they considered their advantage, a consideration certainly not lost on the networks. Frequently, the students in the embassy would schedule "events" to meet satellite deadlines and nightly news broadcasts in the United States. From time to time Iranian officials indicated that it was their plan thus to turn the American people against the policy of their government. This was a bad miscalculation at the outset. Later on the policy had a peculiar, not altogether unwelcome effect, which was to stimulate the media to a more genuinely investigative attitude. But what I want to discuss here is how Iran appeared to Americans during the most intense period of crisis; the other side of the story has to be subordinated to this concern.

As I said in Chapter One, much of the most dramatic, usually bad, news of the past decade, including not only Iran but the Arab-Israeli conflict, oil, and Afghanistan, has been news of "Islam." Nowhere was this more evident than in the long Iranian crisis during which the American consumer of news was given a sustained diet of information about a people, a culture, a religion—really no more than a poorly defined and badly misunderstood abstraction—always, in the case of Iran, represented as militant, dangerous, and anti-American.

What makes the Iran crisis a good occasion for examining the media's performance is exactly what made it understandably agonizing for so many Americans: its duration and the fact that what Iran came to symbolize represented American relations with the Muslim world. Nevertheless, I think we must look carefully at what, over the initial period of two or three months, became apparent in the media's attitudes and in their doing things in such a way as simply to perpetuate these attitudes, despite the new challenges, the unprecedented political changes and crises the West will have to face from now on. In time, though, there were changes in media reporting, and these on the whole tell a slightly more encouraging story than what appeared at the outset.

To sift through the immense amount of material generated by the takeover of the United States Embassy in Teheran is to be struck by a number of things. First of all, it seemed that "we" were at bay, and with us the normal, democratic, rational order of things. Out there, writhing in self-provoked frenzy was "Islam" in general, whose manifestation of the hour was a disturbingly neurotic Iran. "An Ideology of Martyrdom" ran the title of a prominent box about Iranian Shi'a Islam in *Time*'s November 26 issue; concurrently, as if copying the same testimony, *Newsweek* featured a page entitled "Iran's Martyr Complex," also on November 26.

There seemed to be plenty of evidence around for that. On November 7 the *St. Louis Post Dispatch* had printed the proceedings of a workshop held in St. Louis on Iran and the Persian Gulf. One expert was quoted as saying that "the loss of Iran to an Islamic form of government was the greatest setback the United States has had in recent years." Islam, in other words, is by definition inimical to United States interests. The *Wall Street Journal* had editorialized on November 20 that "civilization receding" came from "the decline of the Western powers that spread these [civilized] ideals to begin with," as if not to be Western—the fate of most of the world's population, Islam's included—is not to have any civilized ideals. And there was Professor J. C. Hurewitz of Columbia University, who, when asked by an ABC reporter on November 21 whether to be a Muslim Shi'ite meant being "anti-American," responded with a categorical affirmative.

All the major television commentators, Walter Cronkite of CBS and Frank Reynolds of ABC chief among them, spoke regularly of "Muslim hatred of this country" or more poetically of "the crescent of crisis, a cyclone hurtling across a prairie" (Reynolds, ABC, November 21); on another occasion (December 7) Reynolds voiced-over a picture of crowds chanting "God is great" with what he supposed was the crowd's true intention: "hatred of America." Later in the same program we were informed that the Prophet Mohammed was "a self-proclaimed prophet" (which prophet hasn't been?) and then reminded that "Ayatollah" is "a self-styled twentieth-century title" meaning "reflection of God" (unfortunately, neither is completely accurate). The ABC short (three-minute) course of Is-

lam was held in place with small titles to the right of the picture,
and these told the same unpleasant story of how resentment, suspicion, and contempt were a proper response to "Islam": Mohammedanism, Mecca, purdah, chador, Sunni, Shi'ite (accompanied
by a picture of young men beating themselves), mullah, Ayatollah
Khomeini, Iran. Immediately after these images the program
switched to Janesville, Wisconsin, whose admirably wholesome
schoolchildren—no purdah, self-flagellation, or mullahs among
them—were organizing a patriotic "Unity Day."

"Militant Islam: The Historic Whirlwind" announced the *New
York Times Sunday Magazine* on January 6, 1980; "The Islam Explosion" was the contribution of Michael Walzer in the *New Republic*'s December 8 issue. Both essays, like all the others, purported
not only to prove that Islam was one unchanging thing that could
be grasped over and above the remarkably varied history, geography,
social structure, and culture of the forty Islamic nations and the approximately 800,000,000 Muslims who live in Asia, Africa, Europe,
and North America (including many millions in the Soviet Union
and China), but also to reveal—as Walzer has it—that wherever
there has been murder, war, protracted conflict involving special
horrors, "Islam clearly played an important part." It did not seem to
matter that the normal rules for evidence had been suspended, or
that the writer knew neither the languages nor the societies on
which he pronounced, or that common sense simply withdrew
when "Islam" was discussed. The *New Republic*'s lead editorial reduced Iran to "the rage of thwarted religious passion" and to "Islam
amok," arguing learnedly what the Shari'a, "the holy law of Islam,"
has to say on spying, safe-conduct, and the like. All of this reinforced the main point that if Islam is at war with us, we had better
join battle with our eyes open.

There were slightly more subtle ways of incriminating "Islam"
than the *New Republic*'s. One was to put an expert before the public and have him or her suggest that even though Khomeini was not
really "representative of Islamic clergy" (this was L. Dean Brown,

former United States ambassador to Jordan and special envoy to Lebanon, president of the Middle East Institute, speaking on the *MacNeil/Lehrer Report* November 16), the "ironclad" mullah was a throwback to an earlier (obviously more authentic) Islamic age; the mobs in Teheran reminded Brown of Nuremberg, just as the street demonstrations were signs of "the circus as principal entertainment" habitually provided by dictators.

Another method was to suggest that invisible lines connected various other aspects of the Middle East to Iranian Islam, then damn them together, implicitly or explicitly depending on the case. When former Senator James Abourezk went to Teheran, the announcement on ABC and CBS was made with a reminder that Abourezk was "of Lebanese origin." No reference was ever made to Representative George Hansen's Danish background, or to Ramsey Clark's WASP ancestry. Somehow it was considered important to touch on the vaguely Islamic taint in Abourezk's past, although he happens to be of Christian Lebanese stock. (A related matter was the use of bogus Arab "sheiks" as decoys in the Abscam case.)

Much the most flamboyant use of suggestion originated in a small front-page item by Daniel B. Drooz in the *Atlanta Constitution* on November 8, alleging that the Palestine Liberation Organization was behind the embassy takeover. His sources were "diplomatic and European intelligence" authorities. George Ball stated gnomically in the *Washington Post* on December 9 that "there is some basis to believe that the whole operation is being orchestrated by well-trained Marxists." On December 10, NBC's *Today Show* ran an interview with Amos Perlemutter and Hasi Carmel, identified principally as "a professor at American University" and "a correspondent for the Paris weekly *L'Express.*" In fact both men are Israelis. Robert Abernethy questioned them on their allegations about "a coincidence of interests" between the Soviet Union, the PLO, and "radical" Muslims in Iran: was it true, he asked, that all three forces were *actually* involved in the embassy operation? Well, no, they replied, but there was this coincidence of interests. When

Abernethy volunteered politely that what they were saying sounded like some Israeli attempts to "tarnish the image of the PLO," Professor Perlemutter angrily demurred, citing nothing less than "intellectual integrity" as *his* platform.

Not to be outdone, CBS introduced its *Nightly News* on December 12 with Marvin Kalb from the State Department quoting those same (equally unnamed) "diplomatic and intelligence" sources referred to by Drooz a month earlier, in which it was once again affirmed that the PLO, Islamic fundamentalists, and the Soviet Union had cooperated at the embassy. The PLO men were the ones who mined the compound, Kalb said; this was known, he went on sagely, by virtue of "the sounds of Arabic" that could be heard inside the embassy. (A brief report of Kalb's "story" was carried the next day in the *Los Angeles Times*.) It remained for no less a personage than Hudson Institute expert Constantine Menges to argue exactly the same thesis, first in the *New Republic* of December 15, 1979, then twice more on the *MacNeil/Lehrer Report*. No more evidence was given, except of course the diabolism of communism in natural alliance with the devilish PLO and satanic Muslims. (One wonders why MacNeil and Lehrer did not invite Menges back to comment either on the Soviet invasion of Afghanistan or on official Iranian criticism of it.)

"Where there are Shi'ites, there is trouble," Daniel B. Drooz argued in the *Atlanta Journal-Constitution* on November 29. Or as the *New York Times* put it more judiciously in a small headline November 18: "Embassy seizure is linked to both Shi'ite approval of authority and anger over the Shah." Within a week after the embassy occupation took place on November 4, pictures of a scowling Ayatollah Khomeini were as frequent and unchanging in what they were supposed to be telling the viewer as the endless pictures of vast Iranian mobs. The burning (and selling) of Iranian flags by irate Americans became a regular pastime; the press faithfully reported this kind of patriotism. Interestingly, there were frequent reports showing the popular confusion between Arabs and Iranians, such as the one carried by the *Boston Globe* on November 10 of an angry Springfield crowd chanting "Arab go home." Special features on Shi'a Islam proliferated everywhere, although it is surprising how relatively few articles treated Iran's *modern* history, or referred to the singularly important political resistance of the Persian clerics both to foreign intervention and to the monarchy since the late nineteenth century, or even considered how it was that Khomeini was able to bring down the shah and an undefeated army with radio cassettes and largely unarmed popular masses as his major instruments.

Symbolic in a small way, perhaps, was Walter Cronkite's inability to pronounce names correctly. Ghotbzadeh's name was changed nearly every time it was pronounced, usually into something like "Gaboozaday." (On November 28 CBS called Beheshti "Bashati," and not to be left out, ABC on December 7 changed Montazeri's name to "Montessori.") Almost every capsule history of Islam was either so confusing as to be nonsensical or so inaccurate as to appear frightening. Take, as an example, a CBS *Nightly News* segment on Islam November 21. Moharram was described by reporter Randy Daniels as a period when Shi'ite Muslims "celebrated Mohammed's challenge to world leaders"—a statement so wrong as to be silly. Moharram is an Islamic month; Shi'ite Muslims commemorate the martyrdom of Hussein during the first ten days of Moharram. Later we were informed that the Shi'ites have a persecution complex, so "no wonder they produced a Khomeini"; it was reassuring, though no less misleading, to be told that he does not represent Islam as a whole. In the same program I was interviewed for my wisdom, and mistakenly identified as a professor of Islamic studies. On November 27 a CBS reporter informed us that all of Iran was suffering from "revolutionary hangover," as if Iran were the corner drunk.

But it was when the maximum authority of the elite *New York Times* was brought to bear upon Islam that the truly depressing nature of what force "held America hostage" stood forth. The *Times*'s Islam, however, had a great deal to do with what the *Times* is. It is not only that it is America's leading newspaper, but that taken together with its catholicity, level of expert reporting, responsibility, and, most important, its ability to write credibly from the viewpoint of national security give it a force of unique gravity. In others words, the *Times* can speak authoritatively about a subject and also make that subject pertinent to the nation; it does so deliberately and, it seems, successfully. Thus Harrison Salisbury recalls that in the spring of 1961 President Kennedy told Turner Catledge of the *Times* that had the paper printed more details of the impending Bay of Pigs invasion (which the *Times* had gathered on its own), "you would have saved us from a colossal mistake."[1] After the Bay of Pigs, Salisbury says, neither the *Times* nor the world yet understood that Tad Szulc's reporting was not exceptional, and for that matter, that what the newspaper accomplished was not exceptional either. It was simply a matter of routine. The *Times* had become an extraordinarily strong institution functioning as a power almost coeval with the nation itself.

The Times had now reached a critical mass, not a mass in terms of readers and advertisers, although this was inextricably linked to it. No, it had reached a critical mass of reporting and expertise. It now genuinely covered the world, covered Washington, covered the nation and the city with its own staff men and women, and these were not merely journeymen. They were the best reporters and editors who could be obtained. They had gathered on *The Times* not because of monetary rewards—*The Times'* pay scale was good but had never been spectacular. They had gathered because *The Times* offered a unique outlet for reporting and editing. Nowhere were standards of professionalism so high. The critical mass of reporters now [after the Bay of Pigs] was of such size and quality that it functioned almost without conscious direction. All over the world *Times* men were ranging, news tentacles acutely inclined, probing and digging and asking questions.[2]

Thus in due course, wielding power decisively had come to be the paper's collective mission, and reporters did their *Times* reporting more or less as a matter of habit, "without conscious direction." By 1971, when the *Times* began publishing the Pentagon Papers, a hundred years had passed since it had brought down the Boss Tweed clique at Tammany Hall by publishing the relevant government documents. Here it was again, according to Salisbury, going beyond the law with its exemplary moral prescience, acting in the national interest,[3] demonstrating its power to expose the truth and to move governments. Its financial success under its most recent managing editor, A. M. Rosenthal, was, it is true, the result of adding features like the "Home" and "Living" sections to the daily edition; but the added revenue made possible expanded foreign reporting too.

> The new sections had given the paper a financial floor that made its position virtually unassailable, and this at a moment when the *News* and the *Post* were floundering. Now, unlike any other paper in the country, *The Times* could and did throw $30,000 a month, maybe $50,000 a month, over and above salaries and staff into covering the fall of Iran; the money was there, no strain.[4]

At the end of the year during which Iran "fell" the *Times* turned to Islam at last. On December 11 a full two pages were devoted to a symposium entitled "The Explosion in the Moslem World." The seven participants included three scholars from the Muslim world who were now living and working in the United States; the other four were distinguished experts in the modern history, culture, and societies of the Islamic world. Each of the questions they were asked to discuss was political, and all of the questions touched on the threat of Islam to American interests. Here and there the experts would attempt to discuss the Islamic world as if it had different pasts, different political processes, different kinds of Muslims. But these attempts were overridden by the force of questions like the following: "If we are so satanic in the eyes of many Moslems at this point, how should we deal with forces, with leaders, with governments that we feel some affinity to? Bazergan shakes Brzezinski's hand and he's gone. Bani-Sadr says he wants to come to New York and that finishes him. Is there a lesson for us in how we deal with other regimes? Is there a lesson of restraint or what?" The *Times* obviously felt it was going directly to the source: if Muslims were "ruled" by Islam, question Islam face-to-face. The interesting point is that the scholars were trying to subdivide "Islam" into its more important components, whereas the *Times* recomposed these components into powers either "inimical" or "friendly" to United States interests. The net result of the symposium was exasperation, since it was clearly implied in the last set of *Times* questions that persuasion and logic could not work and therefore force might have to be used as a last resort.

Doubts about what "we" were to think about Islam were cleared up when, on the last four days of 1979, the *Times* published a series of four long articles by Flora Lewis, all attempting seriously to deal with Islam in crisis ("Upsurge in Islam," December 28, 29, 30, 31). There are some excellent things in her articles—for example, her success in delineating complexity and diversity—but there are serious weaknesses too, most of them inherent in the way Islam is supposedly viewed nowadays. Not only did Lewis single out Islam in the Middle East (the upsurge in Judaism and Egyptian or Lebanese Christianity, for instance, was scarcely mentioned), but she went on to make statements, particularly in her third article, about the Arabic language (quoting expert opinion that its poetry is "rhetorical and declamatory, not intimate and personal") and the Islamic mind (an inability to employ "step-by-step thinking") that would be considered either racist or nonsensical if used to describe any other language, religion, or ethnic grouping.

A decade later Chris Hedges, also in the *Times*, published an article entitled "A Language Divided Against Itself," which purported to show how Muslim extremists took advantage of Arabic, already corrupted by nationalism, to produce a new language of hatred, simplistic formulas, and religious fervor: "the brutalization of political conversation," he concludes, "has left so few Arabs able to talk to one another."

Too frequently Lewis's authorities were Orientalists who have made known their general views: Élie Kedourie, who in late 1979 did a study of the Islamic revolution purporting to show that it was equivalent to Marxism-Leninism,[5] was quoted as saying that "the disorder of the East is deep and endemic," and Bernard Lewis (not a relative of Flora Lewis) pronounced on "the end of free speculation and research" in the Islamic world, presumably as a result of Islam's "static" as well as "determinist, occasionalist, and authoritarian" theology. Using the authority of his status as a senior Orientalist, Bernard Lewis has kept up his tendentious and general attacks on "Islam" through the 1980s and 1990s. One could not be expected to get a coherent view of Islam after reading Flora Lewis (or Bernard Lewis) whose scurrying about in sources and unfamiliarity with the subject give her readers a sense of a scavenger hunt for a subject that was not one to begin with; after all, how could one get hold of several hundred million people whose words "are an expression of wish rather than a description of fact"? (Compare the following in the *Atlantic Constitution*, November 19: "the subtle and elusive nature of the Persian language.") The point about Islam was made anyway, that even if "it" wasn't clear at all, "our" attitudes to it (or the attitudes "we" had every right to ascribe to it) were.

In a perhaps unintentionally revealing interview published in the May 1980 issue of *Esquire*, Flora Lewis described the assumptions and the work stemming from them that resulted in her Islam articles. The patchwork reporting and the helter-skelter manner suggest that the *Times* could get away with it because Islam is Islam and the *Times*, the *Times*. This is what she says (note the informal authority of the remark "nobody knows what the hell is going on in Islam"):

A few months ago, for instance, I was involved in a project that was absolutely staggering in its proportions. New York had just given me this special assignment on the ferment in the Islamic world. They had a meeting in New York, and someone said, "Jesus, nobody knows what the hell's going on in Islam. Let's send Flora." So they called me up, and I went. It was crazy; I wasn't even sure how to use the material I would gather.

I had to make arrangements frantically so I would be sure of seeing people beforehand. I did not have time to go anywhere and sit around for three days.

I started off in Paris and London. Then I went on to Cairo, because that's where *the* Islamic university is located, and also to Algiers and Tunis. I came back with twenty notebooks and ten pounds of paper and sat down to write.

Of course, all of this does have the advantage that I do learn something. Talk about *formations permanentes* [perpetual studenthood]—*The New York Times* will give you one scholarship after another.

The exception to doing all the reporting myself is when I simply can't make it to a place because of time pressures. On the Islam project, for example, I needed a rather extensive file on the Philippines. It turned out that the Asiatic bureau couldn't spare anyone to do that either—they had their hands full with the Cambodian war and the mess in South Korea and the political crisis in Tokyo—so someone just had to put together a package for me out of New York.

An illuminating comparison can be made between the *Times*'s feature coverage of "Islam" and *Le Monde*'s. The *Times* had it quickly put together by Flora Lewis; she discusses neither the great theological and moral issues debated all across the Islamic world (how can one talk about Islam today and never once mention the conflict raging between partisans of *ijtihad*—individual

interpretation—and partisans of *taqlid*—reliance on the interpretation of authorities—as modes of Koranic interpretation?) nor the
history and structure of the various Islamic schools fueling the
"upheaval" she tries to document. Nor even the way "Islam" became a natural refuge for the poor and dispossessed. Instead she relies on random quotations from even more random people, she uses
anecdotes to do the work of analysis, and she does not so much as
report the actual terms of Islamic life, whether they are doctrinal,
metaphysical, political, and economic.

It is useful to compare the elite American newspaper in this regard with the elite French newspaper. Exactly one year *before* (on
December 6, 7, and 8, 1978) *Le Monde* commissioned Maxime
Rodinson (an eminent French Marxist Orientalist quoted by Flora
Lewis) to study the same phenomenon.[6] The difference could not
be greater. Rodinson completely commands the subject; he knows
the languages, he knows the religion, he understands politics.
There are no anecdotes, no sensational quotations, no "balance" in
relying on "pro" and "anti" Islamic experts. He tries to suggest what
forces in Islamic society and history have cooperated with present
political configurations to produce the current crisis. As a result, it
is a coherent experience—of imperialism, class conflict, religious
dispute, social morality—that emerges in his work, not merely a col-
lection of attitudes displayed for the benefit of suspicious and frightened readers.

II. THE LOSS OF IRAN

A nyone saturated with superficial, loose-tongued reporting on Iran might well be prone to turn for relief and genuine insight to PBS's nightly *MacNeil/Lehrer Report*. Like the *New York Times* in the world of print journalism, the *Report* is acknowledged to be an elite program in broadcast journalism. I have found the *MacNeil/Lehrer* programs strangely unsatisfying, as much for their surprisingly restrictive and even conservative format as for the choice of guests and range of discussion. Take the format first. Given an unconventional news story about as unfamiliar a part of the world as Iran, the viewer will immediately be made to feel an intense disparity between the mobs "out there" and the carefully dressed, carefully balanced cast of guests whose uniform qualification is expertise, not necessarily insight or understanding. There is nothing wrong with trying to grasp a situation rationally, as the show sets out to do, but the questions asked of guests make it evident that

MacNeil and Lehrer tend to look for support of the prevailing national mood: outrage at the Iranians, ahistorical analyses of what makes the Iranians tick, attempts at making discussion fit either cold-war or crisis-management molds. An extremely telling indication of this appeared in the two programs (December 28 and January 4) in which the guests were the two sets of American clergymen recently returned from Teheran. In both programs the clergymen spoke of their compassion for Iranian feelings about what it was like to suffer under twenty-five years of the shah's despotic rule. Lehrer was openly skeptical, not to say dubious, about what they were saying. When then Foreign Minister Bani-Sadr and his successor, Sadegh Ghotbzadeh, appeared (November 23 and 29), the line of questioning stayed very close to what had emerged as the United States government position: when will the hostages be released, and never mind concessions or investigative committees to deal with the ex-shah's misdemeanors and crimes. The irony is that Bani-Sadr for the first time did not insist on the ex-shah's return; he proposed a formula that was to be enacted by the United Nations commission that went to Teheran several months later. At the time, reporters MacNeil and Lehrer were typical in ignoring the proposal.

The guest list during the period 1979 from early November to mid-January 1980 was even more significant. Aside from five appearances by Iranians and one each by Richard Falk and Eqbal Ahmad, who are known supporters of Third World and antiwar causes, all the panelists were newspapermen, government officials, academic Middle East experts, individuals connected to corporate or quasi-governmental institutions, or Middle Easterners known for their essentially antagonistic positions on the Iranian revolution. The same kind of imbalance occurred during the four-month Gulf crisis of 1990. The frequency with which some people appeared left no room for doubt. Menges of the Hudson Institute was on twice, former United States Ambassador to Afghanistan Robert Neumann and L. Dean Brown also twice. The net result was to place everything the Iranians said and did out of moral bounds; this fed our outrage, but did not help us in understanding the news. I was struck by this, and surprised that neither Lehrer nor MacNeil tried to investigate what Bani-Sadr meant, for example, when he evoked "the oppressed of the world" and suggested that the satisfaction of their claims did not demand the former shah's extradition (i.e., it was not a simple matter of the United States backing down) but required only a gesture of recognition from the United States that the oppressed had legitimate grievances.

Thus in the very conduct of its investigation the *MacNeil/Lehrer Report* seemed to censor itself, prevent itself from straying into wider areas of human experience that antagonists or interlocutors thought were important. The tightly organized ranks of participants sitting around a table dominated by a demanding pair of hosts; the over-all balanced point of view, in which no guest could truly communicate the essentially "foreign" language of distant oppressed peoples who had until now silently endured decades of American or local despotic impingement on their lives; the questions that always focused on how to deal with a crisis, not on trying to understand the new horizons being opened up everywhere in the nonwhite, non-European world; the almost instinctive resort to received wisdom about geopolitics, sectarian unrest, Islamic revivalism, balance of power: these were the constraints within which MacNeil and Lehrer operated. And for better or for worse, they happen to be the very constraints within which the government itself operates.

In the context created by a journalism afflicted with supercaution and self-imposed conformity on Iran, we can now begin to appreciate the astonishing prescience of I. F. Stone's piece "A Shah Lobby Next?" which he wrote on January 17, 1979, and which was published by the *New York Review of Books* February 22. He spoke there of how the shah could "rally formidable friends," from the Chase Manhattan Bank to the arms industry, the oil trust, the CIA, and "hungry academia." But with the shah "now here in person" tempting possibilities might arise, even though "we should have learned by now, but haven't, to keep out of Iran's domestic politics, and we may get a parallel lesson soon in keeping Iran's politics out of ours." Why? Because, Stone's uncanny predictions continue: "What if the new Iranian regime makes demands of its own . . . lays claim to the foreign holdings and bank accounts of the Shah and the Pahlevi Foundation? What if it demands the Shah's return for trial on charges of plundering the country? What if it accuses him, as absolute ruler, with absolute responsibility for untold tortures and deaths at the hands of SAVAK?"

I cite Stone not just because he happens to have been right in his predictions but also because he was not, and never pretended to be, an "expert" on Iran, much less a man known for his pro-Islamic sympathies. Look through his article and you will find no references to the Islamic mentality or Shi'a predilections for martyrdom or any of the other nonsense parading as relevant "information" on Iran. He understands politics; he understands and makes no attempt to lie about what moves men and women to act in this as well as other societies; above all, he does not doubt that even though Iranians are not Europeans or Americans they may have legitimate grievances, ambitions, hopes of their own, which it would be folly for Westerners to ignore. No euphemism, no hyperbole there. If Stone cannot read Farsi, he does not allow himself the compensating luxury of generalizations about "The subtle and elusive nature of the Persian language."

With characteristic hard-headedness Joseph Kraft sketched *his* view of the matter in "Time for a Show of Power," written for the *Washington Post* on November 11, and it was what he wrote there, far more than all the standard remarks about diplomatic immunity and the sanctity of our embassy, that illuminated aspects of the underlying, perhaps even unconscious rationale for the media's overall performance. The downfall of the shah, Kraft wrote, was "a calamity for American national interests." Not only did the shah make available regular amounts of oil, he imposed order on the Iranian plateau through "his imperial pretensions." This was good for America: it kept the oil flowing; it kept the region as well as "submerged nationalists" in line; it kept "us" appearing strong. Kraft went on to recommend "finding occasion for an unmistakable, and preferably surprising, assertion of American power on behalf of the regimes that feel menaced by the Ayatollah," as part of the process of "rebuilding American policy toward Iran." How else might this be done?

> [It] might take the form of supporting Iraq in its effort to stir up provincial resistance inside Iran. It might mean giving military assistance to Turkey. . . . To find and exploit such opportunities, there is required a crucial internal change in Washington. The United States needs a capacity to do something besides sending Marines and bombing. It has to rebuild a capacity self-destructed only a few years ago—a capacity for covert intervention.

What is clear in Kraft's piece is his unwillingness to accept the Iranian revolution as having happened in the first place. Therefore it and everything connected to it—the Ayatollah, Islam, the Iranian people—had to be "revised" as the aberrant event he wished his readers to believe it was. In other words, Kraft was projecting his personal version of reality onto a fairly complex Iranian as well as American reality, thereby substituting that version for reality. And Kraft's version had the additional didactic merit of being entirely devoid of morality: it was about power, American power to have the world on "our" terms, as though the result of what were in fact twenty-five years of intervention in Iran had taught us nothing. If in the process he found himself denying that other people have the right to produce a change in their own form of government, denying even that a change had definitely taken place, that did not much matter. He wanted America to know (and be known by) the world because of its power, its needs, its vision. Anything else was an outrage.

The trouble with that view is that even from a pragmatic and totally selfish standpoint, it is both coarse and blind. At the very moment that Kraft and others like him were attacking the Iranian
revolution and lamenting the loss of the shah, the situation in Iran
was highly volatile and uncertain. The masses who had brought
down the shah's regime were in the forefront of a political coalition
with Ayatollah Khomeini at its head. He alone had the authority
and the spiritual as well as political legitimacy to command the
country's attention; yet immediately beneath the surface he dominated, a struggle was going on between several factions, among
them of course the clergy (whose following was organized into the
Islamic Republican Party), the middle-of-the-road liberals (with
Bazergan in their forefront), a broad grouping of liberal to left Islamic parties and personalities (out of which Bani-Sadr emerged),
and the non-Islamic left, itself made up of many different parties
and groupings. For over a year after the revolution—that is, from
February 1979 until at least March or April 1980—the struggle for
power between these different factions was being waged; at moments Bani-Sadr seemed to triumph, then at others—principally
during the late winter and early spring of 1980—the clergy (with Ayatollah Mohammed Beheshti at their head) dominated. *Very little
of this struggle was reported in the United States while it was taking
place.* So strong was the ideological commitment to the idea of a
monolithic and unchanging Islam that no note was taken of the political process *within* this or any other particular Islamic country.
Then, when the conservative Islamic grouping triumphed as the result of a struggle, the earlier descriptions of Islam seemed to have
been right after all. And once the helicopter rescue failed, and after
the Carter administration decided to put Iran on the back burner
for a while (and, in a sense, when it was too late), the press dutifully
started reporting the power struggles between Beheshti and Bani-
Sadr. In typical fashion Bani-Sadr was portrayed as the kind of person we *could* have dealt with had Beheshti not been there, whereas

in fact when Bani-Sadr was in the ascendancy in late 1979, he was either ignored or disdained.

Power, of course, is a complex, not always visible, very protean thing, unless one thinks only in military terms. Yet there are situations where, as Kraft quite accurately observed, it cannot be seen or understood easily, nor can it be employed directly (a raid, CIA subversion, a punitive strike of some sort), but only indirectly ("America held hostage" presented and re-presented by an information apparatus with seemingly limitless resources). The media were interested in asserting *their* direct power for a very long time. I do not think it an exaggeration to say that the feeling of "national impotence" of which Kraft spoke was the temporary eclipse of one kind of American power by another: the military's by the media's. After the occupation of the embassy, the military was stymied by a force which seemed outside the range of direct American power (a fact amply demonstrated by the abortive rescue attempt in late April 1980).

This same force, however, remained vulnerable to the limits placed on it by the rich symbolizing powers of the media. However much the Iranian individual had gained his or her freedom from the shah and the United States, he or she still appeared on American television screens as part of a large anonymous mob, deindividualized, dehumanized, ruled again as a result. Yet whether they did so consciously or not, the news media were in fact using their powers of representation to accomplish a purpose, similar to that intended by the United States government in the past: namely, the extension of an American presence, or what to Iranians amounted to the same thing, negation of the Iranian revolution. This did not mean principally the presentation of news, nor the analysis of or reflection upon an important new juncture in American foreign relations. With very few exceptions, the media's purpose seemed to be to wage a kind of war against Iran.

A remarkable set of investigative reports by Walter Pincus and Dan Morgan of the *Washington Post* in December, January, February, and March 1980 were exceptions. They put overwhelming evidence before the reader of the former shah's lucrative deals with United States arms firms, of his holdings in the Pahlevi Foundation, of his manipulation and repression of his people (some of which had been detailed in Robert Graham's book *Iran: The Illusion of Power*). Yet such articles, as well as Bernard Nossiter's *New York Times* article on November 26, 1979, comparing Khomeini with the shah, were few in comparison to the prevailing, repeatedly proclaimed mood of outrage conveyed by the media. Strangely, no one thought to view United States policy in Iran against the background of so-called capitulations in practice for a century; this policy, by which various powers beginning with England were given extraterritorial economic, diplomatic, and juridical privileges in Iran (Khomeini was able to say in 1964, "If the Shah should run over an American dog, he would be called to account, but if an American cook should run over the Shah . . . no one has any claim against him"[7]), was never mentioned in the media. Yet it clearly could have been used to interpret the peculiar intensity of Iranian feelings against all "foreign devils" particularly foreign diplomats, not just the United States. This might have muted the sanctimonious protestations of many commentators who saw America as both egregiously wronged by Iran and innocent of anything but excessive benevolence towards Iranians.

Not surprisingly, therefore, one did not learn very much from what was published during the first three months of the crisis. The media provided *insistence*, not analysis or in-depth coverage of the story's rich complexities. I think Americans would say that the media gave ample evidence of their power to be there, in Teheran, and of their knack for prodding events into assimilable if rudimentary shape. But there was no help to be had in analyzing the complicated politics of what was taking place, and surely no one came away with a sense that the media were recording the complex and sometimes bewildering processes of history. But one could learn something about how the media went about their work.

Aside from the unrelenting depictions of the confrontational experience I alluded to, there were the expense and the sheer volume of Iran news. For the period of ten weeks during which I monitored eight daily newspapers, the three networks, *Time, Newsweek,* and PBS, it seemed that every leading newspaper in the country prominently carried the Iranian events, plus "backgrounders" and smaller features associated with it. John Kifner of the *New York Times* wrote on December 15, 1979, that there was a corps of no less than three hundred Western reporters (most if not all of whom needed interpreters) on the ground in Teheran, and Col Allen on December 16, 1979, reported for *The Australian* that between them the three major American networks were spending a million dollars a day in Teheran. In addition to its bureau chief, CBS, according to Allen, "Had a team of 23 journalists, a cameraman, audio man and film and technical experts aided by 12 Iranian interpreters, car driver and guide." A $6,000-a-month hotel suite served as operations center, and thirty-five additional rooms at $70 a day each housed journalists, drivers, and interpreters; add to that the cost of private planes, Telex machines, cars, and phones, as well as a telecommunications satellite used four hours a day at $100 a minute, and the costs rise very steeply.

Returning to the United States after a trip abroad, Vermont Royster commented in the *Wall Street Journal* on December 19, 1979, that the accumulated pile of newspapers and television programs he started going through testified to

how little I learned about the Iranian crisis I didn't already know, despite the voluminous coverage given it. Once home I was startled to find myself inundated in a daily tidal wave of television, radio and newspaper stories about Iran. The papers carried long stories under huge headlines, while TV devoted most of the evenings news to the topic and then ran late-evening specials almost every night.

And from that arose another heretical thought, that the news media were engaged in overkill.

This may seem a strange reaction about a story of such obvious importance. . . . But the volume of words to tell a story don't necessarily equate with the information imparted. The truth is that in much of that wordage there was no real news at all.

Day 28 . . . day 38 . . . day 40. Most days there was hardly anything different to report from the day before.

Perhaps Royster was also reacting not so much to the sameness of the news as to the unsatisfactorily narrow and quickly exhausted range of assumptions used in looking for the news. How long is it possible to rely on experts or reporters who are understandably concerned about the hostages, incensed at the impropriety of the thing, perhaps also angry at Islam, and still hope to get fresh information, news, analysis? If one were to read the *Chicago Tribune* on November 18—a longish piece by James Yuenger citing experts who say that "this is not something up for rational discussion" or that Iranians "hunger for martyrdom" and have "a tendency to look for scapegoats"—and then either *Time* or *Newsweek* the week after, and the several features in the *New York Times* the week after that, one would keep coming up against the information that Iranians are Shi'ites who long for martyrdom, led by a nonrational Khomeini, hating America, determined to destroy the satanic spies, unwilling to compromise, and so forth. Were there no events taking place in Iran *before* the embassy takeover that might illuminate things? Was there no Iranian history or society to write and speak about that *wasn't* translatable into the anthropomorphisms of a crazy Iran gratuitously taunting good-guy America? Above all, was the press simply interested in diffusing news seemingly in keeping with a United States government policy to keep America "united" behind the unconditional demand for the hostages' release, a demand—shrewdly assessed by Roger Fisher of Harvard on the *Today Show* December 3—itself subordinate to the real priority, which wasn't their release but "keeping America strong"?

Paradoxically, government and media sometimes appeared to be antagonists. Hence the stir caused by the government's attack on NBC for using the Gallegos interview.[8] Or the frequent refrain coming from quarters speaking either for or like the government that, as George Ball put it during the *MacNeil/Lehrer Report* of December 12, "the greatest communications network in the world has been really at the service of the so-called government in Iran." And related to that theme, there was the constant undermining of testimonials, statements, or declarations broadcast, printed, diffused, or portrayed by the media, either that so-and-so is brainwashed when he speaks, or that X and Y Iranians are propagandizing or fanatical enemies. Reporting for the *Chicago Tribune* on November 22, James Coates said that "hostages held in the United States Embassy in Teheran are undergoing psychological pressures similar to the brainwashing of American POWs during the Korean and Viet Nam wars, administration officials said." The officials later admitted that "they were concerned about some of the statements the freed hostages have made since their release." Lois Timnick reported for the *Los Angeles Times* on November 26 that according to one expert, "the world can expect to see and hear taped interviews with individual hostages in which they 'confess' to all sorts of misdeeds and make statements that are harmful both to themselves and to the United States."

Still another case of the same collegial quarrel was the attack on Senator Kennedy (e.g., "Teddy is the toast of Teheran," *New York Post*, December 5) for proposing an alternative view that did not replicate views held by the government and the media. Or there was the unmerciful drubbing given Representative George Hansen, whose entire past was reproduced in order to give seriousness to the charges made against him by Tip O'Neill.

I am not saying that there was direct collusion between the media and the government, nor am I saying that *everything* reported about Iran was essentially distorted by the ideological hobbles I have been discussing. Nor, certainly, do I believe that there is any way to condone the holding of hostages; even Mansour Farhang, Khomeini's ambassador to the United Nations for a few months before he did a complete about-face, admitted exactly that on the *MacNeil/Lehrer Report* November 5. No one can doubt, however, that the hostage crisis played a still insufficiently analyzed role in the complex dynamics of Iran's continuing revolution, although it has seemed that the cause of retrogressive elements in Iranian society was helped by the protracted embassy holding. Now that the crisis is coming to a close (largely because the war with Iraq has made the hostages no longer useful to Iran's internal politics), a new situation is beginning to emerge. Even so, what I am saying is that the world we live in is much too complex and much too different now and much too likely to go on producing unconventional situations (however little they may be to the United States' liking as a nation) to be treated as if everything could be translated into affronts to or enhancements of American power. Americans cannot continue to believe that the most important thing about "Islam" is whether it is pro- or anti-American. So xenophobically reductive a view of the world would guarantee a continued confrontation between the United States and the rest of an intransigent mankind, a policy of continuing the Cold War Huntington-style to include an unacceptably large portion of the globe. I suppose that such a policy could be considered active advocacy of the "Western way of life," but I believe that an equally good case could be made that the Western way of life does not necessarily involve provoking hostility and confrontation as a means for clarifying our own sense of our place in the world.

My own assumptions about what I suggest is a newly emerging worldwide political situation (of which Iran is a major harbinger) need to be put forward very briefly at this point. Whereas some people argue that American power is declining, I would say instead that more of the world than before is politically aware and therefore less likely to be content with the status either of a satellite colony or of an unthinking ally. Today's Iran, Turkey, and Western Europe respectively illustrate what I mean: each is unwilling to accept unilateral United States actions banning trade with Iran. Moreover, there is no reason to believe that the people of Afghanistan wanted to be invaded by the Soviet Union any more than the Iranians were happy about United States support for the ex-shah. I think it is both wrong and foolish to regard "Islam" as a block, just as I think it is bad political judgment to treat "America" as if it were an injured person rather than a complex system. Therefore I believe that we need to know more about the world, not less; we should consequently expect higher standards of reporting, more sophistication of information, more sensitive and accurate accounts of what is taking place than we are now getting, which, beginning most dramatically with the 1991 Gulf War and the Oslo agreement of 1993, simply follow the main, on the whole anti-Muslim and anti-Arab lines of United States foreign policy. But this certainly means getting well beyond what is commonly available to newsmen and newswomen who work in a society (a) whose awareness of the non-Western world is essentially determined either by crisis or by unconditional ethnocentrism, (b) whose ability to build an elaborate structure of information for itself out of quickly gathered clichés and narrowly defined self-interest is remarkable, and (c) whose history of interaction with the highly diverse Islamic peoples has been shaped recently only by oil and by rulers (like the ex-shah) whose alliance with the United States brings the limited, badly underexamined rewards of "modernization" and anticommunism.

Getting beyond all this will be difficult indeed. Consider that the correspondents of most of the major American newspapers and television networks struggle sometimes heroically to fulfill an unremitting duty to bring back a story. Yet usually they do not know the language of the area they cover, they have no background in the area, they are removed after a short tour of duty even after beginning to make important contributions. No matter how gifted the individual, he or she cannot hope to report places as complex as Iran or Turkey or Egypt without some training and a lengthy term of residence in the place. Consider, for instance, that James Markham, the capable and gifted man who reported the Lebanese civil war for the *Times* in 1975–1976, had just come from Vietnam, and after only a year in the Near East was sent to Spain; that during John Kifner's absence in Teheran the entire Levant was reported intermittently for the *Times* by Henry Tanner, a man stationed in Rome, or by Nicholas Gage, while Marvine Howe, the former Beirut correspondent (who was also supposed to cover Jordan, Syria, Iraq, and the Gulf), spent one year in Beirut right after her stint in Portugal and a year later, in the autumn of 1979, was moved to Ankara. If this sort of thing is compared with the practice in some European publications, the self-inflicted dangers it incurs stand out starkly: *Le Monde* has had Eric Rouleau, who is fluent in Arabic and has reported the region for almost a quarter of a century; the *Manchester Guardian* has David Hirst, also fluent in the languages, also a veteran of at least thirty years experience. (In most other ways, however, European foreign affairs journalism is no less weak than its American counterpart.) The odds against adequate reporting by the network reporter, who is likely to be even more itinerant than the print journalist, makes the latter seem like an encyclopedia of knowledge and serenity in comparison.

I suspect that the extreme unevenness of reporting about the East and "Islam" that we find routinely in the American media would not as readily be tolerated in reporting on Western Europe, which is not to say that the problems of Western European coverage have been resolved. In any event, I find it difficult to understand why radio, television, and newspaper executives all seem to agree that the fresh-eyed school of reporting is more to be trusted than a record of experience in the region being reported. During the Iran crisis, one could watch competent network reporters like Morton Dean, John Cochran, and George Lewis becoming "experts" before our very eyes, not because they knew more, but simply because it was supposed that if you stay in one spot for a brief length of time you will get to know it adequately. In actuality, what one watched was the reporter relying more and more uncritically on the need to make a report—for example, the nightly NBC discussion between John Chancellor in New York and Lewis and Cochran in Teheran—and less and less on analysis or actual news-gathering. Accuracy—never a virtue of the media—was usually sacrificed to getting a report out, whether or not there really was anything new to report.

But other pressures play important roles also. Print journalists are aware that the television network correspondents can produce literally eye-catching stories every night; they then think too in terms of what will draw consumers, which in the end has little to do with actual coverage, accuracy, or real significance. The competition between print and images has made for overemphasis on what is bizarre in Shi'a Islam and for psychological profiles of Khomeini, although the same competition accounts for neglect in coverage of other figures and forces at work in Iran. Still more important—and distorting—is the fact that the media have been used as diplomatic conduits, an aspect of "the Iran story" noted thoughtfully by *Broadcasting* magazine on December 24, 1979. The Iranians as well as the United States government were perfectly aware that statements made on television were aimed not only at people who wanted the news but also at governments, at partisans of one faction or another, at new or emerging political constituencies. No one has studied the effect of this on "deciding what's news," but I believe that a general awareness of it drove United States reporters to think restrictively and reductively in us-versus-them dichotomies. Yet this literalization of group feeling made the reporters' incapacities and inaccuracies more rather than less apparent.

III. UNEXAMINED AND HIDDEN ASSUMPTIONS

Inaccuracy is bad enough, but reporting that is based on assumptions about the status quo is worse in my opinion. In the January–February 1979 issue of the *Columbia Journalism Review* an article appeared about how the United States media reported the shah's regime. The authors of that extraordinarily perceptive piece showed convincingly that "the press, in sum, has by and large accepted the shah's implicit argument that the best his people can muster in the way of ideological resources are religious fanaticism and communism."[9] *Science* magazine in its December 14, 1979 issue also commented on the failure of understanding, but placed the blame rather more squarely on the entire defense and intelligence community; this view was given its most thoughtful and thorough exposition in an article by Herman Nickel in *Fortune*'s March 12, 1979 issue. Nickel's wise conclusion, however, has generally gone unheeded:

The roots of the American failure [in Iran] run deeper than tactical lapses, deeper into the past.

Only a fair-minded and patient tracing of these roots can produce an inquiry of any serious use to the future. It cannot be said too often that such an exercise in self-examination by the US must not traffic in emotional and divisive recrimination over "Who lost China?" so poisonous to the recent politics of the 1940s and 1950s. The recent history of US policies toward Iran is not a tale conspicuous for wise prophets, long ignored, now entitled to raise their voices and point their fingers. Rather, the responsibility for failure seems widely enough shared to encourage some general sense of humility. The grave exaggeration of the personal power of the Shah to govern Iran was a misjudgment embraced with equal confidence by both Republican and Democratic Administrations. And the voices of doubt or dissent were no more audible in the halls of Congress than in the councils of the White House.

Debates weighing constructive political questions, rather than brandishing ad hominem accusations, probably must start with renewed awareness that other nations are not, after all, ours to "lose." If there is one lesson Americans should have learned from the Vietnam tragedy, it is that we do not *possess* the ability to decree the course of events in ancient countries deeply affected by their own histories, cultures, and religions. If the role of Buddhism in Southeast Asia often seemed politically confounding, the role of Islam in Iran has proved even more remarkable and baffling to U.S. policy-makers.

Almost a year later the proprietary, recriminatory attitudes were still prevalent, with the added irony that the media as a whole seemed to find it difficult to concede that changes in countries that the United States believes fall within its direct sphere of authority are permissible. When the 1996 Turkish elections brought a moderate Islamic party to power there was the *Times*'s pundit Thomas L. Friedman writing on "Who Lost Turkey?" (August 21, 1996) as if Turkey and Iran were "ours" to lose. For one, in the case of Iran, most journalists still tended to refer to Mohammed Reza as "the shah" not "the ex-shah." For another, until the middle of 1980 (when it seemed clear that the right wing of the revolution had gained the ascendancy), there was a substantially higher proportion of stories reporting atrocities and executions over those reporting the country's extremely fluid, actually quite open political struggle. One would have thought it a worthwhile effort to report in detail what it means for a country's national existence, after decades of severe oppression, to have a dozen political parties vying for influence and power, relatively free for a while of torture and imprisonment. What does it mean for a nation to have a leader who, although stubborn and in most ways unattractive, has only an unclearly defined official position, who is not too interested in central government, who is clearly venerated, who seems a virtuoso at keeping a dozen factions busy with each other but under his ultimate control, and who speaks with such conviction and severity of *almostazafin* — the weakened and oppressed? Few stories made the point during the early days of the hostage crisis that government in Iran was provisional at best, pending the setting up of a new state, or that for most of 1979 there had been much debate in Iran about the constitution and the structure of government, or that there were numerous parties operating fiercely (religious and secular, right-wing and left-wing), or that dozens of newspapers appeared regularly, or that there were actual political issues (not by any means all reducible to sectarian or ethnic or religious factionalism) exercising large numbers of Iranians, or that the conflict between the ayatollahs (Khomeini and Shariat-Madari, among others) concerned political as well as religious interpretations of Islamic principles, or that the future of Iran need not inevitably fall into patterns viewed as desirable or undesirable by middle-class reporters for American newspapers.

The hardest thing to understand about the editorial and feature-reporting sector of the media is why, almost without exception, it regarded the movement that overthrew the Pahlevi dynasty and brought in different, perhaps more popular, groups with such disdain and suspicion. "The New Barbarians are loose in Iran," wrote Hal Gulliver of the *Atlanta Constitution* on November 13, 1979; he spoke not just of the students holding the hostages but of everyone in Iran. Read a long, apparently expert piece by Youssef Ibrahim in the October 14, 1979 issue of the *New York Times Sunday Magazine*, and you will be convinced that the revolution has already failed, that Iran is a smoldering lava-bed of resentment, fear, and dislike of the revolution. The evidence: basically some impressions, quotations from two government ministers, and for the most part discussions with a banker, a lawyer, and an advertising executive.

Not that reporters should not have opinions and should not let their clients know what those opinions are. But it is when opinion is metamorphosed into reality that journalism suddenly becomes self-fulfilling prophecy. If you assume that the Iranian revolution was a bad thing because it employed a dramatically unfamiliar (to Western eyes) idiom of religious as well as political resistance to oppose tyranny, then what you will look for, and invariably find, is irrational frenzy. Consider Ray Moseley in an article entitled "Conformity, Intolerance Grip Revolutionary Iran" in the November 25 *Chicago Tribune*:

> People who consider dying to be an honor are, by definition, fanatics. Vengeful blood lust and yearning for martyrdom seem especially pronounced among the Shia Moslems of Iran. This is what impelled thousands of citizens to stand unarmed and defiant against troops with automatic weapons during the revolution.

Each of these sentences contains highly debatable suppositions posing as truth, but they seem allowable generally because an

Islamic revolution is in question. They have persisted in reports on Iran in the 1990s, as well as most accounts of the Lebanese Hizbollah movement (always referred to as "Iran-backed"). Most Americans do not consider Patrick Henry a fanatic because he said "give me liberty or give me death." A desire to kill French citizens who collaborated with Nazis (many thousands were killed in a matter of days) does not mean that the French could be characterized in so general a way. And what about the very common admiration for people whose moral courage faces down armed troops?

Moseley's attack on Iran was supported by a truly cosmic editorial in his paper the same day accusing Khomeini of nothing less than "a holy war on the world." The *jihad* (holy war) motif was also given an extraordinary run by the *Los Angeles Times* in an article by Edmund Bosworth on December 12, and has become the single most important motif in Western media representations of Islam. Leaving aside the fact that according to Fazlur Rahman, "among the later Muslim legal schools . . . it is only the fanatic Kharijites who have declared *jihad* to be one of the 'pillars of the Faith,'"[10] Bosworth goes on indiscriminately to adduce a great deal of historical "evidence" to support the theory that *all* political activity for a period of about twelve hundred years in an area that includes Turkey, Iran, Sudan, Ethiopia, Spain, and India can be understood as emanating from the Muslim call for a *jihad*.

If aggressive hyperbole is one journalistic mode commonly used to describe Iran in particular and Islam generally, the other is misapplied euphemism, usually stemming from ignorance but often deriving from a barely concealed ideological hostility. Its most prevalent form is the device of displacing actuality with a plausible "explanation" of the reporter's own. The one subject newspapers and television programs had looked into only superficially for the first three months of the embassy takeover was the previous Iranian regime: for a remarkably long time it was not popular to take seriously current Iranian grievances against both the deposed monarch and a longstanding United States policy to support him without reservation. Somehow, too, the violation of Iranian sovereignty that occurred in August 1953, when (as Kermit Roosevelt details in his recent and precipitately withdrawn book, *Countercoup*) the CIA in conjunction with the Anglo-Iranian Oil Company overthrew Mohammed Mossadegh,[11] merited little investigation, the assumption being that the United States as a great power is entitled to change governments and forgive tyranny when it is inflicted on illiterate nonwhites at our discretion. George E. Gross, a practicing psychiatrist, speculated in a *New York Times* op-ed article on January 11, 1980, that by admitting the former shah to New York the United States in effect pardoned him, an act "devoid of moral principle," just as Gerald Ford's grandiose pardon of Richard Nixon showed "a damaged capacity to form judgments within a moral framework, a loss of empathy with moral outrage in others."

Observations like that were few and far between. Most feature writers and editorialists contented themselves with euphemisms. There seemed to be agreement that the Iranians had committed an act of war against the United States Embassy, although virtually no one also thought that what the United States did to Iran by overthrowing Mossadegh in 1953 was an act of war. Ernest Conine, editorializing for the *Los Angeles Times* on December 10, 1979, was fairly typical:

> News accounts seem to bear out the contention by Middle East scholars that what we are really seeing is a widespread revolt against the unsettling influences that have accompanied the Western-style modernization of recent years.
>
> The Shah is hated not just because his police tortured people but also because he took away government subsidies from Moslem holy men, and presided over an industrial revolution that uprooted Iranians from their traditional life styles in the countryside.

"Satan America" is elected as the chief villain not just in Iran but elsewhere, because for 25 years the United States has been the most visible power in the area, and is therefore a handy symbol of outside forces that have brought unwelcome changes.

Much in this argument is weighted against the Iranians through unspoken assumptions, so it needs to be read carefully. Conine first of all implies that the "unsettling influences" of "Western-style modernization" are the result of trying in good faith to bring Iran and Islam out of the past into the present; in other words, Islam and Iran are backward, the West is advanced, and no wonder that backward people are going to have a hard time keeping up. These are eminently contestable value judgments and derive, as I pointed out in Chapter One, from the ideology of modernization. Moreover, Conine assumes, without any warrant except ethnocentric bias, that Iranians were less troubled by torture than by the insult to their "holy men," a phrase used intentionally to suggest primitive people with their witch doctors. In addition, he suggests that Iranians may not have the same feelings "we" do. His final point develops the others by association, laying the blame on retrograde Iranians for not appreciating well-intentioned American and Pahlevi efforts to get Iran going; thus not only are "we" exonerated, but Iranians as a people are subtly indicted for not knowing the value of our brand of modernity, which is why the ex-shah was a noble figure after all.

Little mention was made of the fact, which is neither esoteric nor hard to come by, that vast profits were reaped by American corporations in the area (it should not have been difficult to connect 200 percent oil company profit increases during the past years with the wealth of the Pahlevi family) and that most Iranians, like the many millions of Arabs who do not directly profit from oil, see American-connected wealth as a burden of sorts. If it was bruited about that the shah occasionally resorted to a little torture—well, said the *Washington Post* on December 16, "it can be argued that it was entirely in the tradition of Iranian history." This would seem to imply that since Iranians have always been tortured, any attempt of theirs to change this foreordained fate is a betrayal of their own history, to say nothing of their own nature.

This irrefutably logical position turned up in a Don A. Schanche story for the *Los Angeles Times,* December 5, 1979, where it was argued that because the new constitution was "one of the most bizarre political documents of modern times" and because it did not happen to resemble closely the United States Constitution (no checks and balances!), Khomeini's ascendancy was at least as bad as the ex-shah's. That in theory at least there would be "provisions for the popular elections of president and parliament and an organized judicial system" was dismissed by Schanche as "the trappings of democracy." He simply omitted to mention what Eric Rouleau analyzed in detail in *Le Monde* on December 2–3, 1979: the very busy, competitive debate about the constitution, disagreements as to Khomeini's exact role, and so forth. In other words, Schanche seemed more interested in passing off his editorializing as the factual truth about the Iranian Constitution, despite what was actually taking place before his eyes. It was only a matter of coincidence and the result of a tough fight, disappointing in its outcome to many Iranian (and non-Iranian) supporters of the revolution, that the new order in Iran by mid-1980 seemed to be so unpromising. But then surely the emergence in the United States of a Republican candidate of the far right was a no less unhappy coincidence!

With the noteworthy exception of Andrew Young, no high public figure in the United States had anything to say in 1979 about what—to observers like the three ministers who held Christmas services in the embassy or the other groups of clergymen who were in Teheran in late December (both groups appeared on the *MacNeil/Lehrer Report* December 28 and January 4)—the previous regime meant to the Iranians as they took action against the United States. And collaborating in this silence, the press treated the ex-shah exclusively as a charity case for at least twenty days after he was admitted to the United States. Stripped of his political past, he appeared to be somehow unconnected to what was happening at the embassy in Iran. A few journalists, Don Oberdorfer of the *Washington Post* chief among them, tried to reconstruct the devious steps by which David Rockefeller, Henry Kissinger, and John McCloy pressured the United States government into bringing the ex-shah here. But these facts, as well as the ex-shah's longstanding association with the Chase Manhattan Bank—which would have helped to explain Iranian animosities—were not connected causally to the embassy takeover. Instead we were given numerous euphemistic explanations of the hostage crisis as the result of Khomeini's manipulation, his need for distracting the populace, economic difficulties at home, and the like (see the *Los Angeles Times* of November 25 and 27, December 7 and 11; also the *Washington Post* of November 15).

I am convinced finally that it is not too cynical to say of the overall United States government position on Iran (as symbolized by President Carter's refusal to discuss the country's past dealings with Iran, which he called "ancient history") that it was a useful device for turning the media's general animosity towards the Iranians, Islam, and generally speaking the non-Western world into political capital during an election year. The president thus appeared to be keeping America strong against base foreign attacks; and this, conversely, was Khomeini's position in Iran. On occasion Carter's refusal to use force earned him the scorn of William Safire and of Joseph Kraft, but on the whole it seems to have assured the public that in comparison with the Islamic "terrorists," as they came to be called, he was upholding Western standards of civilized behavior. Another effect of the crisis was that rulers like President Sadat (whose remark that Khomeini was a lunatic and a disgrace to Islam was repeated *ad nauseam*) were made to seem the desirable Islamic norm. The same was true of the Saudi royal family, although what went unreported in the meantime was a considerable amount of disturbing information and, in the case of Iran, a considerable prolongation of the crisis.

Take Sadat and the Saudis first. Since the Camp David agreements of 1978 there has been a consensus that Sadat was our friend in the region; along with Menachem Begin he had openly proclaimed his willingness to become a regional policeman, give the United States bases on his territory, and so forth. As a consequence, most of what was reported out of Egypt by the media effectively made his point of view on matters Egyptian, Arab, and regional seem like the correct one. Egypt and the Arab world are now reported with an aim to confirming Sadat's perception of things, even though Hosni Mubarak, his successor and still very much in the American camp, is neither as amenable nor pliant as Sadat was. Before his assassination, very little in comparison appeared about him, and it was widely assumed that he was the political norm as well as the main source of news. Exactly the same thing happened during the Pahlevi regime, of course, when, with the exception of a singularly prophetic article by Berkeley scholar Hamid Algar,[12] no one paid the slightest attention to the potential of the shah's religious and political opposition. A great many of the United States' political, military, strategic, and economic investments were made through Sadat, and through Sadat's perspective on things. In part this was due to the media's ignorance, their preference for spectacular "personalities," the almost total absence of investigative reporting in deference to the ideological consensus now operating in Egypt and the Middle East.

There are other reasons too. One is the Middle East's sensitive *domestic* aspects. It is not accident, for example, that after Watergate, various revelations about the CIA, the Freedom of Information Act, there have been no major discoveries about United States involvement in the Middle East except for Irangate. This is obvious as concerns Iran, not simply because so many Americans were illegally involved there as a way of supporting the Nicaraguan contras, but also because of Israel's extremely close involvement with the United States there under the shah's regime as well as after it. SAVAK was set up with the direct help of the Mosad, and as in many other cases, the CIA and the FBI cooperated willingly with the Israeli secret services.[13] A series of revealing articles in the Israeli press in 1979 and early 1980 were written by Uri Lubrani and others who were charged with maintaining Israeli-Iranian cooperation before the revolution (see *Davar*, March 20, 1980, and *Ha'aretz*, January 10, 1979); none of this appeared in the American press, probably because it might appear embarrassing to Israel's image as democratic and freedom-loving. The Israeli involvement in the Iran-Contra affair was very much played down. At the very moment that the entire United States establishment was up in arms against any talk of extraditing the ex-shah to Iran, a poor Palestinian youth, Ziad Abu Ain, was undergoing the prolonged agony of extradition proceedings (plus the denial of bail and of a habeas corpus writ) with the active collaboration of the State Department, just because (and only because) the Israeli government had claimed—with a third-party confession extracted from and later recanted by another Palestinian in an Israeli jail in Hebrew, a language he did not know—that he was a terrorist, responsible for a bomb incident two years before. Very little of this caught the media's attention except for an important article by the *New Statesman*'s Claudia Wright, "Toying with Extradition," *Inquiry*, January 7 and 21, 1980.

In addition, widespread concern with the stability of places like Saudi Arabia and Kuwait has produced no news reporting commensurate with that concern, except for the constrained, and highly selective, criticism of Saudi Arabia's vulnerability that I described in Chapter One. Of the major networks and newspapers, only CBS's Ed Bradley noted, on November 24, 1979, that all information about the mosque takeover in Mecca came from the government; no other news was permitted, but the *Christian Science Monitor's* Helena Cobban reported from Beirut on November 30 that the mosque's seizure had a very definite *political* meaning; that far from being simply Islamic fanatics the attackers were part of a political network having a secular as well as an Islamic program, pointedly directed at the monopoly on power and money held by the Saudi royal family. Over the years, this network has considerably expanded, as witness the Riyadh and Khoban bombings of late 1995 and the summer of 1996. A few weeks later Cobban's source, a Saudi Arabian resident in Beirut, disappeared; Saudi intelligence is believed to have been responsible.

Following the invasion of Afghanistan, we are probably going to have an even more dramatic cleavage separating good Muslims from bad, more news hailing the achievements of good Muslims like Hosni Mubarak, Benazir Bhutto, and Yasir Arafat's anti-Hamas security forces, and more equating of good Islam with "moderation," if possible, with freedom and democracy, which principally mean a "free" market economy, not an enhanced human rights situation in countries like Saudi Arabia, Kuwait, Egypt, and Jordan. Few people, however, equate Afghanistan's resistance to Soviet occupation with Palestinian resistance to Israeli occupation, a point made by King Hussein of Jordan when he appeared on *Meet the Press* June 22, 1980. In the case of Saudi Arabia, the dangers of massive United States investment have only been paid attention to (not surprisingly) by American supporters of Israel, who feel that American patronage ought not to be deflected from Israel to the Arabs. A case in point is Peter Lubin's December 22, 1979 *New Republic* article, "What We Don't Know About Saudi Arabia." He makes a plausible if overstated case for dismissing much of what is written or taught in universities about the Gulf oil states either as propaganda for ruling houses or as ignorance. Nevertheless, he is wholly unable to extend his criticisms to what is written about Israel or to the not very subtle pro-Israeli bias found in many Middle Eastern studies programs in various universities. Likewise, in rightly insisting that journalists ought to be more demanding in what passes for information about our oil-rich allies, Lubin does not also say, as he should, that there is a notorious absence of rigor and fairness in writing about Israel.

IV. ANOTHER COUNTRY

All of what I have been saying about media treatment of Islam and Iran during the first, most intense and anguished months of the hostage crisis comes down finally to a few main points. The most useful way of illustrating and formulating these points is to check the over-all American version of the Iran story against a European version, Eric Rouleau's series of daily articles in *Le Monde*, which ran from the first week of the crisis through the end of December; later, after most American reporters were asked to leave Iran in January, the *Times* carried Rouleau's reports for a few days. Of course, it is important to keep in mind that Rouleau is not an American, that no French hostages were being held, that Iran has never been in the French sphere of influence, and that aside from what Rouleau himself produces, the French media are not necessarily better in foreign policy reporting than their American counterparts. It is also important to say again that the prodigious amount of media coverage allowed a certain number of extremely valuable, generally (but not always) anticonsensus items to appear. Op-ed pieces on the *Los Angeles Times* and the *Boston Globe*, imaginative articles on alternatives to force and attempts to take Iranian realities seriously (e.g., Richard Falk in the *Atlanta Constitution* December 9, Roger Fisher in *Newsweek* January 14), excellent background reporting on the shah's admission to this country, good political analysis intermittently and well-narrated news stories (Doyle McManus in the *Los Angeles Times*, Kifner in the *New York Times*): These were some of the high spots more or less available to any reader during the first few weeks of the hostage crisis who was looking for something beyond the narrowly patriotic line generally hewed to most of the time. One should also mention two powerful articles on the new jingoism of Americans wearing "Iran Sucks" and "Nuke Iran" buttons that appeared in *Inquiry* magazine (December 24 and January 7–21), or the very timely information contained in Fred J. Cook's piece for *The Nation* December 22, about how a congressional investigation into Iranian kickbacks that began in 1965 was mysteriously dropped and has just as mysteriously been kept from restarting now when it is of urgent relevance. This was prophetic, given the secret negotiations with the Iranians conducted by Robert McFarlane and Oliver North in 1986, negotiations that illegally swapped American arms for the release of hostages held by Iranian allies in Lebanon.

But all in all, television, the daily press, and the weekly news magazines reported Iran with nowhere near the insight and impressive understanding of what was taking place there that is displayed in Rouleau's sequence for *Le Monde* during the same period. If I were to put matters very strongly, I would have to say that what he wrote made Iran seem like a different country from the one represented by the American media. Rouleau never lost sight of the fact that Iran was still undergoing massive revolutionary change, and that being without a government it was consequently in the process of creating a completely new set of political institutions, processes, and actualities. Therefore the United States Embassy crisis had to be viewed within that often confusing, always complicated process, not isolated from it. He never used Islam to explain events or personalities; he seems to have viewed his reporter's mandate as comprising the analysis of politics, societies, and histories—complex enough as they are—without resorting to ideological generalizations and mystifying rhetoric, even if, as later happened, things did not work out as had been hoped, nor in a way one was able to understand. No United States reporter spent any time to speak of reporting the extended debate in Iran over the constitutional referendum; there have been few analyses of the various parties, scarcely a reference to the important ideological struggles separating Beheshti, Bazergan, Bani-Sadr, and Ghotbzadeh, no reporting of the various tactics of struggle employed in Iran, no detailed itemizing (at least until mid-1980) of the numerous political personalities, ideas, and institutions vying for power and attention; for almost a decade after the revolution and the hostage crisis, no American journalist has even suggested that Iran's political life outside the question whether the hostages were going to be released, or whether someone was pro- or anti-American, had enough intrinsic interest to make it worth some study. Even crucial events like Bani-Sadr's visit to the students in the embassy on December 5, 1979, were ignored, just as no one has so much as mentioned the important role played in the embassy by Hajitolislam Khoeiny, who also happens to have been a candidate for Iran's presidency. These are some of the things treated by Rouleau.

What is more important is that Rouleau seemed to be able to grant in advance that personalities or currents of ideas at work in the crisis might have a potentially serious role. He did not judge things impetuously, did not prejudice something in advance, did not jump to conclusions encouraged by officials, did not leave stories uninvestigated. Representative Hansen's visit emerges as a much more successful undertaking in what Rouleau tells us about it than one could have suspected; there is even substantial evidence given by

Rouleau on November 24, 1979, that Hansen's success with the Iranians was deliberately allowed to shrivel up by the White House (and the United States media), just as a possible congressional investigation into United States–Iranian banking procedures (sought by the Iranians, possibly as an exchange for the hostages' release) was snuffed out by the White House. The struggle through the latter part of 1979 between Bani-Sadr and Ghotbzadeh, the former a determined socialist and anti-imperialist, the latter a conservative on political and economic issues, was described by Rouleau in detail, just as the apparently paradoxical positions they took on the hostage crisis in November and December (Bani-Sadr for defusing it, Ghotbzadeh for escalating it) are chronicled.

What we can also surmise—although no United States journalist mentioned it at the time—is that the United States preferred dealing with Ghotbzadeh and seemed to encourage Bani-Sadr's removal from the Foreign Ministry (by not taking him seriously, by actively derogating his suggestions, by actually calling him a "kook"). Clearly, too, future United States government positions towards Iran (and the decided preference for dealing with conservatives rather than socialists) given the presidential contest handily won by Bani-Sadr are relevant to this period, as is the real reason for Bazergan's fall: certainly not the fact that he was a liberal democrat as the United States media liked to argue, or that he had shaken hands with Brzezinski in Algiers, but that he was inefficient and incompetent in fulfilling his government's stated "Islamic" policies. In one of his more important articles (reproduced in abridged form in the *Manchester Guardian* of December 2, 1979) Rouleau also shows how the United States conducted a sustained economic war against Iran well before the embassy takeover in November; a sinister aspect of this is that the Chase Manhattan Bank continued to play a leading part.

Rouleau's performance can be explained in part because he is a capable man, in part because he has a long history of experience in

the Middle East, and in part because, like his American counterparts, he reports with a home constituency very much in mind. *Le
Monde*, after all, is not just a French newspaper; it is *the* French
journal of record, and it certainly views itself as representing the
world in accordance with a specific conception of what French interests are. It is this conception that partly accounts for the difference between Rouleau's Iran and that, for example, of the *New York
Times*. The French view is consciously an *alternative* one, neither
like a superpower's nor like the other Europeans' view. Moreover,
France's (and by extension *Le Monde*'s) attitude to the East is an old
and experienced one: studiously postcolonialist yet with colonialist
attitudes toward its former colonies and protectorates; concerned
less with brute power than with deployment, strategy, and process;
focused more on the cultivation of interest rather than on protect-
ing top-heavy investments in isolated regimes; selective, provisional, and nuanced (some would say opportunist) in the choice of
what to regard with favor, what to criticize. *Le Monde*, after all, is
collectively owned; it is the newspaper of the French bourgeoisie,
and so far as the non-French world is concerned, it expresses a politics that has been characterized variously as missionary, pastoral,
paternalistic, "socialism with soul," eighteenth-century Enlighten-
ment, and progressively Catholic (Louis Wiznitzer in the *Christian
Science Monitor* May 13, 1980; Jane Kramer in the *New Yorker*, June
30, 1980).[14] Be that as it may, what counts is how *Le Monde* attempts, no doubt consciously, to cover the world. Whereas the *New
York Times* seems guided principally by crisis and newsworthiness,
Le Monde tries to record or at least to note most of what takes place
abroad. Opinion and fact are not so rigorously separated as they seem
(formally, at least) to be in the *Times:* the result, when stories or issues of unusual complexity are concerned, is a far greater flexibility
in length, detail, sophistication of reporting. *Le Monde* in its reporting suggests worldliness, the *Times* a grave, rather selective concern. Consider now Rouleau's report on December 2 and 3, 1979.

Rouleau begins by mentioning that for the past three months there had been extraordinary attention given to the discussion of the Constitutional Assembly; hundreds of open meetings were held, many of them televised; the press and partisan journals analyzed the issues, and much time was spent denouncing "antidemocratic" elements in the proposed text. (Very little of this was ever treated in the American media, by the way.) Next, Rouleau comments on the paradoxical rift between Khomeini and a major part of the country's *political class*, and proceeds then in great detail to show how Khomeini nevertheless managed to work his will immediately by risking direct appeals to the country rather than by temporizing delays. For this, of course, Rouleau must analyze both the constitutional debate (its issues, partisans, and style) and then the actual *forces* involved, keeping clear the rift between power and constitution. In the end Khomeini's "Islamic" partisans are seen to be a heterogeneous group, marshaled and dispersed throughout the polity by Khomeini's remarkable awareness of the "permanent revolution" in course, which only he, a "fastidious legalist" by nature, has been able quite paradoxically to master. After listing the various parties of left and right and quoting a few positions of each, Rouleau locates a number of inconsistencies in the proposed constitution: women are not to be mere objects of sexual pleasure or economic profit, although their rights are not spelled out; syndicates are denounced as Marxist inventions, yet workers' councils are to play an important role in economic life; all citizens have equal rights, but Shi'ism is the religion of the state; and so on. All this leads to the following paragraphs:

It is indispensable for Imam Khomeini without delay to adopt so discussable a constitution. Many people have advised him to postpone the referendum until after the end of the test of strength with the US. A country in revolution, it was said, could very well accommodate itself to a transitional regime for a long period. But the Imam put aside all the advice and objections offered him.

Paradoxically, to those who do not know him well, the patriarch of Qum is a fastidious legalist. He insists on resting his power on juridical bases. The immense popularity he has acquired during the past few weeks has given him direct satisfaction. As for the future, this popularity will be modulated less by the constitution's text than by the balance of political forces to emerge from the "second revolution" now in progress.

Rouleau here makes no effort to judge matters overtly (compare with the superficial *Los Angeles Times* Don Schanche analysis referred to above); he shows instead the disjunctions between appearance and power, between text and readers, between personalities and parties, locating them all exactly within what is essentially a setting in turbulent flux. What he tries to communicate is some sense not only of the process but of the emphases and contests within the process. At most, Rouleau offers a cautious assessment. Never does he resort to patriotic comparisons, nor to ignorant value judgments.

After he retired from 'Le Monde', Rouleau was made French Ambassador to Tunisia, the Arab league, and the PLO, by François Mitterand, and then between 1989 and 1991 he was ambassador to Turkey. Thereafter he returned to private life and freelance writing on the Middle East. In what seemed a continuation of the perceptively subtle analyses he produced during the hostage crisis, Rouleau made a visit to Iran in early 1995, the result of which was a magisterial survey of the complex changes in Iranian society since the death of Khomeini (*Le Monde diplomatique*, May 1995). Among other matters not even mentioned in the mainstream United States press, he alluded to the effect of computers and the Internet on the transmission, interpretation, and accessibility of religious texts in Qom. He also characterized what he called the second Islamic republic as undergoing a series of remarkable transformations as a result of all kinds of internal debates and clashes: there are now sixty extremely articulate and well-staffed feminist organizations that press for women's rights, a large number of preachers, filmmakers, scholars, and independent-minded clerics, who challenge the still powerful administration of *vilayet el faqih*, and on the whole he gives one the impression of a volatile Islamic state, markedly more democratic than all but one or two of its Arab neighbors, resolutely disproving, or at least disputing, the formulas and stereotypes still put forward with few exceptions in the United States media about demonized Iran.

In sum, Rouleau's reporting on Iran for *Le Monde* was political in the best sense of the word. For several months the American media's simply was not; or one could say it was political in the bad sense. What seemed unfamiliar or strange to American (and other Western) reporters was branded "Islamic" and treated with commensurate hostility or derision. Iran as a contemporary society going through extraordinarily important change had little impact on the Western press generally; certainly Iranian history for at least the first year of the revolution was rarely allowed to appear with much integrity. Clichés, caricatures, ignorance, unqualified ethnocentrism, and inaccuracy were inordinately evident, as was an almost total subservience to the government thesis that the only things that mattered were "not giving in to blackmail" and whether or not the hostages were released. Conclusions were given recklessly; a contest in progress was rashly decided by the reporter, with the result that the distinctive continuities and discontinuities of Iranian revolutionary life never emerged. Along with this went a troubling assumption that if the United States had forgiven the former shah and declared him a charity case, it did not matter what Iranians (or Iranian history itself) said. During this period I. F. Stone had the courage to say forthrightly that the necessity for a United States apology to Iran for "our restoration of the Shah in 1953 . . . is not ancient history for the Iranians, and it may not be ancient history for us either" (*Village Voice*, February 25, 1980).

So poorly and with such antagonism did the press report Islam and Iran during 1979 that it can be suspected that a number of opportunities for resolving the hostage crisis were lost, and perhaps this is why the Iranian government suggested early in 1980 that fewer reporters in Iran might quiet the tension and produce a peaceful resolution. What is most serious about the media's failure, and what does not augur well for the future, is that so far as urgent international issues during a period of acute crisis are concerned, the media do not securely and easily see themselves as performing an independent, truly informational task. There seems to be little awareness that the new era we have entered in the 1980s and 1990s cannot with impunity be represented in confrontational dichotomies — "us" versus "them," the United States versus the Soviet Union, followed by the West versus Islam, the media always siding with the "good" side — unless we get to the point of believing it inevitable that between them the two superpowers will destroy the world.

And yet, fairness enjoins us to note the changes taking place in the media as the hostage crisis wore on during 1980. There were deeper investigations of the United States' role in Iran: CBS, for example, allocated a major part of two *Sixty Minutes* shows to torture under the shah's regime and to Henry Kissinger's machinations on behalf of the shah. The *New York Times* and the *Washington Post* dutifully reported (on March 7 and March 6, respectively) the government's effort to quash the CBS story, and as was to be expected by then, all the major newspapers did skeptical, disenchanted stories on the late-April rescue effort. More willingly than before, the consensus widened to admit the possibility of different views on Iran. Criticism of the stonewalling government position increased, as did the sense among citizens (expressed principally in letters to the editor) that we were not being told the full story on Iran. Hostility to and misunderstanding of Islam persisted, however, led (predictably) by conservative journals like the *New Republic*: "The West Defers," argued Élie Kedourie in its June 7, 1980 issue; "Western" power had to be made "visible and respected," he said, otherwise endemic disorder would continue. Periodically, the rigid consensus would make itself felt in dispiriting ways. When Ramsey Clark was interviewed on ABC's *Issues and Answers* (June 8, 1980) upon his return from the "Crimes of America" conference in Teheran, his interviewers did not allow themselves *one single genuinely exploratory question*; everything they asked was profoundly unfriendly, and reflected unhesitating compliance with the administration position that Clark had done a treasonous thing in going.[15]

From time to time, for example in John Kifner's intelligent four-part series on the Iranian revolution (*New York Times*, May 29, 30, 31, June 1, 1980) and in Shaul Bhakhash's essay on the Iranian revolution for the *New York Review of Books* (June 26, 1980), one would encounter serious, reflective efforts at coming to grips with what was both a continuing revolution and one whose energies were still not graspable in simple conceptual or strictly empirical terms. Yet I believe there is little doubt that such articles would not have been written if in fact the hostages had been released. The embassy seizure—immoral, illegal, and outrageous, politically useful in the short run but wasteful for Iran in the long run—had quite literally forced a crisis of awareness in the United States. From being an almost forgotten, taken-for-granted colony in Asia, Iran had intermittently become an occasion for self-examination on the part of the United States. The Iran story's very persistence, its anxious, unseemly duration, gradually had modified the media's early single-mindedness and narrow focus into something more critical and useful. In short, the embassy seizure instituted *process* where there had only been static anger; in time this process acquired a history of its own, through which the media—and Americans generally—saw more of themselves than they had hitherto. Whether this was what the militants had intended, or whether this has delayed rather than encouraged the return of normal conditions in Iran, it is too early to tell. Certainly more Americans now understand what a struggle for power means (who has not felt the conflict between Bani-Sadr and

Beheshti, with Khomeini lurking mysteriously behind them?), and certainly, too, more Americans than before appreciate the futility of trying to impose "our" order on that upheaval, or, for that matter, on the battle between Iraq and Iran. Many questions remain unanswered—the circumstances of Beheshti's ascendancy, the modes of struggle between the left and the right, the state of the Iranian economy—and many possible outcomes remain imminent.[16]

What has been left unexplored, and what we must try now to broach, is the question underlying the crisis. Why does Iran matter, why does Islam matter, and what sort of knowledge, or coverage, of both do we require? This tripartite question is not an abstract one. It must be seen not only as an integral part of contemporary politics but as a vital part of scholarly pursuits and interpretative activities involving the knowledge of other cultures. But without a demystifying look at the relationship between power and knowledge in this context, we will have dodged the central nub of things. That is what must orient our investigation from this point on.

CHAPTER
THREE

KNOWLEDGE AND POWER

I. THE POLITICS OF INTERPRETING ISLAM: ORTHODOX AND ANTITHETICAL KNOWLEDGE

Given the present circumstances, with neither "Islam" nor "the West" at peace with each other or with themselves, it may seem exceptionally futile to ask whether, for members of one culture, knowledge of other cultures is really possible. Seek knowledge even as far as China, runs a well-known Islamic precept, and at least since the Greeks it has been a common practice in the West to assert that so long as knowledge pertains to what is human and natural, knowledge must be sought. But the actual result of this search, so far as thinkers in the West are concerned, has usually been believed to be flawed. Even Bacon, whose *Advancement of Learning* is considered to have inaugurated modern Western thought in its most enthusiastic, self-encouraging modes, in effect expresses all sorts of doubts that the various impediments to knowledge (the Idols) can ever really be removed. Bacon's respectful disciple Vico says explicitly that human knowledge is only what human beings have made;

external reality, then, is no more than the "modifications of the human mind."[1] The prospects for objective knowledge of what is distant and alien diminish still further after Nietzsche.

As against this skeptical and pessimistic current, students of Islam in the West (and, though I shall not discuss them, students of the West within the Islamic world) have generally tended to be disquietingly optimistic and confident. Early modern Orientalists in Europe seemed to have had little doubt that the study of the Orient, of which the Islamic world was a part, was the royal road to universal knowledge. One of them, the Baron d'Eckstein, wrote in the 1820s that

> in the same way that Cuvier and Humboldt discovered the mysteries of [nature's] organization in the earth's entrails, so too would Abel Rémusat, Saint-Martin, Silvestre de Sacy, Bopp, Grimm, and A. W. Schlegel trace and discover in the words of a language all of the internal organization and the primitive bases of human thought.[2]

A few years later Ernest Renan prefaced his discussion of "Mahomet et les origines de l'islamisme" with remarks on the possibilities opening up before what he called "la science critique." Geologists, historians, and linguists, Renan said, can get at "primitive"—that is, basic and original—natural objects by examining their traces delicately and patiently: Islam is a particularly valuable phenomenon because its birth was comparatively recent and unoriginal. Therefore, he concluded, to study Islam is to study something about which one can acquire both a certain and a scientific knowledge.[3]

Perhaps because of this happy attitude, the history of Islamic Orientalism is relatively free from skeptical currents and until quite recently has been almost entirely free from methodological self-questioning. Most students of Islam in the West have not doubted that despite the limitations of their time and place, a genuinely objective knowledge of Islam, or of some aspect of Islamic life, is achievable. On the other hand, few modern scholars would be as explicitly arrogant as Renan in their views of what Islam is: no professional scholar, for instance, would candidly say like Renan that Islam is knowable because it represents a fundamental case of arrested human development. Yet I have not been able to find any contemporary example of the Islamic scholar for whom the enterprise itself was a source of doubt. In part, I think, the guild tradition of Islamic studies, which has been handed down genealogically for about two centuries, has both protected and confirmed individual scholars in what they did, regardless of the methodological perils and innovations challenging scholars in most other humanistic fields.

A representative instance of what I mean is a recent essay, "The State of Middle Eastern Studies," published in the summer 1979 issue of the *American Scholar* by a well-known British scholar of Islam, now resident and working in the United States. Taken as a whole the essay is the product of a mind going over routine things in a lazy, not particularly interesting way. What still strikes the nonspecialist, however, aside from the surprising indifference of this writer to intellectual issues, is the account of Orientalism's supposed cultural pedigree. It deserves quotation at length.

The Renaissance initiated an entirely new phase in the development of Islamic and Middle Eastern studies in the Western world. Perhaps the most important new factor was a kind of intellectual curiosity that is still unique in human history. For until that time, no comparable desire had been felt and no effort made to study and understand alien, still less hostile, civilizations. Many societies have tried to study their predecessors, those to which they feel they owe something, those from which they perceive themselves to be derived. Societies under the domination of an alien and stronger culture have usually been impelled, by force or otherwise, to learn the language and try to understand the ways of those who dominate them.

Societies, in a word, have studied their masters, in both senses of the word. . . . But the kind of effort to study remote and alien cultures made by Europe (and later by the overseas daughters of Europe) from Renaissance times onward, *represents something new and totally different.* It is significant that today the peoples of the Middle East show little interest in each other and even less in the non-Islamic cultures of Asia and Africa. The only serious attempts to study the languages and civilizations of India and China in the universities of the Middle East have been made in Turkey and Israel—the two countries in the region which have consciously chosen a Western way of life.

Even now, non-European civilizations still have the greatest difficulty in understanding intellectual curiosity of this kind. When the first European Egyptologists and other archeologists began to dig in the Middle East, many of the local people found it impossible to believe that foreigners would be willing to spend so much time, effort, and money and undergo so many risks and hardships merely to dig up and decipher the ancient relics of their own forgotten ancestors. They therefore sought other, more rational explanations. For the simple villagers, the archeologists were seekers after buried treasure. For the more sophisticated townspeople, they were spies or other agents of their governments. The fact that some few archeologists did, indeed, render such services to their governments does not make this interpretation of their science any less mistaken, and reveals a sad inability to understand an enterprise that has added new chapters to the history of mankind and new dimensions to the self-awareness of Middle Eastern nations. *This difficulty of perception continues to the present day,* and even affects some academics, who persist in regarding orientalists as either treasure seekers or agents of imperialism.

The gratification of *this new intellectual curiosity* was greatly helped by the voyages of discovery which brought Europeans to new and strange lands beyond the ocean. These helped break intellectual molds and provided both a stimulus and an opportunity for further study.[4]

Employing little more than unsupported assertion this writing directly contravenes everything that has ever been written either by a fair number of Orientalists themselves, or by historians of Europe from the Renaissance to the present, or by students of the history of interpretation, from Augustine onwards. Even if we leave aside "the new and totally different" and therefore (by assumption) pure intellectual curiosity—which no one else who has tried to read and interpret a text has ever been fortunate enough to possess—there is much too much to be accepted on faith here. From reading such cultural and colonial historians as Donald Lach or J. H. Parry, one would conclude that European interest in alien cultures was based on actual encounters with those cultures usually as a result of trade, conquest, or accident.[5] "Interest" derives from need, and need rests on empirically stimulated things working and existing together—appetite, fear, curiosity, and so on—which have always been in play wherever and whenever human beings have lived.

Besides, how does one interpret another culture unless prior circumstances have made that culture available for interpretation in the first place? And these circumstances, so far as the European interest in alien cultures is concerned, have always been commercial, colonial, or military expansion, conquest, empire. Even when Orientalist scholars in nineteenth-century German universities studied Sanskrit, codified the *hadith*, or explained the caliphate, they relied less on the fiction of pure curiosity than on the universities themselves, the libraries, other scholars, the social rewards that made their careers possible. Only Dr. Pangloss or a member of Swift's Academy of Projectors at Lagado in *Gulliver's Travels* would locate the drive for acquiring enormous European empires and the knowledge that went with them principally in "the gratification of new intellectual curiosity." Small wonder, then, that benighted non-European natives have viewed the scholars' "intellectual curiosity" with such suspicion, for when was a Western scholar ever in a non-Western country except by dint, however symbolic and indirect, of Western power over that country?[6] It is an indication of *this* Orientalist's peculiar ignorance and conceit that he seems unaware of the debate raging within the field of anthropology over the complicity between imperialism and ethnology; even so mandarin a figure as Lévi-Strauss has expressed misgivings, if not regrets, about imperialism being a constitutive aspect of ethnological field work.

If we dismiss out of hand the protestations about pure curiosity, we will still conclude, I believe, that the whole argument being advanced about Middle East studies is actually a defense of their essentially unflawed capacity—historically and culturally—for telling the truth about distant and alien societies. Later in the same essay this point is further elaborated with reference to the dangers of "politicizing" the field, which, it is alleged, only some scholars and some departments have managed to avoid. Politics here seems associated with narrow partisanship, as if the real scholar is above petty squabbles, being preoccupied only with ideas, eternal values, and high principles; significantly, no examples are given. The interesting point about this entire essay, nevertheless, is how it calls for science and scientific procedures in name only. When it comes to *what* the truth of nonpolitical Middle East studies is, or could be, the author simply says nothing. In other words, the attitudes, the postures, the rhetoric—in fine, the ideology—of scholarship is what counts. Its content is simply not spelled out, and what is worse, there is a deliberate attempt to conceal the connections between scholarship and what we might call worldliness, for the sake of maintaining the fiction of nonpartisan and unpolitical scholarly truth.

This tells us more about the author than it does about the field he purportedly is writing about, an irony that has dogged all modern

European or Western attempts to write about non-Western societies. Not that all other scholars have been aware of the difficulty. In 1973 the Middle East Studies Association (MESA), in collaboration with the Ford Foundation, commissioned a team of experts to survey the entire field in order to assess its current state, its needs, its prospects, and its problems.[7] The result was a large, densely written volume called *The Study of the Middle East: Research and Scholarship in the Humanities and the Social Sciences*, edited by Leonard Binder and published in 1976. Since the book is a collective work it is inevitably uneven in quality, but one is struck throughout by the general air of crisis and urgency, something totally missing from the essay in the *American Scholar*. For this group of scholars, no less distinguished than their British colleague, Middle East studies is an embattled field: there is not enough attention devoted to it, not enough money, not enough scholars. (Ironically, one member of MESA's Research and Training Committee, which first conceived the study, had written a study of the Middle East studies field a mere handful of years earlier for the United States government, in which he had derogated the need for specialized studies on Islam or the Arabs: this was a field, he said, that was culturally and politically of only secondary importance to the United States.[8]) But underlying all the problems they mention is one which Leonard Binder treats candidly in his introduction.

"The basic motive in the development of area studies in the United States," runs Binder's very first sentence, "has been political."[9] He then proceeds to go through all the organizational and philosophical issues facing the modern specialist in the Middle East, never losing sight of the fact—for it is a fact—that Middle East studies are a part of the society in which, so to speak, they occur. At the end of his survey, after saying quite frankly that even the most basic questions about the field—whether, for instance, one should begin by studying social structures or by studying religion, or whether for a scholar political structures are more or less important than per capita incomes—are not value-free, and after also saying that even if the "value-orientations of Middle East studies are manifestly more subtle in most cases than the perspectives of government informa-tion . . . the problem cannot be avoided,"[10] Binder tries at last to summarize the effects of politics upon the truth of what is produced by Western students of alien cultures.

He grants at once that every scholar has "value orientations" that come into play when scholarship is produced. But then, he says, "the normative orientations of the disciplines" reduce the distract-ing effect of personal "ad hoc judgments."[11] Binder neither explains how "the disciplines" do things, nor does he specify what it is about "the disciplines" that so easily transforms human judgments into Olympian analyses. As if somehow to deal with these questions, he tacks on a statement at the end of his argument that is unnecessar-ily opaque and totally discontinuous with what has come before it: The disciplines, he says, "also present us with methods for exploring those moral issues which arise in the context of the area." Which moral issues? What methods? What context of which area? No ex-planation is given. His conclusion instead is of such utterly bewil-dering seriousness that one is left with a reassuring sense of confidence in "the disciplines"—and no sense at all of what "the disciplines" are really about.

Even when the coarse political pressures impinging upon Mid-dle East studies are acknowledged, there is a disquieting tendency to spirit those pressures away and reestablish the canonical au-thority of Orientalist discourse. It bears repeating that that author-ity comes directly from a power within Western culture allowing students of the Orient or Islam to make statements about Islam and the Orient that, for a great many years, have been virtually unchal-lengeable. For who except the Orientalists spoke and continue to speak for the Orient? Neither the nineteenth-century Orientalist nor, in the twentieth century, a scholar like Leonard Binder has doubted that "the field"—and not, it must be noted, the Orient it-self or its people (except as objects or informants)—has always sup-plied Western culture with all that it needed to know about the

Orient; consequently anyone who spoke the discipline's language, deployed its concepts, managed its techniques, and acquired its credentials would be able to get beyond prejudice and immediate circumstances in order to make scientific statements. And that sense of self-sufficient, self-correcting, self-endorsing power gave and still gives Orientalism its remarkably unself-conscious rhetoric. According to Binder, the disciplines, not the people of the Orient, state the normative issues in general terms; the disciplines, not the desires of the people of that area nor the morality of everyday life, "present us with methods for exploring those moral issues which arise in the context of the area."

On the one hand, therefore, "the disciplines" are institutions more than they are activities; on the other hand, they regulate and normalize what they study (which in a sense they have also created) far more readily than they analyze themselves or reflect on what they do. The net result, I think, could only by a kind of tautological indulgence be described as full knowledge of another culture. True, there have been important achievements in the study of Islam: texts have been established and positivistic descriptions of classical Islam have been made very precise. But so far as the *human* dimension of contemporary Islam or the predicament of any interpretative activity is concerned, neither has been greatly illuminated or helped by "the disciplines" of contemporary Middle East studies.

Virtually nothing about the study of Islam today is "free" and undetermined by urgent contemporary pressures. This is very far from the unpolitical objectivity alleged by many Orientalist scholars about their work; and it is almost as far both from the mechanical determinism of vulgar materialists, who see all intellectual and cultural activity as determined in advance by economic forces, and from the happy confidence of specialists who put all their faith in the technical efficiency of "disciplines." Somewhere between those extremes the interpreter's "interests" work themselves out and are reflected out into the culture at large.

But here, too, there is less diversity and freedom than we would like to believe. For what is it that makes a topic of interest out of what might otherwise be an academic or antiquarian concern if not power and will, both of which in Western society (as in all others in differing degrees) tend to be organized, to be capable of certain kinds of implementation, to exercise a redoubtable institutional authority of their own over and above narrow and pragmatic immediacy? A simple instance will make the point quickly: then we can go on to discuss one or two elaborations.

For the general public in America and Europe today, Islam is "news" of a particularly unpleasant sort. The media, the government, the geopolitical strategists, and—although they are marginal to the culture at large—the academic experts on Islam are all in concert: Islam is a threat to Western civilization. Now this is by no means the same as saying that only derogatory or racist caricatures of Islam are to be found in the West. I do not say that, nor would I agree with anyone who did. What I am saying is that negative images of Islam continue to be very much more prevalent than any others, and that such images correspond not to what Islam "is" (given that "Islam" is not a natural fact but a composite structure created to a certain extent by Muslims and the West in the ways I have tried to describe), but to what prominent sectors of a particular society take it to be. Those sectors have the power and the will to propagate *that* particular image of Islam, and this image therefore becomes more prevalent, more present, than all others. As I said in Chapter One, this is done through the workings of a consensus, which sets limits and applies pressures.

Consider, as a useful case, a series of four seminars held between 1971 and 1978 and funded by the Ford Foundation at Princeton University, which for many social and political reasons is an obviously eye-catching place for academic seminars. In addition to its general fame, Princeton has a renowned and very respectable Program in Near East Studies; called until recently the Department of Oriental Studies; it was founded by Philip Hitti almost half a century ago. Today, the program's orientation—like that of many other Near East programs—is dominated by social and policy scientists. Classical Islamic, Arabic, and Persian literature, for instance, are less well represented in the curriculum and on the faculty than are modern Near Eastern economics, politics, history, and sociology. The cooperation of this program with the Ford Foundation, the country's premier social science foundation, argues—and I would add, is meant to argue—authoritative power of a very high sort in the United States. Any subject focused on under such auspices is thereby given undoubted prominence, for what Princeton proposes and what Ford finances suggests (and is meant to suggest) emphases, priorities, stresses of major consequence. In short, although they were formulated and conducted by academics, these seminars were held with the national interest in mind. Scholarship was thought of as serving that interest, and as we shall see, the choice of subject matter indicated that political preferences actually resulted in the formulation of scholarly imperatives. It is worth noting in this regard that the Ford Foundation and Princeton were not and are unlikely to be interested in deluxe seminars dealing with medieval Arabic grammatical theories, even though on strictly intellectual grounds a much stronger case can be made for such a seminar than for any of the ones that were held.

Be that as it may, what were the seminars about and who attended them? One of them dealt with "slavery and related institutions in Islamic Africa." In the proposal for that seminar much was made of African fear and resentment of Arab Muslims, and it was also noted that "some Israeli scholars" have tried to warn African countries against depending too much on Arab nations "who depopulated their countries in time past."[12] By choosing slavery in Islam the sponsors were highlighting a subject certain to worsen relations between African and Arab Muslims: it was as part of achieving this aim that no scholars from the Arab Muslim world were invited.

A second seminar dealt with the *millet* system, and its main theme was "the position of minorities and in particular of religious minorities within the Muslim state in the Middle East."[13] *Millets* were the relatively autonomous minority groupings that existed within the Ottoman Empire. After the breakup of the empire and the end of the various French and British colonial regimes, a series of new states emerged in the Near East around the time of the Second World War. Most of them were, or attempted to be, nation-states: one (Israel) was a minority religious state in the surrounding Islamic context; another (Lebanon) was to be torn apart in large measure by a militant non-Muslim minority armed and supported by both Israel and the United States.

Far from being a neutral academic topic, "the *millet* system" was in its very formulation the expression of a preferred policy solution for the complex nationality and ethnic problems of the contemporary Islamic world. Whatever the academic reasons for studying it, the *millet* system represents a throwback to an earlier time, by which imperial powers (whether Ottoman or Western) divided and ruled a large and potentially fractious population. To the majority Sunni inhabitants of the region as well as to some of the minorities, the recent history of the modern Islamic world has been a struggle to progress beyond ethnic and religious divisions toward some sort of (perhaps unitary) secular democracy. None of the states of the region has achieved this except in the realm of declared (but usually nonimplemented) policy, but only Israel and the far-right-wing Maronites in Lebanon have actively waged a campaign to revert to a state structure based principally upon minority ethnic autonomy with bilateral links to an outside patron or great power. That this also happens to be the solution proposed for the Palestinians was not a fortuitous matter for the seminar planners, since the person brought to Princeton to speak about the Palestinian Arab "minority" (how many ironies in that designation!) was an Israeli professor. It is also a remarkable fact that as in the case of the slavery conference, no members of the majority Sunni community were invited. That a seminar on so sensitive a topic was held in the United States at such a time (1978), and that so many members of religious and ethnic minorities essentially hostile to what was designated as Islamic rule (and therefore potentially useful to United States policy planners) participated, can hardly be ascribed to scholarly interest. It was no accident that the seminar's principal convener was the same scholar to whom I referred above, the very same person who praised Western intellectual curiosity and derided those academics and all those non-Europeans who saw a political plot in everything.

The first seminar had dealt with the application of psychoanalytic and behavioral techniques of analysis to the understanding of modern Middle Eastern societies. Subsequently a volume based on that seminar's proceedings was published.[14] In the main, the seminar was as one might have expected. There was a central emphasis upon national character studies (though with a rigorous and perspicacious critique by Ali Banuazizi of Iranian character studies so-called, which he very correctly connected to the manipulative aims of imperial powers with designs on Iran[15]). The results were drearily predictable. In the book we are told many times that Muslims live in a make-believe world, that the family is repressive, that most leaders are psychopathological, that the societies are immature, and so on. All of this is not presented from the point of view of scholars interested in changing these societies into "mature" ones, but from the perspective of neutral, objective, and value-free scientists. No allowances are made for what positions such scientists (however neutral and value-free they may be) occupy in relation to corporate and governmental powers, what roles their investigations play in the conduct of governmental policies towards the Muslim world, what the methodological implications of psychology are for the study of a weak society by a stronger one.

No investigation of these matters was to be found in the fourth seminar, whose title was "Land, Population, and Society in the Near East: Studies in Economic History from the Rise of Islam to the Nineteenth Century." Like the others, this seminar also presented itself as scholarly and impartial, although beneath the surface could be seen a quite pressing policy concern: in this instance, it was an interest in the relationship between landholding, demographic patterns, and state authority as indices of stability (or instability) in modern Muslim societies. We should not conclude that every contribution to the seminar was objectively valueless, nor that each participating scholar was a party to a nefarious conspiracy. The organizers had very sagely seen to it that there was "balance" between views, and that, taken as a whole, the seminar should appear responsible and serious. On the other hand, we ought not to fall into the trap of regarding the enterprise itself as being only the mechanical sum of its many discrete parts. In the choice of over-all topics and trends the four seminars undertook to shape awareness of Islam in terms that either distanced it as a hostile phenomenon or highlighted certain aspects of it that could be "managed" in policy terms.

In this regard the Princeton seminars on Islam conformed to the history of other Third World area-studies programs in the United States—for example, the immediate postwar period in the academic study of China.[16] The difference is that Islamic programs have yet to be "revised": they are still dominated by outmoded, impossibly vague concepts (like "Islam" itself) and an intellectual idiom that are out of touch with what has gone on generally in the human sciences and in the society as a whole. It is still possible to say things about Islam that are simply unacceptable for Judaism, for other Asians, or for blacks, and it is still possible to write studies of Islamic history and society that blithely ignore every major advance in interpretative theory since Nietzsche, Marx, and Freud.

The result is that very little of what goes on in the study of Islam has much to say to scholars interested in the methodological problems of general historiography, say, or in textual analysis. Instead, if we take the Princeton seminars as a perfect case in point, a scholarly work on Islam appears (as the volume on psychology in Middle East studies appeared), it is reviewed by one or two highly specialized publications of limited circulation, and then it disappears. Precisely this marginality, this willed irrelevance for the general culture, of Islamic studies makes it possible for scholars to go on doing what they have been doing, and for the media to take over the dissemination of racist caricatures of the Islamic peoples. Since the middle 1980s, however, studies of political Islam — most of them aggressive studies of fundamentalism, terrorism, and antimodernism as principal aspects of Islam — have flooded the market. Most of them draw on a handful of scholars (like Bernard Lewis) to mobilize popular opinion against the "threat" of Islam. In this way the scholarly constituency perpetuates itself, while the clientele for Islam as news continues to get the massive doses of Islamic punishment, gratuitous violence, terrorism, and harem capers it has been fed for decades.

When the experts venture into the public eye it is as experts, brought in because an emergency has caught "the West" unprepared. Their pronouncements are neither cushioned nor refined by any residual cultural feeling for Islam, as in Britain or France. They are viewed as technicians with "a solid set of 'how-tos'" (the phrase is Dwight MacDonald's)[17] to present to the anxious public. And the public takes kindly to them, for they are an answer to what Christopher Lasch has called

> an unprecedented demand for experts, technicians and managers [created by what Lasch calls "the postindustrial order"]. Both business and government, under the pressure of technological revolution, expanding population, and the indefinitely prolonged emergency of the Cold War, became increasingly dependent on a vast apparatus of systematized data intelligible only to trained specialists; and the universities, accordingly, became themselves industries for the mass production of experts.[18]

The market for expertise is so attractive and lucrative that work done on the Middle East is directed almost exclusively at it. This is one reason that in none of the established journals (nor for that matter in recent books by established scholars) is there any attention paid to the basic questions *Why* Middle East and Islamic studies? and *For whom* are they being transacted? The obliteration of the methodological consciousness is absolutely coterminous with the presence of the market, for news as well as whole clienteles of security-conscious consumers (governments, corporations, foundations): one simply does not ask why one does what one does if there is an appreciative, or at least a potentially receptive, clientele. Worse yet, the scholar stops thinking in terms of the region and the people about whom studies are being conducted. Islam, if it is "Islam" that is being studied, is not an interlocutor but in a sense a commodity. The overall result is a kind of institutional bad faith. The scholarly honor and integrity of the field are upheld against critical outsiders, scholarly rhetoric is willfully arrogant about denying political partisanship, and scholarly self-congratulation fortifies present practices (principally in popular journalism) indefinitely.

What I have been describing is an essentially lonely enterprise, which means in this case that the scholar works reactively in answer to what various interests seem to require of him or her; he or she is guided more by a guild orthodoxy than by the exigencies of genuine interpretation, and, above all, the general culture ghettoizes his or her work, rendering it marginal except during times of crisis. Neither of the two necessary conditions for knowing another culture— uncoercive contact with an alien culture through real exchange, and self-consciousness about the interpretative project itself—is present, and this absence enforces the solitude, the provinciality, and the circularity of covering Islam. Significantly, these things also make it evident that covering Islam from the United States, the last superpower, is not interpretation in the genuine sense but an assertion of power. The media say what they wish about Islam because they can, with the result that Islamic fundamentalism and terrorism and "good" Muslims (in Bosnia, for instance) dominate the scene indiscriminately; little else is covered because anything falling outside the consensus definition of what is important is considered irrelevant to United States interests and to the media's definition of a good story. The academic community, on the other hand, responds to what it construes as national and corporate needs, with the result that suitable Islamic topics are hewn out of an enormous mass of Islamic details, and these topics (extremism, violence, and so forth) define both Islam and the proper study of Islam so as to exclude everything not fitting neatly between them. Even when on occasion the government or one of the university Middle East departments or one of the foundations organizes a conference to deal with the future of Middle East studies (which is usually a euphemism for "What are we going to do about the Islamic world?"), the same battery of concepts and goals keeps turning up. Little is changed.

A great deal is staked on this repetition, not least a fairly well run system of patronage. The senior experts in the field, whether from the government, the corporation world, or the university, tend to have connections with one another and with compliant donors. A young scholar depends on this network for his or her subventions, to say nothing of employment and the possibility of publication in the established journals. To venture unfriendly critiques of the recognized scholars or of their work, in this field more than in the fields of general history or literature, is to risk too much. Book reviews as a result are insipid and mainly complimentary; criticism is uniformly couched in the most pedantic language possible, and nothing is ever said about methodology or assumptions. The most curious omission — and the most routine — is the analysis of the connection between scholarship and the various forms of power in the society for which this scholarship is produced. And the moment a voice is heard that challenges this conspiracy of silence, ideology and ethnic origins become the main topic: He (or she) is a Marxist; or, he (or she) is a Palestinian (or an Iranian, or a Muslim, or a Syrian) — and we know what *they're* like.[19] As for the sources themselves, they are always treated as if they were inert; thus in discussing a contemporary Islamic society or a movement or a figure, the scholar refers to what is being discussed mainly as *evidence*, rarely as something entitled to its own integrity or to its right, in a sense, to reply. Interestingly, there has never been any systematic attempt by Western experts on Islam to deal methodologically with Islamic writing on Islam: Is it scholarship? Is it evidence? Is it neither?

Yet despite this rather arid state of affairs, or perhaps even because of it, some knowledge of value about Islam is produced, and some independent minds manage to get through the desert. In the main, however, the over-all marginality, the overall *intellectual* incoherence (as opposed to guild consensus), the overall interpretative bankruptcy of most—though by no means all—writing on Islam can be traced to the old-boy corporation-government-university network dominating the whole enterprise. Look at the way in which the *same* basically anti-Muslim figures keep turning up on the *MacNeil/Lehrer Report, Nightline*, or *Charlie Rose*. And that, finally, determines the way the United States views the Islamic world. For why else could so peculiar a structure of knowledge about Islam develop and thrive, so intertwined, well established, untroubled by one failure after another?

The most effective way of understanding the precise quality of this vision, which has the force of unquestioned faith, is to compare it once again with the situation obtaining in Britain and France, those two predecessors of the United States in the Islamic world. In both countries there has always been a cadre of Islamic experts, of course, with a longstanding advisory role in formulating—and even executing—government as well as commercial policy. But in both instances there was an immediate task at hand: the administering of rule in colonies. This was the case until the end of World War II. The Islamic world was viewed as a discrete series of problems, and knowledge about those problems was on the whole positivistic as well as directly engaged. Theories and abstractions about the Islamic mind, in France about the *mission civilisatrice*, in Britain about self-rule for subject peoples, intervened here and there in the conduct of policy, but always after the policy was in place and on the ground, so to speak. Discourse about Islam played the role essentially of justifying the national (or even a private economic) interest in the Islamic world. This is why today in France and Britain great scholars of Islam are public figures whose *raison d'être*, even now that the colonial empires have been dissolved, is to maintain a French or a British interest in the Islamic world. For a number of other reasons such scholars on the whole tend to be humanists, not social scientists, and their support in the general culture comes less from the postindustrial cult of expertise (which exists in both countries) than from broad intellectual and moral currents in the society. Rodinson in France is a great philologist who is also a well-known Marxist; the late Hourani in England was a famous historian and a man whose work represents an evident liberalism.[20] Such persons are disappearing, however, and in both France and England, American-style social scientists or specialized antiquarians are likely to replace them in the future.

Similar scholars in the United States are known only as Middle East or Islamic experts; they belong to the class of experts, and their domain, insofar as they are concerned with modern societies in the Islamic world, can be regarded as the intellectual equivalent of crisis management. Much of their status derives from the notion that for the United States the Islamic world is a strategic area, with all sorts of *possible* (if not always actual) problems. During their many decades of administering Islamic colonies, both Britain and France naturally produced a class of colonial experts, but this class did not in turn produce an adjunct to it equivalent to the network of the Middle East studies-government-corporate alliance that exists in the United States. Professors of Arabic or Persian or Islamic institutions did their work in British and French universities; they were called on for advice and even participation by the colonial departments and by private business enterprises; they occasionally held congresses; but they do not seem to have created an independent structure of their own, sustained and even maintained by the private business sector or directly by foundations and the government.

Knowledge and coverage of the Islamic world, therefore, are defined in the United States by geopolitics and economic interests on—for the individual—an impossibly massive scale, aided and abetted by a structure of knowledge production that is almost as vast and unmanageable. What is the student of Arabian or Trucial States tribes to do about the interposition between him or her and those tribes of the oil company's presence, about the active talk and promotion of rapid-deployment forces (see the *Newsweek* cover story, "Defending the Oilfields: The U.S. Military Buildup," on July 14, 1980) for the Gulf area, about the whole apparatus of Middle East "hands" at the State Department, the corporations and foundations, the array of senior Orientalist professors? Of what sort can knowledge of another culture actually be when it is so hemmed in by the hypothetical urgencies of "the crescent of crisis" on the one hand and by the thriving institutional affiliations between scholarship, business, and the government on the other?

Let me conclude this section by trying to answer the question very concretely in two parts. First, the actual conditions and the facts and figures governing what might be called orthodox working coverage of Islam. I shall concentrate on the United States, but a very similar situation is gradually coming to obtain in Europe as well. According to a useful French survey of American Middle East studies centers, about 1,650 Middle East specialists in 1970 taught the area's languages to 2,659 graduate students and 4,150 undergraduates (respectively, 12 percent and 7.4 percent of the total number of graduates and undergraduates majoring in "area studies"[21]). Area courses on the Middle East enrolled 6,400 graduates and 22,300 undergraduates (which was 12.6 percent of the total). Yet in recent years the number of Ph.D.s produced in Middle East studies has been a proportionately small one—less than 1 percent of the nation's Ph.D. graduates.[22] According to a perspicacious study of Middle East centers at American universities done by Richard Nolte (commissioned, interestingly enough, by Esso Middle East, a division of Exxon) and published in 1979, the Office of Education supported area studies "to develop experts and specialists quickly and in large numbers for government, corporate and educational purposes." The universities have complied with this outlook: "From a university point of view," Nolte writes appropriately, "the [Middle East] centers can be seen as a promising new marketing mechanism for university output—helping not only to produce a more marketable product, area-trained specialists of useful disciplines and professionals for potentially huge new markets, but also to create the markets." And he says in connection with M.A. programs, "The governmental, corporate, banking and other professional markets for appropriately trained M.A.s with a Middle East dimension is comparatively brisk, thanks to economic and political factors similar to all."[23]

Just as the Princeton seminars I referred to help to shape intellectual concerns in the scholarly community, so too do these market realities affect the scholarly curriculum. Heaviest emphasis in Middle East studies is placed on fields like Islamic law and the Arab-Israeli conflict: their relevance is obvious on the face of it. But a concomitant is that literature, according to Nolte, is neglected, as are the reasonably large groups of Middle Eastern students enrolled in American universities. Moreover, Nolte says, center directors he interviewed

mentioned incidents involving organized political pressure often of off-campus origin, to prevent or discredit Arab-connected activities regarded as academically legitimate and desirable by the centers concerned. Arab cultural events, film showings, visiting speakers, acceptance of Arab budgetary support funds—anything could become a target. Awareness of this has imposed a pervasive inhibition which few directors fail to resent—or can afford to ignore. Some directors felt matters were improving, others were not so sure.[24]

All these things—politics, pressures, markets—make themselves felt in various ways. The need for expertise about the contemporary Middle East produces many courses, many students, and a marked

emphasis upon accepting and maintaining the instrumental perspectives of knowledge that are both lucrative and immediately ap-
plicable. Another result is that methodological investigations simply
do not occur: a student wishing to make a career in Middle East
studies will first of all dread the long and arid years necessary for obtaining a Ph.D. (with no certainty that he or she will get a teaching
job as a result); then he or she will acquire an M.A. or an international-
studies diploma in a subject attractive to the biggest employers (the
government, the oil companies, the international investment houses,
contracting firms); finally, the work will tend to be done as quickly
as possible in the form of a case study. All this isolates study of Islam
or the Middle East from other intellectual and moral currents in
the scholarly community. The media will seem like a more promising stage upon which to display expertise than, for instance, a general
intellectual journal, and in the media, as habitués know, you are either a partisan (an extremely limiting thing) or you are an expert,
called on to make judgments about Shi'ism and anti-Americanism.
The role of expert furthers one's career obviously enough, unless
one has already done well in business or in the government.

This may seem like a parody of how knowledge gets produced,
but it fairly describes the extreme narrowing of focus and the disastrous thinning of substance in knowledge of Islam. Above all, it explains why it is that far from challenging the vulgar stereotypes
circulated in the media. The academic experts on Islam are as a
body neutralized in their isolated, immediately functional role as
status symbols of relevant authority on Islam, and also dependent
on the whole system constituting and legitimating their function
within it; and it is this system which the media, in their reliance
upon stereotypes based on fear and ignorance, reflect.

If what I have been describing seems intellectually restrictive —
as indeed it is — it does not prevent the production of a huge
amount of material on the Middle East, on Islam, and indeed on
other parts of the Third World. In other words, we have to do with
what Foucault, in another connection, has called "an incitement to

discourse."²⁵ Very different from a simple interventionary censorship, the intellectual regulation of discourse about distant and alien
cultures positively and affirmatively encourages more of itself. This
is why it has persisted despite changes taking place in the world,
and this is why it has continued to draw recruits to its service.

All in all, present coverage of Islam and of non-Western societies
in effect canonizes certain notions, texts, and authorities. The idea
that Islam is medieval and dangerous, as well as hostile and threatening to "us," for example, has acquired a place both in the culture
and in the polity that is very well defined: Authorities can be cited
for it readily, references can be made to it, arguments about particular instances of Islam can be adduced from it—by anyone, not just
by experts or by journalists. And in turn such an idea furnishes a
kind of *a priori* touchstone to be taken account of by anyone wishing to discuss or say something about Islam. From being something
out there, Islam—or rather, the material invariably associated with
it—is turned into an orthodoxy of *this* society. It enters the cultural
canon, and this makes the task of changing it very difficult indeed.

So much for the orthodox coverage of Islam, coverage whose affiliations with power give it strength, durability, and above all, *presence*. Yet there is another view of Islam circulating which belongs to
the category of what might be called *antithetical knowledge*.²⁶

By antithetical knowledge I mean the kind of knowledge produced by people who quite consciously consider themselves to be
writing in opposition to the prevailing orthodoxy. As we shall see,
they do so for varying reasons and in different situations, but all of
these people have a pronounced sense that how and for what reason
they study Islam are questions that require deliberation and explic-
itness. In these antithetical interpreters, the methodological silence
of Orientalism, which has usually been overlaid by layers of optimistic confidence in value-free objectivity, is replaced by urgent discussion of the political meanings of scholarship.

There are three main types of antithetical knowledge of Islam
and, producing it, three forces within the society in a position to

challenge the orthodoxy. One is a group of younger scholars. They tend to be more sophisticated, and more honest politically, than their elders in the field; they see work on Islam as in some way connected to the political activities of the state and therefore make no pretense of being "objective" scholars. For them the fact that the United States is involved in a global politics, a great deal of it having to do with the Muslim world, is not something to be silent about or to accept as a neutral truth. Unlike the older Orientalists they are specialists rather than generalists, and they have welcomed such innovative methodological instruments as structural anthropology, quantitative methods, and Marxist modes of analysis with real interest and often successful applications.[27] They seem especially sensitive to the ethnocentric forms of Orientalist discourse, and most of them—because they are young—are relative outsiders to the patronage system that keeps the senior members of the profession in Scotch and tweed suits. From their ranks have appeared the Alternative Middle East Studies Seminar (AMESS) and the Middle East Research and Information Project (MERIP), both of which were founded as organizations specifically designed to avoid complicity with the government and the oil companies; similar groups have been formed in Europe, and all of them have links to each other. Not all of the younger scholars I am referring to belong in these groups, but most of them are avowedly revisionist in their aims. All of them seek to cover Islam from perspectives either neglected by or unknown to their seniors.

A second group is made up of older scholars whose own work, for too many reasons to summarize schematically, runs counter to the orthodox scholarship dominating the field. Hamid Algar of Berkeley and Nikki Keddie of UCLA, for example, were two of the very few Iranologists who for some years before the Iranian revolution had taken seriously the political role of the 'ulama (the Shi'ite clergy in Iran). Algar and Keddie are very different from each other, even though both of them voiced considerable doubts about the stability of the Pahlevi regime. Similarly, Ervand Abrahamian of Baruch

College, whose studies of the secular opposition to the shah provided a brilliant series of insights into the revolution's political dynamics; or more recently, Michael G. Fischer of Harvard and, in England, Fred Halliday, both of them scholars who for intellectual as well as academic reasons stood away from the majority view of Iran and, as a result, did extraordinarily valuable work on contemporary Iran.[28] Fischer has stopped writing about Islam and Iran, while Halliday has become a conventional, on the whole, predictable figure.

The interesting thing about this group of antithetical writers on Islam is that they cannot be reduced to a methodological and ideological characterization that does them any sort of justice. Nevertheless, it is a striking fact that almost none of them belongs to the establishment in Middle East studies. This is not to say that they are not distinguished and respected figures; they are, but few if any of them have been actively and institutionally involved as consultants to governments or to corporations. Perhaps this fact has freed them from obligation to the status quo and enabled them to see things that conventional writers on Islam have bypassed. Yet it must be said about them, and about the group of younger scholars referred to above, that in order for their work to have the effect it potentially can have, they must become more political in this society. It is not enough for them to have views that distinguish them from orthodox experts; they must try to give their views currency, and because such an effort will have to go considerably beyond writing things and getting them published, they have a long political and organizational struggle ahead of them.

Lastly, there is a group of writers, activists, and intellectuals who are not accredited experts on Islam but whose role in society is determined by their overall oppositional stance: these are the antiwar and anti-imperialist militants, the dissenting clergy, the radical intellectuals and teachers, and so on. Their insight into Islam has very little to do with the wisdom of Orientalists, although some of them have been influenced by the cultural Orientalism that is to be found everywhere in the West. Nevertheless—if we consider a man like I. F. Stone as an example—the cultural distrust of and antipathy towards Islam is tempered by an even stronger feeling about what imperalism is like and what, no matter whether it is Jews, Muslims, or Christians who are involved, human suffering is like. Stone was unique in predicting the consequences of continuing United States support for the shah after the revolution, and it was people like him and not the governmental and academic experts on Iran who advocated a conciliatory policy towards the revolutionary regime.

The impressive thing about such people is how, despite their lack of expert certification, they seem to understand certain dynamics within the postcolonial world and hence within large portions of the Islamic world. For them human experience, and not limiting labels like "the Islamic mind" or "the Islamic personality," defines the unit of attention. Moreover, they are genuinely interested in exchange, and have made it a matter of conscious choice to overstep the rigid lines of hostility put down between peoples by governments. One thinks quintessentially here of Ramsey Clark going to Teheran and of the courageous role played during the worst days of the Iran crisis by individuals like Richard Falk, William Sloane Coffin, Jr., Don Luce, and others too numerous to mention, as well as organizations such as the Friends Service Committee, Clergy and Laity Concerned, and other groups like them. In addition, as a part of this dissenting configuration we ought to include various publications and alternative news organizations, among them *The Progressive, Mother Jones, The Nation,* who opened their pages and made their resources available to oppositional views on Iran and—less frequently, alas—on Islam. The same phenomenon is repeated in Europe.

What is most important, in my opinion, about these three groups is that for them knowledge is essentially an actively sought out and contested thing, not merely a passive recitation of facts and "accepted" views. The struggle between this view, as it bears upon other cultures and beyond that into wide political questions, and the specialized institutional knowledge fostered by the dominant powers of advanced Western society is an epochal matter. It far transcends the question whether a view is pro- or anti-Islamic, or whether one is a patriot or a traitor. As our world grows more tightly knit together, the control of scarce resources, strategic areas, and large populations will seem more desirable and more necessary. Carefully fostered fears of anarchy and disorder will very likely produce conformity of views and, with reference to the "outside" world, greater distrust: this is as true of the Islamic world as it is of the West. At such a time—which has already begun—the production and diffusion of knowledge will play an absolutely crucial role. Yet until knowledge is understood in human and political terms as something to be won to the service of coexistence and community, not of particular races, nations, classes, or religions, the future augurs badly.

II. KNOWLEDGE AND INTERPRETATION

All knowledge that is about human society, and not about the natural world, is historical knowledge, and therefore rests upon judgment and interpretation. This is not to say that facts or data are nonexistent, but that facts get their importance from what is made of them in interpretation. No one disputes the fact that Napoleon actually lived and was a French emperor; there is however, a great deal of interpretative disagreement as to whether he was a great or in some ways a disastrous ruler of France. Such disagreements are the stuff out of which historical writing is made and from which historical knowledge derives. For interpretations depend very much on who the interpreter is, who he or she is addressing, what his or her purpose is in interpreting, at what historical moment the interpretation takes place. In this sense, all interpretations are what might be called *situational*: they always occur in a situation whose bearing on the interpretation is *affiliative*.[29] It is related to what other interpreters have said, either by confirming them, or by disputing them, or by continuing them. No interpretation is without precedents or without some connection to other interpretations. Thus anyone writing seriously about Islam, or China, or Shakespeare, or Marx must in some way take account of what has been said about these subjects, if only because he or she wishes not to be irrelevant or redundant. No writing is (or can be) so new as to be completely original, for in writing about human society one is not doing mathematics, and therefore one cannot aspire to the radical originality possible in that activity.

Knowledge of other cultures, then, is especially subject to "unscientific" imprecision and to the circumstances of interpretation. Nevertheless, we can say tentatively that knowledge of another culture is possible, and it is important to add, desirable, if two conditions are fulfilled—which, incidentally, are precisely the two conditions that today's Middle East or Islamic studies by and large do not fulfill. One, the student must feel that he or she is answerable to and in uncoercive contact with the culture and the people being studied. As I said earlier, most of what the West knew about the non-Western world it knew in the framework of colonialism; the European scholar therefore approached his subject from a general position of dominance, and what he said *about* this subject was said with little reference to what anyone but other European scholars had said. For the many reasons I have enumerated earlier in this book and in *Orientalism*, knowledge of Islam and of Islamic peoples has generally proceeded not only from dominance and confrontation but also from cultural antipathy. Today Islam is defined negatively as that with which the West is radically at odds, and this tension establishes a framework radically limiting knowledge of Islam. So long as this framework stands, Islam, as a vitally lived experience for Muslims, cannot be known. This, unfortunately, is particularly true in the United States, and only slightly less true in Europe.

The second condition complements and fulfills the first. Knowledge of the social world, as opposed to knowledge of nature, is at bottom what I have been calling interpretation: it acquires the status of knowledge by various means, some of them intellectual, many of them social and even political. Interpretation is first of all a form of making: that is, it depends on the willed intentional activity of the human mind, molding and forming the objects of its attention with care and study. Such an activity takes place perforce in a specific time and place and is engaged in by a specifically located individual, with a specific background, in a specific situation, for a particular series of ends. Therefore the interpretation of texts, which is what the knowledge of other cultures is principally based on, neither takes place in a clinically secure laboratory nor pretends to objective results. It is a social activity and inextricably tied to the situation out of which it arose in the first place, which then either gives it the status of knowledge or rejects it as unsuitable for that status. No interpretation can neglect this situation, and no interpretation is complete without an interpretation of the situation.

It will be evident that such unscientific nuisances as feelings, habits, conventions, associations, and values are an intrinsic part of any interpretation. Every interpreter is a reader, and there is no such thing as a neutral or value-free reader. Every reader, in other words, is both a private ego and a member of a society, with affiliations of every sort linking him or her to that society. Working through national feelings like patriotism or chauvinism to private emotions like fear or despair, the interpreter must seek in a disciplined way to employ reason and the information he or she has gained through formal education (itself a long interpretative process) so that understanding may be achieved. A great effort has to be made to pierce the barriers that exist between one situation, the situation of the interpreter, and another, the situation that existed when and where the text was produced. It is precisely this conscious willed effort of overcoming distances and cultural barriers that makes knowledge of other societies and cultures possible—and at the same time limits that knowledge. At that moment, the interpreter understands himself or herself in his or her human situation and the text in relation to *its* situation, the human situation out of which it came. This can occur only as the result of self-awareness animating an awareness of what is distant and alien but human nonetheless. It scarcely needs to be said that this whole process has very little to do either with "the new and totally different knowledge" alluded to by the conventional Orientalist, or with Professor Binder's self-correcting "disciplines."

One thing more needs to be said in this rather abstract description of the interpretative process at the end of which knowledge — by no means a stable thing — is arrived at. There is never interpretation, understanding, and then knowledge where there is no *interest*. This may seem like the most pedestrian truism, but it is exactly this fairly obvious truth that is usually ignored or denied. For an American scholar to read and decode a contemporary Arabic or Japanese novel involves a totally different sort of engagement with an alien object than that of a chemist decoding a chemical formula. Chemical elements are not intrinsically affective and do not engage one's human feelings, though of course even they may trigger emotional associations in the scientist for wholly extrinsic reasons. The opposite is true in what might be called humanistic interpretation, which according to many theorists actually begins in awareness of the interpreter's prejudices, sense of alienation from the text to be interpreted, and so on. As Hans-Georg Gadamer has written:

> A person trying to understand a text is prepared for it to tell him something. That is why a hermeneutically trained mind must be, from the start, sensitive to the text's quality of newness. But this kind of sensitivity involves neither "neutrality" in the matter of the object nor the extinction of one's self, but the conscious assimilation of one's own foremeanings [that is, those meanings or interpretations that already exist as a result of past experiences] and prejudices. The important thing is to

be aware of one's own bias, so that the text may present itself
in all its newness and thus be able to assert its own truth
against one's own foremeanings.[30]

Therefore, the first thing to be aware of in reading a text produced in an alien culture is its distance, the main condition of its
distance (in both time and space) being quite literally, although not
exclusively, the presence of the interpreter in his or her time and
place. As we saw, the orthodox Orientalist or "area studies" approach is to equate distance with authority, to incorporate the foreignness of a distant culture into the authoritative rhetoric of a
scholarly discourse, which has the social status of knowledge, with
no acknowledgment of what that foreignness exacted from the interpreter and no acknowledgment of what structure of power made
the interpreter's job possible. I mean quite simply that, almost without exception, no writer on Islam in the West today reckons explicitly with the fact that "Islam" is considered a hostile culture, or that
anything said about Islam by a professional scholar is within the
sphere of influence of corporations, the media, and the government, all of which in turn play a very large role in making interpretations and, subsequently, knowledge of Islam desirable and "in the
national interest." In the argument that I analyzed above, Leonard
Binder is typical: he mentions these matters, then he makes them
disappear in a sentence paying homage to professionalism and "the
disciplines," whose collective function is an efficient way of dismissing whatever disturbs their mask of rational objectivity. This is an instance of socially acceptable knowledge erasing the steps by which
it was produced.

As an aspect of intepretation, "interest" can be glossed a good
deal further and much more concretely. No one simply happens
upon Islam, Islamic culture, or Islamic society. For the citizen of a
Western industrial state today, Islam is encountered by virtue either
of the political oil crisis, or of fundamentalism and terrorism, or of
intense media attention, or of the longstanding tradition of expert—

that is, Orientalist—commentary on Islam in the West. Take the case of a young historian who wishes to specialize in modern Middle Eastern history. He or she comes to study that subject with all three factors in play, all of them molding and shaping the situation in which "the facts"—the supposedly raw data—are apprehended. In addition, there are the individual's own history, sensibility, and intellectual gifts to be figured in. Taken together these constitute a significant measure of his or her interest in the subject: sheer curiosity is tempered by such things as the promise of consulting work for the State Department, the military, or oil companies, a wish to appear at conferences, on television, on lecture platforms, and to become a famous scholar, a desire to "prove" that Islam is a wonderful (or for that matter, a terrible) cultural system, an ambition to serve as a bridge of understanding between this culture and that, a desire to know. The texts, the professors, the scholarly tradition, the specific moment, add their imprint to what this young historian is going to study. In the end there are other things to be considered too. If one has studied the history of nineteenth-century Syrian land tenure, for instance, it is extremely likely that even the driest and most "objective" treatment of the subject will have some contemporary policy relevance, particularly for a government official who is anxious to understand the dynamics of traditional authority (which is connected to land ownership) as a counterweight to Baath party power in contemporary Syria.

But if, in the first place, some effort is made to have uncoercive contact with a distant culture, and secondly, if the interpreter is consciously aware of the interpretative situation in which he or she is to be found (that is, if the interpreter understands that knowledge of another culture is not absolute but is relative to the interpretative situation in which that knowledge gets produced), then it is more than likely that the interpreter will feel the orthodox view of Islam and of other "alien" cultures to be an acutely limited one. By comparison, antithetical knowledge of Islam seems to go a reasonable distance toward overcoming the limitations of orthodox views.

Precisely because the antithetical scholars reject the notion that knowledge of Islam ought to be subservient to the government's immediate policy interests, or that it should simply feed into the media's image of Islam as supplying the world with terrifying militancy and violence, they highlight the complicity between knowledge and power. And in doing so they seek to establish other relationships with Islam than those ordained by the imperatives of power. Looking for alternative relationships means looking for other interpretative situations; hence, a far more scrupulous methodological sense is developed.

In the end, though, there is never any simple escape from what some critics have called the interpretative circle. Knowledge of the social world, in short, is *always* no better than the interpretations on which it is based. All our knowledge of so complex and elusive a phenomenon as Islam comes about through texts, images, experiences that are not direct embodiments of Islam (which is after all apprehended only through instances of it) but representations or interpretations of it. In other words, all knowledge of other cultures, societies, or religions comes about through an admixture of indirect evidence with the individual scholar's personal situation, which includes time, place, personal gifts, historical situation, as well as the overall political circumstances. What makes such knowledge accurate or inaccurate, bad, better, or worse, has to do mainly with the needs of the society in which that knowledge is produced. There is, of course, a level of simple factuality without which no knowledge can occur: after all, how can one "know" Islam in Morocco without knowing Arabic, Berber, and something about the country and its society? But beyond that, knowledge of Moroccan Islam is not a mere matter of correspondence between there and here, an inert object and its beholder, but an interaction of the two (usually) for a purpose *here*: for example, a learned article, a lecture, an appearance on television, advice to the policymaker. Insofar as the purpose is fulfilled, knowledge is considered to have been produced. There are other uses for knowledge (including even the use of uselessness), but the main ones tend to be very functional or instrumental.

What passes for knowledge, therefore, is a very mixed thing indeed, and is determined less by intrinsic needs (which are rarely intrinsic anyway) than by extrinsic ones. A study of the Iranian elite under the Pahlevis done by an American academic with good credentials may be useful for policymakers having to deal with the imperial regime; to an unorthodox expert on Iran, the very same study will be riddled with errors and misjudgments.[31] The radically differing standards of judgment do not, however, suggest the need for still better touchstones, still firmer absolutes; rather, they ought to remind us that it is the nature of interpretation to send us back to the problems raised by interpretation itself, to asking the questions for whom, for what purpose, and why such an interpretation is more convincing in this context than in that. Interpretation, knowledge, and, as Matthew Arnold said, culture itself are always the result of contests and not simply a gift from heaven.

My thesis in this book has been that the canonical, orthodox coverage of Islam that we find in the academy, in the government, and in the media is all interrelated and has been *more* diffused, has seemed *more* persuasive and influential, in the West than any other "coverage" or interpretation. The success of this coverage can be attributed to the political influence of those people and institutions producing it rather than necessarily to truth or accuracy. I have also argued that this coverage has served purposes only tangentially related to actual knowledge of Islam itself. The result has been the triumph not just of a particular *knowledge* of Islam but rather of a particular *interpretation* which, however, has neither been unchallenged nor impervious to the kinds of questions asked by unorthodox, inquiring minds.

It is therefore just as well that "Islam" has not been particularly useful in explaining the Gulf War, any more than ideas about "the Negro mentality" were useful in explaining the twentieth-century experiences of black Americans. For aside from giving narcissistic satisfaction to the expert who employs them and whose livelihood often depends on them, these totalitarian concepts have kept up neither with the sheer force of events nor with the complex forces that produced the events. The result has been an ever-widening rift between the assertions of homogenizing concepts and the far more powerful assertions and discontinuities of actual history. And into this rift has occasionally stepped an individual who asks pertinent questions and expects reasonable answers.

No one can know everything about the world we live in, and so the division of intellectual labor will have to continue foreseeably. The academy requires that division, knowledge itself demands it, society in the West is organized around it. But most knowledge about human society is, I think, finally accessible to common sense—that is, the sense that grows out of the common human experience—and is, indeed must be, subject to some sort of critical assessment. These two things, common sense and critical assessment, are in the final analysis social and generally intellectual attributes available to and cultivatable by everyone, not the privilege of a special class nor the possession of a handful of certified "experts." Yet special training is necessary if one is to learn Arabic or Chinese, or if one is to understand the meaning of economic, historical, and demographic trends. And the academy is the place for making that training available: of this I have no doubt at all. The trouble comes when training produces guilds and journalistic "experts" who, losing touch with the realities of community, good sense, and intellectual responsibility, either promote the special interest group at all costs or put it too willingly and uncritically at the service of power. In both instances, foreign societies or cultures like Islam end up being covered more than elucidated or understood. There is even the danger that new fictions will be invented and unheard-of varieties of disinformation circulated.

At almost any given moment during the past few years there has been considerable evidence, available to anyone, that the non-Western world generally and Islam in particular no longer conform to the patterns mapped out by American or European social scientists, Orientalists, and area experts in the immediate postwar years. This, I think, has best been formulated by the distinguished Algerian scholar and critic Mohammed Arkoun, Sorbonne Professor of Islamic Thought:

> The academic discourse on "Islamic studies" has still to proffer explanation as to how so many diverse fields, theories, cultural spheres, disciplines, and concepts came to be associated with a single word "Islam" and why the discussion remains so one-dimensional where Islam is concerned. In contrast, the study of Western society is characterised by careful scrutiny, attention to precise detail, meticulous distinctions, and theory-building. Indeed, the study of Western cultures continues to develop along such lines and to move in a different direction altogether from the unfortunate approach adopted in the area of "Islam" and the so-called "Arab world." (Quoted by Malise Ruthven, *London Review of Books*, August 1, 1996, p. 27).

It is certainly true that the Islamic world as a whole is neither completely anti-American and anti-West nor unified and predictable in its actions. Without trying to give an exhaustive account of these changes, I have been saying that this has meant the emergence of new and irregular realities in the Islamic world; it is no less true that similar irregularities, disturbing the calm theoretical descriptions of earlier years, have emerged in other parts of the post-colonial world. Merely to reassert the old formulas about "underdevelopment" and "the Afro-Asian mentality" is foolish enough; but to connect these causally with notions about the sad decline of the West, the unfortunate end of colonialism, and the regrettable diminishment of American power is, I must say as strongly as possible, rank folly. There is simply no way in which societies thousands of miles away from the Atlantic world in both space and identity can be made to conform to what we want of them. One can consider this a neutral fact without also regarding it (as I happen to) as a good thing. In any event, the danger in talking about the loss and therefore threat of Iran and the decline of the West in the same breath is that we immediately foreclose the possibility of most courses of action—except the ascendancy of the West and the regaining of places like Iran and the Gulf, which has been the pattern of the last two decades. The recent success of "experts" who in their work bewail the end (or argue for the extension) of British or American or French dominion in the Islamic world is, in my opinion, frightening testimony to what might be lurking in the minds of policymakers, and to what deep needs for aggression and reconquest these "experts," consciously or unconsciously, really serve.[32] That there are compliant natives who play in the same orchestra belongs to the shabby history of collaboration and is not (as some would have it) a sign of new maturity in the Third World.

Except for the purposes of conquest, "Islam" is not what it is generally said to be in the West today. Immediately, then, we must provide an alternative: if "Islam" tells us far less than it ought to, if it covers up more than it covers, where—or rather, how—are we to look for information that encourages neither new dreams of power nor old fears and prejudices? In this book I have mentioned and sometimes described the kinds of investigations that are most useful at this point, and I have also said that all of them begin with the idea that all knowledge is interpretation, and that interpretation must be self-conscious in its methods and its aims if it is to be vigilant and humane, if it is also to arrive at knowledge. But underlying every interpretation of other cultures—especially of Islam—is the choice facing the individual scholar or intellectual: whether to put intellect at the service of power or at the service of criticism, community, dialogue, and moral sense. This choice must be the first act of interpretation today, and it must result in a decision, not simply a postponement. If the history of knowledge about Islam in the West has been too closely tied to conquest and domination, the time has come for these ties to be severed completely. About this one cannot be too emphatic. For otherwise we will not only face protracted tension and perhaps even war, but we will offer the Muslim world, its various societies and states, the prospect of many wars, unimaginable suffering, and disastrous upheavals, not the least of which would be the victory of an "Islam" fully ready to play the role prepared for it by reaction, orthodoxy, and desperation. By even the most sanguine of standards, this is not a pleasant possibility.

NOTES

INTRODUCTION TO THE VINTAGE EDITION

1. Lustick, "Fundamentalism, Politicised Religion and Pietism," *MESA Bulletin* 30, 1996, p. 26.

INTRODUCTION

1. Edward W. Said, *Orientalism* (New York: Pantheon Books, 1978; reprint ed., New York: Vintage Books, 1979).

2. Edward W. Said, *The Question of Palestine* (New York: Times Books, 1979; reprint ed., New York: Vintage Books, 1980).

3. For a reference to this see Robert Graham, "The Middle East Muddle," *New York Review of Books*, October 23, 1980, p. 26.

4. J. B. Kelly, *Arabia, The Gulf, and the West: A Critical View of the Arabs and Their Oil Policy* (London: Weidenfeld & Nicolson, 1980). p. 504.

5. Thomas N. Franck and Edward Weisband, *Word Politics: Verbal Strategy Among the Superpowers* (New York: Oxford University Press, 1971).

6. See Paul Marijnis, "De Dubbelrol van een Islam-Kennen," *NRC Handelsblad*, December 12, 1979. Marijnis's article is a report of research done on Snouck Hurgronje by Professor van Koningveld of the Theologi-

cal Faculty at the University of Leiden. I am grateful to Jonathan Beard for bringing this item to my attention, and to Professor Jacob Smit for his help in translating it.

7. For a very full account of the overall context, see Noam Chomsky and Edward S. Herman, *The Washington Connection and Third World Fascism* and *After the Cataclysm: Postwar Indochina and the Reconstruction of Imperial Ideology*, vols. 1 and 2 of *The Political Economy of Human Rights* (Boston: South End Press, 1979). For a valuable analysis of the nineteenth-century picture see Ronald T. Takaki, *Iron Cages: Race and Culture in 19th Century America* (New York: Alfred A. Knopf, 1979).

8. For a well-presented account of how giant corporations intervene in the university, see David F. Noble and Nancy E. Pfund, "Business Goes Back to College," *The Nation*, September 20, 1980, pp. 246–52.

CHAPTER ONE: ISLAM AS NEWS

1. See Edward W. Said, *Orientalism*, pp. 49–73.

2. See Norman Daniel, *The Arabs and Medieval Europe* (London: Longmans, Green & Co., 1975); also his earlier and very useful *Islam and the West: The Making of an Image* (Edinburgh: University Press, 1960). There is a first-rate survey of this matter, set in the political context of the 1956 Suez War, by Erskine B. Childers in *The Road to Suez: A Study of Western-Arab Relations* (London: MacGibbon & Kee, 1962), pp. 25–61.

3. I have discussed Naipaul in "Bitter Dispatches From the Third World," *The Nation*, May 3, 1980, pp. 522–25.

4. Maxime Rodinson, *Marxism and The Modern World*, trans. Michael Palis (London: Zed Press, 1979). See also Thomas Hodgkin, "The Revolutionary Tradition in Islam," *Race and Class* 21, no. 3 (Winter 1980): 221–37.

5. There is an elegant account of this theme, done by a contemporary Tunisian intellectual: see Hichem Djaït, *L'Europe et l'Islam* (Paris: Éditions du Seuil, 1979). A brilliant psychoanalytic/structuralist reading of one "Islamic" motif in European literature—the seraglio—is to be found in Alain Grosrichard, *Structure du sérail: La Fiction du despotisme asiatique dans l'Occident classique* (Paris: Éditions du Seuil, 1979).

6. See Maxime Rodinson, *La Fascination de l'Islam* (Paris: Maspéro, 1980).

7. Albert Hourani, "Islam and the Philosophers of History," in *Europe and The Middle East* (London: Macmillan & Co., 1980), pp. 19–73.

8. As an instance, see the penetrating study by Syed Hussein Alatas, *The Myth of the Lazy Native: A Study of the Image of the Malays, Filipinos, and Javanese from the 16th to the 20th Century and in the ideology of Colonial Capitalism* (London: Frank Cass & Co., 1977).

9. Not that this has always meant poor writing and scholarship: as an informative general account which answers principally to political exigencies and not mainly to the need for new knowledge about Islam, there is Martin Kramer, *Political Islam* (Washington, D.C.: Sage Publications, 1980). This was written for the Center for Strategic and International Studies, Georgetown University, and therefore belongs to the category of policy, not of "objective," knowledge. Another instance in the January 1980 (vol. 78, no. 453) special issue on "The Middle East, 1980" of *Current History*.

10. *Atlantic Community Quarterly* 17, no. 3 (Fall 1979): 291–305, 377–78.

11. Marshall Hodgson, *The Venture of Islam*, 3 vols. (Chicago and London: University of Chicago Press, 1974). See the important review of this by Albert Hourani, *Journal of Near Eastern Studies* 37, no. 1 (January 1978): 53–62.

12. One index of this is the report "Middle Eastern and African Studies: Developments and Needs" commissioned by the U.S. Department of Health, Education and Welfare in 1967, written by Professor Morroe Berger of Princeton, also president of the Middle East Studies Association (MESA). In this report Berger asserts that the Middle East "is not a center of great cultural achievement . . . and therefore does not constitute its own reward so far as modern culture is concerned. . . . [It] has been receding in immediate political importance to the U.S." For a discussion of this extraordinary document and the context that produced it, see Said, *Orientalism*, pp. 287–93.

13. Quoted in Michael A. Ledeen and William H. Lewis, "Carter and the Fall of the Shah: The Inside Story," *Washington Quarterly* 3, no. 2 (Spring 1980): 11–12. Ledeen and Lewis are supplemented (and supported to a degree) by William H. Sullivan, "Dateline Iran: The Road Not Taken," *Foreign Policy* 40 (Fall 1980): 175–86; Sullivan was United States ambassador to Iran before and during the revolution. See also the six-part series by Scott Armstrong, "The Fall of the Shah," *Washington Post*, October 25, 26, 27, 28, 29, 30, 1980.

14. Hamid Algar, "The Oppositional Role of the Ulama in Twentieth Century Iran," in Nikki R. Keddie, ed., *Scholars, Saints, and Sufis: Muslim Religious Institutions Since 1500* (Berkeley, Los Angeles, and London: Uni-

versity of California Press, 1972), pp. 231–55. See also Ervand Abrahamian, "The Crowd in Iranian Politics, 1905–1953," *Past and Present* 41 (December 1968): 184–210; also his "Factionalism in Iran: Political Groups in the 14th Parliament (1944–46)," *Middle Eastern Studies* 14, no. 1 (January 1978): 22–25; also "The Causes of the Constitutional Revolution in Iran," *International Journal of Middle East Studies* 10, no. 3 (August 1979): 381–414; and "Structural Causes of the Iranian Revolution," *MERIP Reports* no. 87 (May 1980), pp. 21–26. See also Richard W. Cottam, *Nationalism in Iran* (Pittsburgh, Pa.: University of Pittsburgh Press, 1979).

15. This is especially true of Fred Halliday, *Iran: Dictatorship and Development* (New York: Penguin Books, 1979), which is nevertheless one of the two or three best studies of Iran done since World War II. Maxime Rodinson, in *Marxism and the Muslim World*, has nearly nothing to say about the Muslim religious opposition. Only Algar (note 14 above) seems to have been right on this point—a remarkable achievement.

16. This is the argument put forward in Edward Shils, "The Prospect for Lebanese Civility," in Leonard Binder, ed., *Politics in Lebanon* (New York: John Wiley & Sons, 1966), pp. 1–11.

17. Malcolm Kerr, "Political Decision Making in a Confessional Democracy," in Binder, ed., *Politics in Lebanon*, p. 209.

18. See the extraordinarily rich material found in the Moshe Sharett *Personal Diary* (Tel Aviv: Ma'ariv, 1979); Livia Rokach, *Israel's Sacred Terrorism: A Study Based on Moshe Sharett's Personal Diary and Other Documents*, intro. by Noam Chomsky (Belmont, Mass.: Association of Arab-American University Graduates [AAZG], 1980). See also the revelations about the CIA role in Lebanon by former CIA advisor Wilbur Crane Eveland, *Ropes of Sand: America's Failure in the Middle East* (New York: W. W. Norton & Co., 1980).

19. Élie Adib Salem, *Modernization Without Revolution: Lebanon's Experience* (Bloomington and London: Indiana University Press, 1972), p. 144. Salem is also the author of "Form and Substance: A Critical Examination of the Arabic Language," *Middle East Forum* 33 (July 1958): 17–19. The title indicates the approach.

20. Clifford Geertz, "The Integrative Revolution: Primordial Sentiments and Civil Politics in the New States," in *The Interpretation of Cultures* (New York: Basic Books, 1973), p. 296.

21. For an interesting description of "expert" illusions about Lebanon on the eve of the civil war, see Paul and Susan Starr, "Blindness in Lebanon," *Human Behavior* 6 (January 1977): 56–61.

22. I have discussed this in *The Question of Palestine*, pp. 3–53 and *passim*.

23. For a brilliant account of this collective delusion see Ali Jandaghi (pseud.), "The Present Situation in Iran," *Monthly Review*, November 1973, pp. 34–47. See also Stuart Schaar, "Orientalism at the Service of Imperialism," *Race and Class* 21, no. 1 (Summer 1979): 67–80.

24. James A. Bill, "Iran and the Crisis of '78," *Foreign Affairs* 57, no. 2 (Winter 1978–79): 341.

25. William O. Beeman, "Devaluing Experts on Iran," *New York Times*, April 11, 1980; James A. Bill, "Iran Experts: Proven Right But Not Consulted," *Christian Science Monitor*, May 6, 1980.

26. As opposed to scholars during the Vietnam War who made a stronger case for themselves as "scientists" willingly serving the state: here it would be good to know why Vietnam specialists were consulted (with no less disastrous results) and Iran experts not. See Noam Chomsky, "Objectivity and Liberal Scholarship," in *American Power and the New Mandarins: Historical and Political Essays* (New York: Pantheon Books, 1969), pp. 23–158.

27. See Said, *Orientalism*, pp. 123–66.

28. On the connection between scholarship and politics as it has affected the colonial world, see *Le Mal de voir: Ethnologie et orientalisme: politique et épistémologie, critique et autocritique*, Cahiers Jussieu no. 2 (Paris: Collections 10/18, 1976). On the way in which "fields" of study coincide with national interests are "Special Supplement: Modern China Studies," *Bulletin of Concerned Asia Scholars* 3, nos. 3–4 (Summer–Fall, 1971): 91–168.

29. See Edmund Ghareeb, ed., *Split Vision: Arab Portrayal in the American Media* (Washington, D.C.: Institute of Middle Eastern and North African Affairs, 1977). For the British counterpart see Sari Nasir, *The Arabs and the English* (London: Longmans, Green & Co., 1979), pp. 140–72.

30. James Peck, "Revolution Versus Modernization and Revisionism: A Two-Front Struggle," in Victor G. Nee and James Peck, eds., *China's Uninterrupted Revolution: From 1840 to the Present* (New York: Pantheon Books, 1975), p. 71. See also Irene L. Gendzier, "Notes Toward a Reading of *The Passing of Traditional Society*," *Review of Middle East Studies* 3 (London: Ithaca Press, 1978), pp. 32–47.

31. An account of the Pahlevi regime's "modernization" is to be found in Robert Graham, *Iran: The Illusion of Power* (New York: St. Martin's Press, 1979). See also Thierry-A. Brun, "The Failures of Western-Style De-

velopment Add to the Regime's Problems," and Eric Rouleau, "Oil Riches Underwrite Ominous Militarization in a Repressive Society," in Ali-Reza Nobari, ed., *Iran Erupts* (Stanford, Calif.: Iran-American Documentation Group, 1978). Also Claire Brière and Pierre Blanchet, *Iran: La Révolution au nom de Dieu* (Paris: Éditions du Seuil, 1979); this book has an interview with Michel Foucault appended to it.

32. There has been an extraordinary reluctance on the part of the press to say anything about the explicitly *religious* formulation of positions and policies inside Israel, especially when these are directed at non-Jews. There would be interesting material found in the Gush Emunim literature, or the pronouncements of the various rabbinic authorities, and so on.

33. See Garry Wills, "The Greatest Story Ever Told," subtitled "Blissed out by the pope's U.S. visit—'unique,' 'historic,' 'transcendent'—the breathless press produced a load of papal bull," *Columbia Journalism Review* 17, no. 5 (January–February 1980): 25–33.

34. See the excellent and exhaustive study by Marwan R. Buheiry, *U.S. Threats Against Arab Oil: 1973–1979*, IPS Papers no. 4 (Beirut: Institute for Palestine Studies, 1980).

35. This is a peculiarly American syndrome. In Europe, the situation is considerably more fair, at least as far as journalism on the whole is concerned.

36. Fritz Stern, "The End of the Postwar Era," *Commentary*, April 1974, pp. 27–35.

37. Daniel P. Moynihan, "The United States in Opposition," *Commentary*, March 1975, p. 44.

38. Robert W. Tucker, "Oil: The Issue of American Intervention," *Commentary*, January 1975, pp. 21–31.

39. Tucker, "Further Reflections on Oil and Force," *Commentary*, January 1975, p. 55.

40. In *Encounter*, 54, no. 5 (May 1980): 20–27.

41. Gerard Chaliand, *Revolution in the Third World: Myths and Prospects* (New York: Viking Press, 1977).

42. See Christopher T. Rand, "The Arabian Fantasy: A Dissenting View of the Oil Crisis," *Harper's Magazine*, January 1974, pp. 42–54, and his *Making Democracy Safe for Oil: Oilmen and the Islamic East* (Boston: Little, Brown & Co., 1975). For authoritative work on the true oil picture see John M. Blair, *The Control of Oil* (New York: Pantheon Books, 1976), and Robert Engler, *The Brotherhood of Oil: Energy Policy and the Public Interest* (Chicago and London: University of Chicago Press, 1977).

43. *Ayatollah Khomeini's Mein Kampf: Islamic Government by Ayatollah Ruhollah Khomeini* (New York: Manor Books, 1979), p. 123. For a careful, prorevolutionary critique of repression in Khomeini's Iran, see Fred Halliday, "The Revolution Turns to Repression," *New Statesman*, August 24, 1979, pp. 260–64; also his comments in *The Iranian*, August 22, 1979. See also Nikki R. Keddie, *Iran, Religion, Politics, and Society: Collected Essays* (London: Frank Cass & Co., 1980).

44. C. Wright Mills, "The Cultural Apparatus," in *Power, Politics and People: The Collected Essays of C. Wright Mills*, ed. Irving Louis Horowitz (London, Oxford, New York: Oxford University Press, 1967), pp. 405–6.

45. See Herbert I. Schiller, *The Mind Managers* (Boston: Beacon Press, 1973), pp. 24–27.

46. Herbert Gans, *Deciding What's News: A Study of "CBS Evening News," "NBC Nightly News," "Newsweek," and "Time"* (New York: Pantheon Books, 1979).

47. Gay Talese, *The Kingdom and the Power* (New York: New American Library, 1969); Harrison Salisbury, *Without Fear or Favor: The New York Times and Its Times* (New York: Times Books, 1979); David Halberstam, *The Powers That Be* (New York: Alfred A. Knopf, 1979); Gaye Tuchman, *Making News: A Study in the Construction of Reality* (New York: Free Press, 1978); Herbert I. Schiller, *Mass Communications and American Empire* (Boston: Beacon Press, 1969), *Communication and Cultural Domination* (White Plains, N.Y.: International Arts and Sciences, 1976), *The Mind Managers*; Michael Schudson, *Discovering the News: A Social History of American Newspapers* (New York: Basic Books, 1978); Armand Mattelart, *Multinational Corporations and the Control of Culture: The Ideological Apparatus of Imperialism*, trans. Michael Chanan (Brighton, Sussex: Harvester Press, 1979).

48. Robert Darnton, "Writing News and Telling Stories," *Daedalus* 104, no. 2 (Spring 1975): 183, 188, 192.

49. This is convincingly demonstrated by Todd Gitlin, *The Whole World Is Watching: Mass Media in the Making and Unmaking of the New Left* (Berkeley, Los Angeles, and London: University of California Press, 1980).

50. See in particular Sacvan Bercovitch, "The Rites of Assent: Rhetoric, Ritual, and the Ideology of American Consensus," in Sam Girgus, ed., *Myth, Popular Culture, and the American Ideology* (Albuquerque: University of New Mexico Press, 1980), pp. 3–40.

51. This is well described by Raymond Williams, "Base and Super-structure in Marxist Cultural Theory," *New Left Review* 82 (November-December 1973): 3–16.

52. A series of recent studies dealing with American experiences involving Indians, various foreign groups, and "empty" territory make this point tellingly: see Michael Paul Rogin, *Andrew Jackson and the Subjugation of the American Indian* (New York: Alfred A. Knopf, 1975); Ronald T. Takaki, *Iron Cages*; Richard Drinnon, *Facing West: The Metaphysics of Indian-Hating and Empire-Building* (Minneapolis: University of Minnesota Press, 1980); Frederick Turner, *Beyond Geography: The Western Spirit Against the Wilderness* (New York: Viking Press, 1980).

53. See the recent account of this dissimulation by Chomsky and Herman, *After the Cataclysm*.

54. In particular see the works by Herbert Schiller and Armand Mattelart cited above, note 47.

55. For a description of the same verbal action-reaction paradigm, see Franck and Wiesband, *Word Politics*.

56. On the role of Western-style elites in Muslim/Arab societies, see John Waterbury and Ragaci El Mallakh, *The Middle East in the Coming Decade: From Wellhead to Well-Being?* (New York: McGraw-Hill Book Co., 1978).

57. Rodinson, "Islam and the Modern Economic Revolution," in his *Marxism and the Muslim World*, p. 151.

58. *Ibid.*, pp. 154–55.

59. As a particularly noteworthy example see the recent work of Mohammed Arkoun: *Contribution à l'étude de l'humanisme arabe au IVe/Xe siècle: Miskawayh, philosophe et historien* (Paris: J. Vrin, 1970); also *Essais sur la pensée islamique* (Paris: Maisonneuve & Larose, 1973); and "La Pensée" and "La vie," in Mohammed Arkoun and Louis Gardet, *L'Islam: Hier. Demain* (Paris: Buchet/Chastel, 1978), pp. 120–247.

60. Albert Hourani, "History," in Leonard Binder, ed., *The Study of the Middle East: Research and Scholarship in the Humanities and the Social Sciences* (New York: John Wiley & Sons, 1976), p. 117.

61. See the very useful analysis of this subject as an aspect of the State in dependent societies, by Eqbal Ahmad, "Post-Colonial Systems of Power," *Arab Studies Quarterly* 2, no. 4 (Fall 1980): 350–63.

62. A good sense of this activity is provided for Iran by Michael M. G. Fischer, *Iran: From Religious Dispute to Revolution* (Cambridge: Harvard University Press, 1980). But see also Marshall Hodgson, *The Venture of Islam*.

63. The key ideological document is Bernard Lewis, "The Return of Islam," *Commentary*, January 1976, pp. 39–49; see my discussion of this in *Orientalism*, pp. 314–20. In comparison with Élie Kedourie, however, Lewis is mild indeed: see Kedourie's extraordinary attempt to show that Islamic resurgence is principally a variant of "Marxism-Leninism" in his *Islamic Revolution*, *Salisbury Papers* no. 6 (London: Salisbury Group, 1979).

64. W. Montgomery Watt, *What Is Islam?* 2nd ed. (London and New York: Longmans, Green & Co., 1979), pp. 9–21.

65. There is an especially cogent description of this in Albert Hourani, *Arabic Thought in the Liberal Age, 1798–1939* (1962; reprint ed., London and Oxford: Oxford University Press, 1970).

66. For a recent, albeit partisan, instance see Adonis (Ali Ahmad Said), *Al-Thabit wal Mutahawwil*, vol. 1, *Al-Usul* (Beirut: Dar al Awdah, 1974). See also Tayyib Tizini, *Min al-Turath ilal-Thawra: Hawl Nathariya Muqtaraha fi Qadiyyat al-Turath al-'Arabi* (Beirut: Dar Ibu Khaldum, 1978). There is a good account of Tizzini's work by Saleh Omar, *Arab Studies Quarterly* 2, no. 3 (Summer 1980): 276–84. For a recent European view of the matter see Jacques Berque, *L'Islam au défi* (Paris: Gallimard, 1980).

67. Hodgson, *Venture of Islam*, 1: 56 ff.

68. Ali Shariati, "Anthropology: The Creation of Man and the Contradiction of God and Iblis, or Spirit and Clay," in *On the Sociology of Islam: Lectures by Ali Shari'ati*, trans. Hamid Algar (Berkeley, Calif.: Mizan Press, 1979), p. 93.

69. Shariati, "The Philosophy of History: Cain and Abel" in *On the Sociology of Islam*, pp. 97–110.

70. See Thomas Hodgkin, "The Revolutionary Tradition in Islam," and Adonis, *Al-Thabit wal Mutahawwil*, on the conflict between official cultures and countercultures.

71. Said, *Orientalism*, pp. 41 ff.

72. Until recently the situation was no different in the representation of other "Oriental" groups: see Tom Engelhardt, "Ambush at Kamikaze Pass," *Bulletin of Concerned Asia Scholars* 3, no. 1 (Winter–Spring 1971): 65–84.

73. Eric Hoffer, "Islam and Modernization: Muhammad, Messenger of Plod," *American Spectator* 13, no. 6 (June 1980): 11–12.

74. According to L. J. Davis, "Consorting with Arabs: The Friends Oil Buys," *Harper's Magazine*, July 1980, p. 40.

CHAPTER TWO: THE IRAN STORY

1. Salisbury, *Without Fear or Favor*, p. 158.

2. *Ibid.*, p. 163.

3. *Ibid.*, p. 311.

4. *Ibid.*, pp. 560–61.

5. Kedourie, *Islamic Revolution*.

6. These articles are conveniently found in translation: Rodinson, "Islam Resurgent?" *Gazelle Review* 6, ed. Roger Hardy (London: Ithaca Press, 1979), pp. 1–17.

7. Quoted in Roy Parriz Mottahedeh, "Iran's Foreign Devils," *Foreign Policy* 38 (Spring 1980): 28. See also Eqbal Ahmad, "A Century of Subjugation," *Christianity and Crisis* 40, no. 3 (March 3, 1980): 37–44.

8. See Robert Friedman, "The Gallegos Affair," *Media People*, March 1980, pp. 33–34.

9. William A. Dorman and Ehsan Omeed, "Reporting Iran the Shah's Way," *Columbia Journalism Review* 17, no. 5 (January–February 1979): 31.

10. Fazlur Rahman, *Islam* (Chicago: University of Chicago Press, 1979), p. 37.

11. Kermit Roosevelt, *Countercoup: The Struggle for the Control of Iran* (New York: McGraw-Hill Book Co., 1979).

12. Hamid Algar, "The Oppositional Role of the 'Ulama in Twentieth-Century Iran," in Keddie, *Scholars, Saints, and Sufis*, pp. 231–55.

13. See Richard Deacon, *The Israeli Secret Service* (New York: Taplinger Publishing Co., 1978), pp. 176–77.

14. For alternative views of *Le Monde*, see Aimé Guedj and Jacques Girault, *"Le Monde": Humanisme, objectivité et politique* (Paris: Éditions Sociales, 1970), and Philippe Simonnot, *"Le Monde" et le pouvoir* (Paris: Les Presses d'aujourd'hui, 1977).

15. See Clark's proposal for solving the Iran-American crisis: "The Iranian Solution," *The Nation*, June 21, 1980, pp. 737–40.

16. Almost alone, the Middle East Research and Information Project (MERIP) has attempted to do this: see *MERIP Reports*, no. 88 (June 1980), "Iran's Revolution: The First Year," pp. 3–31, or the study of Afghanistan in no. 89 (July–August 1980), pp. 3–26.

CHAPTER THREE: KNOWLEDGE AND POWER

1. Giambattista Vico, *The New Science*, trans. T. G. Bergin and Max Fisch (Ithaca, N.Y.: Cornell University Press, 1968), p. 96.

2. Quoted in Raymond Schwab, *Le Renaissance orientale* (Paris: Payot, 1950), p. 327.

3. Ernest Renan, "Mahomet et les origines de L'islamisme," in *Études d'histoire religieuse* (Paris: Calmann-Lévy, 1880), p. 220.

4. Bernard Lewis, "The State of Middle East Studies," *American Scholar* 48, 3 (Summer 1979), 366–67; emphasis added. It is interesting to compare Lewis's disingenuous assertions with Bryan S. Turner, *Marx and the End of Orientalism* (London: George Allen & Unwin, 1978).

5. See, for example, Donald F. Lach and Carol Flaumenhaft, eds., *Asia on the Eve of Europe's Expansion* (Englewood Cliffs, N. J.: Prentice-Hall, 1965); Donald F. Lach, *Asia in the Making of Europe*; vol. 1, *The Century of Discovery* (Chicago and London: University of Chicago Press, 1965), and vol. 2, *A Century of Wonder* (1977); J. H. Parry, *Europe and a Wider World* (London: Hutchinson & Co., 1949), and *The Age of Reconnaissance* (London: Weidenfeld & Nicolson, 1963). Certainly one should also consult K. M. Panikkan, *Asia and Western Dominance* (London: George Allen & Unwin, 1959). For interesting accounts of Asians "discovering" the West in modern times, see Ibrahim Abu-Lughod, *Arab Rediscovery of Europe: A Study in Cultural Encounters* (Princeton, N.J.: Princeton University Press, 1963), and Masao Miyoshi, *As We Saw Them: The First Japanese Embassy to the United States (1860)* (Berkeley, Los Angeles, and London: University of California Press, 1979).

6. There are numerous examples of this, from the career of William Jones, to the Napoleonic expedition to Egypt, to a whole series of nineteenth-century scholar-traveler-agent types: see Said, *Orientalism, passim*. See also the revelations about Snouck Hurgronje, note 6, Introduction.

7. See the penetrating review of the work by Bryan S. Turner, *MERIP Reports* no. 68 (June 1978), pp. 20–22. Following Turner's review, in the same issue of *MERIP Reports*, James Paul estimates the cost of the MESA volume at $85.50 per page.

8. See Said, *Orientalism*, pp. 288–90.

9. Leonard Binder, "Area Studies: A Critical Assessment," in Binder, ed., *Story of the Middle East*, p. 1.

10. *Ibid.*, p. 20.

11. *Ibid.*, p. 21.

12. *Proposal to the Ford Foundation for Two Seminar-Conferences*, Program in Near Eastern Studies, Princeton University (1974–75), pp. 15–16.

13. *Ibid.*, p. 26.

14. L. Carl Brown and Norman Istkowitz, *Psychological Dimensions of Near Eastern Studies* (Princeton, N.J.: Darwin Press, 1977).

15. Ali Banuazizi, "Iranian 'National Character': A Critique of Some Western Perspectives," in Brown and Istkowitz, eds., *Psychological Dimensions of New Eastern Studies*, pp. 210–39. For similar work on a directly related subject, see the important articles by Benjamin Beit-Hallahmi, "National Character and National Behavior in the Middle East: The Case of the Arab Personality," *International Journal of Group Tensions* 2, no. 3 (1972): 19–28; and Fouad Moghrabi, "The Arab Basic Personality," *International Journal of Middle East Studies* 9 (1978): 99–112; also Moghrabi's "A Political Technology of the Soul," *Arab Studies Quarterly* 3, no. 1 (Winter 1981).

16. See "Special Supplement: Modern China Studies," *Bulletin of Concerned Asia Scholars* 3, nos. 3–4 (Summer–Fall 1971).

17. Dwight Macdonald, "Howtoism," in *Against the American Grain* (New York: Vintage Books, 1962), pp. 360–92.

18. Christopher Lasch, *The New Radicalism in America, 1889–1963: The Intellectual as Social Type* (New York: Vintage Books, 1965), p. 316.

19. For an instance of how ethnic origins are cited as "credentials" by a typical Middle East studies expert, see J. C. Hurewitz, "Another View on Iran and the Press," *Columbia Journalism Review* 19, no. 1 (May–June 1980): 19–21. For a response, see Edward W. Said, "Reply," *Columbia Journalism Review* 19 no. 2 (July–August 1980): 68–69.

20. See my comments on recent books by Rodinson and Hourani in *Arab Studies Quarterly* 2, no. 4 (Fall 1980): 386–93.

21. Irène Ferrera-Hoeschstetter, "Les Études sur le moyen-orient aux États-Unis," *Maghreb-Mashrek* 82 (October–November 1978): 34.

22. Richard H. Nolte, *Middle East Centers at U.S. Universities*, June 1979, p. 2 (courtesy of Mr. Don Snook of Esso Middle East, who very kindly sent me a copy of Nolte's report).

23. *Ibid.*, pp. 40, 46, 20.

24. *Ibid.*, pp. 43, 24.

25. Michel Foucault, *The History of Sexuality, Volume One: An Introduction*, trans. Robert Hurley (New York: Pantheon Books, 1978), p. 34.

26. The phrase is partly Harold Bloom's, although of course he uses it in a very different context and calls it "antithetical criticism": see his book

The Anxiety of Influence: A Theory of Poetry (New York: Oxford University Press, 1973), pp. 93–96.

27. The work of Peter Gran, Judith Tucker, Basem Musallem, Eric Davis, and Stuart Schaar, among others, is representative of this group.

28. See notes 14, 15, and 62, Chapter One.

29. I have discussed the notion of *affiliation* in "Reflections on Recent American 'Left' Literary Criticism," *Boundary* 2 8, no. 1 (Fall 1979): 26–29.

30. Hans-Georg Gadamer, *Truth and Method* (New York: Seabury Press, 1975), p. 238.

31. See Ali Jandaghi's comments on Marvin Zonis's study of the Iranian elite, in "The Present Situation in Iran," *Monthly Review*, November 1973, pp. 34–47.

32. As instances, there is J. B. Kelly, *Arabia, the Gulf and the West*, who bewails the departure of the British east of Suez; there is Élie Kedourie, who attacks de Gaulle for having "given up" Algeria—see his review of Alistair Horne, *A Savage War of Peace: Algeria, 1954–1962* in the *Times Literary Supplement*, April 21, 1978, pp. 447–50; and there is Robert W. Tucker and a whole string of followers who have been advocating an American invasion of the Gulf for at least five years (see notes 34 and 38, Chapter One). Behind much of this is the work of Edward N. Luttwak: see the model presented in his book *The Grand Strategy of the Roman Empire: From the First Century A.D. to the Third* (Baltimore and London: Johns Hopkins University Press, 1976).

INDEX

Copyright © 1980 by The New York Times Company. Reprinted by permission.

Oxford University Press: Excerpt from *Power, Politics and People* by C. Wright Mills. Reprinted by permission of Oxford University Press.

Harry Stein: Excerpt from an interview, "A Day in the Life: Flora Lewis" by Harry Stein, first published in *Esquire* Magazine, May 1980. Reprinted by permission.

John Wiley & Sons, Inc. Publishers: Excerpt from "History" by Albert Hourani in *The Study of the Middle East*, edited by Leonard Binder. Copyright © 1976. Reprinted by permission of John Wiley & Sons, Inc.

Zed Press: Excerpt from *Marxism and the Muslim World*, translated by Michael Palis, 1979. Published by Zed Press, 57 Caledonian Road, London N1. Reprinted by permission.